Irish Literature in the Celtic Tiger
Years 1990 to 2008

Continuum Literary Studies Series
Also available in the series:

Irish Literature in the Celtic Tiger Years 1990 to 2008

Gender, Bodies, Memory

Susan Cahill

continuum

Continuum International Publishing Group

The Tower Building   80 Maiden Lane
11 York Road   Suite 704
London SE1 7NX   New York NY 10038

www.continuumbooks.com

British Library Cataloguing-in-Publication Data
A catalogue record for this book is available from the British Library.

ISBN: 978-1-4411-5202-2 (hardcover)

Library of Congress Cataloging-in-Publication Data
A catalog record for this book is available from the Library of Congress

Typeset by Newgen Imaging Systems, Pvt Ltd, Chennai, India.
Britain

Contents

Acknowledgements

I would like to thank a number of people for all their advice, support, inspiration, and good humour, which made this book possible. I am extremely grateful to Claire Bracken, Claire Connolly, Anne Fogarty, Gerardine Meaney, John O'Neill, and Emma Radley for reading several drafts of various chapters. Their encouragement, advice, and incisive comments are hugely appreciated. Gerardine Meaney has been a constant source of encouragement and enthusiasm and I am extremely thankful to her for all her help. Emma Radley deserves particular thanks for sharing an office with me throughout this process and the many conversations I have had with her, Claire Bracken, and Anne Mulhall have been invaluable to this project.

I am very grateful to all my colleagues in the School of English, Drama and Film, UCD and the UCD John Hume Institute for Global Irish Studies and former colleagues in the School of English, Queen's University Belfast and the Department of Languages and Cultural Studies, University of Limerick. Particular thanks are due to colleagues and friends, Pat Coughlan, Anne Mulhall, Tina O'Toole Gerardine Meaney, Brian Jackson, and Moynagh Sullivan for continued support and friendship. There are many others who have helped in various ways throughout the project including Oriana Corbett, Anna Crudge, Claudia Fontéyne, Emma Hegarty, Paul Keegan, Susan O'Grady, Catherine O'Leary Pauline Power, Dave O'Leary, and Emma Tobin.

I wish to gratefully acknowledge funding from the Irish Research Council for the Humanities and Social Sciences and the UCD John Hume Institute for Global Irish Studies.

My family also deserves special thanks for their support: my mother, Mary; sisters, Roisín and Alice; brother, Robert; and grandparents, Ita and Con Power.

Thanks especially to John O'Neill for constant support, encouragement, kindness, and good humour.

Previous versions of Chapters 1, 2, 3, and 4 have been published in part in the following forms: "'The 'Other' that Moves and Misleads": Mapping and Temporality in Éilís Ní Dhuibhne's *The Dancers Dancing' Liminal Borderlands: Ireland Past, Present, Future*. Eds. Irene Gilsenan Nordin and Elin Holmsten (Oxford: Peter Lang, 2009, 69–83); 'Corporeal Architecture: Body and City in Colum McCann's This Side of Brightness', *Études Irlandaises* 32.1 (2007): 43–58; '"A Greedy Girl" and "A National Thing": Gender and History in Anne Enright's *The Pleasure of Eliza Lynch' Irish Literature: Feminist Perspectives.* Eds. Patricia Coughlan and Tina O'Toole (Dublin: Carysfort Press, 2008, 203–22); and '"Dreaming of upholstered breasts", or, how to find your way back home: dislocation in *What Are You Like?' Anne Enright.* Eds. Claire Bracken and Susan Cahill (Dublin: Irish Academic Press, 2011). I would like to thank the editors for permission to reprint these revised versions.

Finally, I would like to thank my editor at Continuum, Colleen Coalter, for all her support and assistance, and the production team at Newgen.

Timeline

	Political	Cultural
1990	Mary Robinson elected as first female President	Dermot Bolger, *The Journey Home*
	Second Commission on the Status of Women established	Roddy Doyle, *The Snapper*
		John McGahern, *Amongst Women* (shortlisted for the Booker)
	Brian Keenan released after four and a half years of being held hostage in Beruit	Éilís Ní Dhuibhne, *The Bray House*
		Colm Toibín, *The South*
		Ireland reaches the quarter-final in the World Cup but are defeated by the hosts, Italy
1991	Father Brendan Smyth charged with sexual abuse of minors.	Roddy Doyle, *The Van* (shortlisted for the Booker)
	Birmingham Six are released	Anne Enright, *The Portable Virgin* (won the Rooney Prize for Irish Literature)
		Jennifer Johnston, *The Invisible Worm*
		Éilís Ní Dhuibhne, *Eating Women is Not Recommended*
		William Trevor, *Reading Turgenev (from Two Lives)* (shortlisted for the Booker)
		Field Day Anthology of Irish Writing, Vols. I, II, III
		Irish Museum of Modern Art opened
1992	Referendum to ratify Maastricht Treaty passed	Patrick McCabe, *The Butcher Boy* (shortlisted for the Booker)
	Supreme Court decision in 'X Case' established right to abortion where mother's life under threat	Edna O'Brien, *Time and Tide*
		Glenn Patterson, *Fat Lad*

Continued

	Political	Cultural
	Referendum on right to travel for an abortion passed Referendum on right to acquire information on abortion passed. Eamonn Casey, Bishop of Galway, revealed to have fathered a child	
1993	Decriminalization of homosexuality Downing Street Declaration	John Banville, *Ghosts* Roddy Doyle wins the Booker Prize for *Paddy Clarke Ha Ha Ha* Colm Toibín, *The Heather Blazing* Irish Film Board re-established Introduction of tax breaks for film makers
1994	Father Brendan Smyth tried in Belfast Crown Court, pleaded guilty to seventeen charges of sexual abuse of minors. Controversy over delay of extradition of Smyth leads to collapse of Fianna Fáil/Labour coalition. Albert Reynolds resigns as Taoiseach and leader of Fianna Fáil The Tribunal of Inquiry into the Beef Processing Industry Ireland's economic growth termed the "Celtic Tiger" by a London-based economist IRA / Loyalist Military ceasefires	Emma Donoghue, *Stir Fry* Colum McCann, *Fishing the Sloe Black River* (won the Rooney Prize for Irish Literature) Edna O'Brien, *The House of Splendid Isolation* William Trevor, *Felicia's Journey* wins Costa Book of the Year Award and Novel Award UTV *Counterpoint* documentary about Brendan Smyth scandal, reveals extent of collusion and cover-up by the Church authorities "Riverdance" first performed during the interval of the Eurovision Song contest, held in Ireland
1995	Referendum to grant divorce after four years of separation passed IRA ceasefire ends	John Banville, *Athena* Emma Donoghue, *Hood* Anne Enright, *The Wig My Father Wore* Jennifer Johnston, *The Illusionist*

Political	Cultural
	Mary Morrissy, *Mother of Pearl*
	Patrick McCabe, *The Dead School*
	Colum McCann, *Songdogs*
	Seamus Heaney awarded Nobel Prize for Literature
	Artist Kathy Prendergast wins Premio Demila award at Venice Biennale
1996 Last Magdalene laundry closed	John Banville, *The Ark*
	Seamus Deane *Reading in the Dark* (shortlisted for the Booker)
	Roddy Doyle, *The Woman Who Walked Into Doors,*
	Lia Mills, *Another Alice*
	Edna O'Brien, *Down by the River* (based on events surrounding the X case)
	Nuala O'Faolain, *Are You Somebody?: The Life and Times of Nuala O'Faolain*
	Teilifís na Gaeilge starts broadcasting
1997 150th anniversary of the Famine	John Banville, *The Untouchable*
McCracken Tribunal established to investigate payments to politicians implicating Ben Dunne and Charles Haughey	Anne Haverty, *One Day as a Tiger*
	Bernard MacLaverty, *Grace Notes* (shortlisted for the Booker)
Moriarty Tribunal established to further investigate these payments	Frank McCourt wins the Pulitzer Prize (Biography and Autobiography) for *Angela's Ashes*
Flood Tribunal (later Mahon Tribunal) began investigating planning decisions and payments	Éilís Ní Dhuibhne, *The Inland Ice*
	Colm Toibín, *The Story of the Night*
The Tribunal of Inquiry into the Blood Transfusion Service Board (Finlay Tribunal) revealed that large number of people had been infected with contaminated blood in the 1970s and 1980s	

Continued

	Political	Cultural
	Mary Robinson takes up post as UN High Commissioner Mary McAleese elected as President Second IRA ceasefire announced	
1998	Bicentenary of 1798 Rebellion Good Friday Agreement Northern Ireland Assembly established Omagh bombing	Sebastian Barry, *The Whereabouts of Eneas McNulty* Jennifer Johnston, *Two Moons* Eugene McCabe, *Death and Nightingales* Patrick McCabe, *Breakfast on Pluto* (shortlisted for the Booker) Colum McCann, *This Side of Brightness* Keith Ridgeway, *The Long Falling*
1999	Republic of Ireland joins single European currency, the Euro Cross-party Executive established in Northern Ireland Moriarty Tribunal exposed Charles Haughey as having lived beyond his means, relying on payments from developers and businessmen	Roddy Doyle, *A Star Called Henry* Claire Keegan, *Antarctica* Brian O'Doherty, *The Deposition of Father McGreevey* (shortlisted for the Booker in 2000) Éilís Ní Dhuibhne, *The Dancers Dancing* Edna O'Brien, *Wild Decembers* Colm Toibín, *The Blackwater Lightship* (shortlisted for the Booker) RTÉ broadcast of *States of Fear*, three-part documentary about abuse in Irish industrial schools
2000	The Commission to Inquire into Child Abuse established	John Banville, *Eclipse* Michael Collins, *The Keepers of Truth* (shortlisted for the Booker) Emma Donoghue, *Slammerkin* Anne Enright, *What Are You Like?* (shortlisted for the Whitbread Novel Award) Anne Haverty, *The Far Side of a Kiss* Jennifer Johnston, *The Gingerbread Woman* Colum McCann, *Everything in This Country Must*

	Political	**Cultural**
		Mary Morrissy, *The Pretender*
		Éilís Ní Dhuibhne, *The Pale Gold of Alaska*
2001	Nice Treaty rejected	Patrick McCabe, *Emerald Germs of Ireland*
		Mary Morrissy, *The Pretender*
		Jamie O'Neill, *At Swim, Two Boys*
2002	Changeover to Euro complete	John Banville, *Shroud*
	Referendum to remove threat of suicide as ground for legal abortion rejected	Sebastian Barry, *Annie Dunne*
		Emma Donoghue, *The Woman Who Gave Birth to Rabbits*
	Bishop Brendan Comiskey, of the Diocese of Ferns in County Wexford, resigns due to allegations of child sexual abuse.	Anne Enright, *The Pleasure of Eliza Lynch*
		Jennifer Johnston, *This is not a Novel*
		John McGahern, *That They May Face the Rising Sun*
	Nice Treaty accepted	Edna O'Brien, *In the Forest*
	General election returns Fianna Fáil/ Progressive Democrat coalition to government	Joseph O'Connor, *Star of the Sea*
		William Trevor, *The Story of Lucy Gault* (shortlisted for the Booker)
		The Field Day Anthology of Irish Writing, Vols. IV and V: Irish Women's Writing and Traditions
		The Magdalene Sisters, directed by Peter Mullan released
		Suing the Pope, documentary by Colm O'Gorman broadcast on BBC, the documentary revealed the failure of Bishop Brendan Comiskey to deal with widespread sexual abuse of children by Fr Fortune and a number of other priests in the Diocese of Ferns in County Wexford
		Cardinal Secrets, documentary broadcast on RTÉ, investigated the handling of allegations of clerical child sex abuse in Dublin Archdiocese

Continued

	Political	Cultural
2003	Ferns Inquiry established to investigate allegations of child sexual abuse made against Ferns diocesan clergy	Hugo Hamilton, *The Speckled People* Claire Kilroy, *All Summer* (won the Rooney Prize for Irish Literature in 2004) Patrick McCabe, *Call Me the Breeze* Colum McCann, *Dancer* Éilís Ní Dhuibhne, *Midwife to the Fairies* Keith Ridgeway, *The Parts* Paul Muldoon awarded Pulitzer Prize for Poetry and the Griffin International Prize for Excellence in Poetry
2004	Citizenship Referendum Luas, Dublin's light rail system launched Ireland holds EU presidency overseeing entry of ten new member states	Roddy Doyle, *Oh, Play that Thing* Emma Donoghue, *Life Mask* Anne Enright, *Making Babies: Stumbling into Motherhood* Colm Toibín, *The Master* (shortlisted for the Booker, wins the Los Angeles Times Book Prize)
2005	The Ferns Report presented to Minister for Health and Children Irish language becomes an official language of the European Union IRA decommissioning complete	John Banville wins the Booker Prize for *The Sea* Sebastian Barry, *A Long Long Way* (shortlisted for the Booker) Jennifer Johnston, *Grace and Truth* Lia Mills, *Nothing Simple*
2006	St Andrews Agreement 90th anniversary of the 1916 Rising Commission of Investigation, Dublin Archdiocese set up to investigate the handling of allegations of clerical child sex abuse	Anne Haverty, *The Free and Easy* Claire Kilroy, *Tenderwire* Patrick McCabe, *Winterwood* Colum McCann, *Zoli* Edna O'Brien, *The Light of Evening* Colm Toibín, *Mother and Sons* Colm Toibín, *The Master* (published 2004) is awarded IMPAC Dublin Literary Award Death of John McGahern

	Political	Cultural
2007	Direct rule over Northern Ireland by Westminster ends General election returns Fianna Fáil/ Green/ Progressive Democrat coalition to government	Anne Enright wins Booker Prize for *The Gathering* Emma Donoghue, *Landing* Jennifer Johnston, *Foolish Mortals* Claire Keegan, *Walk the Blue Fields* Joseph O'Connor, *Redemption Falls* Éilís Ní Dhuibhne, *Fox, Swallow, Scarecrow*
2008	Bertie Ahern resigns as Taoiseach, Brian Cowen takes over Lisbon Treaty rejected Economy announced to be officially in recession, Ireland becomes first Eurozone country to enter recession Bank deposit guarantee scheme extended Beginning of Anglo Irish Bank hidden loans controversy An Bord Snip Nua (Special Group on Public Service Numbers and Expenditure Programmes) established	Sebastian Barry, *The Secret Scripture* (shortlisted for the Booker, wins Costa Book of the Year award and Novel award) Anne Enright, *Taking Pictures* Anne Enright, *Yesterday's Weather* Patrick McCabe, The Holy City
2009	Anglo Irish Bank nationalized Commission to Inquire into Child Abuse (Ryan Report) published National Asset Management Agency established Second referendum on Lisbon Treaty is passed McCarthy Report, findings of An Bord Snip Nua, published	John Banville, *The Infinities* Claire Kilroy, *All Names Have Been Changed* Colum McCann, *Let The Great World Spin* Colm Toibín's *Brooklyn* wins Costa Novel Award

Introduction:
Irish Literature in the Celtic Tiger Years:
Gender, Bodies, Memory

At the beginning of Anne Enright's most recent novel, *The Gathering*, the narrator, Veronica, describes her need to 'bear witness' to events in her childhood that may explain her brother's suicide: 'I write it down, I lay them out in nice sentences, all my clean, white bones' (Enright, 2007, 1, 2). Veronica's desire to unearth clean, manageable skeletons from the past ultimately proves unsustainable and the novel consistently troubles the boundaries between history and memory, and the possibility of accurately representing either, undermining Veronica's ossified model of historiography. By the end of the novel Veronica accepts a messier, more fleshy version of human relations:

> And I think we make for peculiar refugees, running from our own blood, or towards our own blood; pulsing back and forth along ghostly veins that wrap the world in a skein of blood. (Enright, 2007, 258)

I will come back to *The Gathering* in Chapter 5, but it is worth noting that recourse to the body is often the means by which contemporary Irish novelists structure engagements with the past, in particular the novelists that this book focuses on: Anne Enright, Éilís Ní Dhuibhne, and Colum McCann.

The body is what we cannot get away from. It is the place from which we perceive the world. This book focuses on three contemporary Irish novelists who engage in their fiction with the inescapability of the body in order to raise questions concerning nation, gender, race and memory. This approach highlights common concerns for the writers – the relationships between past and present, between generations and between memory and history. All three novelists articulate these concerns through sustained literary engagements with the body. These relationships become particularly pertinent for the writers in the context of Celtic Tiger Ireland, a historical moment that reveals complex attitudes towards relationships between past, present and future.

In her introduction to a collection entitled *Literature and the Body: Essays on Populations and Persons*, published in 1988, Elaine Scarry identifies a turn to materialism that underlies contemporaneous attention to the corporeal (vii). This emphasis on the material, and consequently on the body, highlights an ethical consideration that underpins this book. To consider how authors use the body in their writing is to think about their attempts to intervene in political and cultural placements of corporeality in the milieu in which they write. To focus on the body is to ask how it matters; materialist criticism insists that we pay attention to how bodies are configured and what impact this might have for embodied individuals. As Scarry writes: 'The notion of "consequence," of "mattering," is nearly inseparable from the substantive fact of "matter"' (xxii). It is also important to ask the question: which bodies matter? In other words, which types of corporeality are granted material presence in hegemonic narratives and which are rendered invisible? The writers on which I focus in this book engage with these crucial questions in their fiction.

In the last three decades there has been an explosion of work on the body in sociology, philosophy, literary criticism, and feminist theory. However, this interest has only recently filtered through to the field of Irish Studies. This absence misrepresents the importance of the body as a potent source of metaphor and identity construction, particularly in terms of nationalist discourses. Ireland's corporeal figurations and body politic have been fraught ones historically and, as many critics have noted, issues relating to landscape became imbricated with constructions of the 'national body' (see Nash, 1997). The dominance of Catholicism as a set of moral principles, an ideology, and a collection of imagery, despite being one of the more bodily oriented religions, contributed to a repression of the physical on a widespread scale in Ireland's independent nation. Though this morality has loosened its hold in the Irish cultural arena, issues pertaining to the body and reproductive rights remain bastions of conservative opinion. It is no accident that the corporeal is situated at the crux of conflict. Metaphors of the body form the basis of our ordering of the world and are forceful means of structuring concepts of nation and history. However, in contrast to a focus on the body in disciplines such as sociology, feminism, and literary criticism from the early-modern period to the nineteenth century, Irish Studies tends to avoid explicit focus on the corporeal.

Contemporary Irish poetry has, however, received a critical focus on the body which is reflected in Irene Gilsenan Nordin's edited collection, *The Body and Desire in Contemporary Irish Poetry* (2006). Broadly speaking, this criticism has divided into two categories. The first would include critics who focus on poets such as Eavan Boland, Nuala Ní Dhomhnaill, Eiléan Ní Chuilleanáin, and Medbh McGuckian in terms of the concerns linking body and nation. The second category I would distinguish is made up of critics who focus particularly on Northern Irish male poets in terms of political violence inflicted upon the body, resulting in a traumatic dispersed, fragmented, or dismembered corporeality. Rand Brandes, in an article on the body in poetry by Seamus Heaney and Ciaran Carson, argues that 'there appears to be a correlation between how one constructs the physical body in the tropic discourse of the poem and how one constructs the body of History itself, that is, History as an integrated corpus' (Brandes, 1994, 178). Heaney, for Brandes, envisages the body, history, and memory as total, coherent, and whole, whereas Carson revels in their fragmentation and incomprehensibility. Brandes's argument concerning the link between conceptualizations of the body and attitudes towards conflict in Northern Ireland is based on the identification by Peter Stallybrass and Allon White of the crucial connection between the morphology of corporeality and social topography (Stallybrass and White 1986). Brandes's extension of this connection to cover notions of history and memory is an important one. In the work of the writers discussed in this thesis, the body and its configurations bear crucial relations to how these novelists engage with questions of history and temporality. However, in contrast to the writers discussed in this book, Brandes understands corporeality either in terms of wholeness and coherence or in terms of fragmentation, which implies an original unity. This appears to be the dominant mode for conceptualizing the body in this strand of Irish criticism.[1]

Contemporary Irish fiction has expanded in recent decades alongside attempts to catalogue it, such as Dermot Bolger's *The New Picador Book of Contemporary Irish Fiction* (2000) and Colm Tóibín's *The Penguin Book of Irish Fiction* (1999), the latter of which devotes a substantial amount of its collection to the contemporary. The intensity and speed of changes is a constant sentiment in criticism focusing on contemporary Irish fiction. Dermot Bolger, for example, in his introduction to *The New Picador Book of Contemporary Irish Fiction*, claims that Ireland exhibits a more profound sociological change in the past twenty-five years than most other European countries (Bolger, 2000, xii). Anne Fogarty uses the example of Bolger's publication to illustrate 'the difficulty of constructing reliable guides to the protean unwieldiness and ever-mutating phenomenon of contemporary Irish fiction' (2000, 59). Bolger's revision of the book in the year following its initial publication to include fifteen new writers illustrates, for Fogarty, the 'rapidly changing nature of Irish society and the perpetually fluctuating map of contemporary Irish fiction which has to be constantly re-drawn' (2000, 59). Liam Harte laments the impossibility of writing 'purposefully, let alone comprehensively, about the swirling abundance of themes and trends in contemporary Irish fiction' (2009, 201).

The contemporary is also notoriously difficult to define. Anthony Roche, in his introduction to a special issue of the *Irish University Review* on the subject, rails against its categorization as including all 'living' authors and instead dates the term to 1970 (Roche, 2000).[2] For the purpose of this project, I date the contemporary as even more recent, partly due to the fact that Enright, McCann, and Ní Dhuibhne have all written and published within the late 1980s, 1990s, and early 2000s, and partly because I would mark the last decades of the twentieth century and the initial years of the twenty-first century as offering these writers a milieu different in kind from that which had preceded it. In 1994, Kevin Gardiner, an economist at Morgan Stanley in London, coined the term 'Celtic Tiger' to describe Ireland's rapid economic growth as similar to fiscal advancement in East Asia's 'tiger' economies. The term took hold to designate Ireland's years of prosperity in which low corporation tax, aid from the European Union, a boom in the United States' economy, and the attraction to multinational corporations of a well-educated workforce who spoke English all contributed towards Ireland's boom (Brown, 2004, 381–3; Parker, 2009, 6–7). This period of economic prosperity facilitated major developments in Ireland's social, cultural, and ideological landscapes and, as Patricia Coughlan points out, 'caused questioning of the hitherto dominant image (and self-image) of Irishness as essentially rooted in the land, the West, and traditional ways of life' (Coughlan, 2004, 178), though this construction of Irishness maintained purchase in much advertising, particularly for the Irish tourist board and the Gaelic Athletic Association (GAA), promoting conceptions of Irish identity that were often conservative, reactionary, and exclusionary in terms of gender, race and ethnicity (Cronin, 2007; Negra, 2006; 2007).

The rapidity of social change in the 1990s and 2000s has been well rehearsed (Brewster, 2009; Brown, 2004; Coughlan, 2004; Parker, 2009). Ireland did display significant reforms in social and legal terms in these decades, particularly impacting on the perceived sanctity of the family as enshrined in De Valera's 1937 Constitution and positively affecting the lived experience of women and the gay community. Mary Robinson's presidency, which began in 1990 and marked the first female to hold this role, heralded a significant symbolic development particularly in relation to issues of sexuality and women's lives. Robinson's career in law preceding the presidency saw her taking leading roles in the changing of legislation relating to contraception and to free legal aid, and working with the Campaign for Homosexual Law Reform (see Brown, 2004, 358–9). These decades saw the decriminalization of homosexuality in 1993, divorce laws in 1995, and most recently the Civil Partnership Bill in 2010, which although promising legal recognition and equal rights to same-sex couples, fails to offer legal security for children of civil partners.

Despite Derek Hand's proclamation that 'all such "pivotal" moments must be seen in retrospect as utterly arbitrary' (Hand, 2001), I would agree with Anne Fogarty's reading of Gerry Smyth's coinage of the term 'Robinsonian' as an 'instructive' concept to describe the Ireland of the 1990s in which these authors write:

> The forces of feminist radicalism and political innovation with which Mary Robinson is associated provide resonant metaphors for the new perspectives, themes and aesthetics of contemporary Irish fiction. (Fogarty, 2000, 60)

The decades of the 1990s and 2000s have seen real and profound changes in women's economic power and position in public life. However, as Patricia Coughlan cautions, the picture is far from liberatory:

> Women are typically required, in a painful contradiction, both to sustain care and nurture at home and to meet the instrumental demands of increasingly pragmatic workplaces. The inherited cultural construction of the Irish mother still functions as a powerful background ideal, intensifying this strain. (Coughlan, 2004, 177)

As previously stated, it is particularly in relation to issues surrounding the female body, especially the reproductive body, that repression and regulation become most profound, seen especially clearly in debates relating to abortion and the Citizenship Referendum of 2004 (see Conrad, 2001; Sullivan, 2005).

In tandem with such developments in legal and social reforms, these decades also witnessed a series of tribunals investigating the financial dealings of politicians, developers, and businessmen, as well as revelations concerning the sexual behaviour of Catholic clergy, the cruelty of the Magdalene laundries as well as cases involving 'multiple paedophile rape, parental cruelty, and family dysfunction, [...] breaking the previous shamed silence of female rape victims' (Coughlan, 2004, 176). These disclosures related to

Ireland's not so distant past complicate any linear, progressive paradigm of modernity. As Coughlan elaborates:

> it would be misleading to accept a simple before-and-after narrative of enlightenment, or to posit a completely clear liberal-conservative and urban-rural divide in Ireland, especially where questions of women's status and freedoms are concerned. (176)

All three writers on whom this book focuses contend with this complicated relationship between past and present. Enright, McCann, and Ní Dhuibhne attempt in their writing to formulate innovative and connective means of thinking about the relationships between temporalities highlighting the occlusions and absences of Celtic Tiger culture. All place the body, its configurations and associations, at the centre of their efforts to reconsider paradigms between the past and the present, particularly in relation to the female body and maternal genealogies. These authors foreground the materiality of the body; their writing is material in its interests and concerns.

Contemporary Enough?

In early 2010, Irish novelist Julian Gough posted his heated response, on his blog, to a question about the state of the contemporary Irish novel: 'If there is a movement in Ireland, it is backwards. Novel after novel set in the nineteen seventies, sixties, fifties. Reading award-winning Irish literary fiction, you wouldn't know television had been invented' (2010). Gough's invective against a contemporary Irish literature that does not engage sufficiently with its Celtic Tiger present and is instead obsessed with the past is not a new complaint. In 2001, Fintan O'Toole described what he saw as a crisis in Irish literature: 'the difficulty of creating stories of the boomtime' due to 'the emergence of a frantic, globalised, dislocated Ireland [which] has deprived fiction writers of their traditional tools', whatever these tools might be (O'Toole, 2001). Declan Kiberd repeated the criticism in a lecture given in 2003 (published in 2005): 'There has been no really major art-work about the Tony O'Reilly dynasty or about a conflicted, interesting figure such as Dermot Desmond' (Kiberd, 2005, 278). John Banville, in response to Gough's piece, also concurred: 'it is true, as the critic Declan Kiberd remarks, that no contemporary Irish writer has yet attempted the Great Irish Novel on social and political themes. Where is our *Middlemarch*, our *Doctor Zhivago*, our Rabbit trilogy?' (Banville qtd in Flood, 2010). That *Middlemarch* and *Doctor Zhivago* are themselves historical novels does not seem to worry Banville, and Gough and O'Toole seem unaware of the position that historical fiction most often engages with the time at which it is written.[3] Enright's *The Pleasure of Eliza Lynch*, which I will deal with in more detail in Chapter 4, is a case in point. The excessive consumption of Eliza Lynch, the nineteenth-century protagonist, (her 'talent' is 'for shipping' consumer goods from Europe to Paraguay (Enright, 2002, 225)) can be read as a direct comment on the consumerism of the Celtic Tiger period.

The comments of these critics point to a tendency towards reductive models of past-present relations which privilege rigid distinctions between temporalities. The issues of time, the relationship between past and present, history and memory continuously recur in commentary concerning contemporary Ireland and its literature and culture. Terence Brown notes that a 'curious obsession with the past [. . .] was [. . .] a characteristic of much cultural production in the period' of the 1990s, the result of a combination of millennial retrospection and continued revelations concerning the endemic corruption of both the state and church (2004, 403). For Fogarty, on the other hand, the rapid social change and economic prosperity led, instead, to a tendency to efface and resist the past:

A by-product of the accelerated changes in Irish society in the 1990s, chiefly as a result of the short-lived economic phenomenon of the Celtic Tiger, has been the disavowal of the past on many fronts. (2003, xii)

Indeed, in Anne Haverty's novel, *The Free and Easy* (2007), set during and commenting directly on the prosperity years (despite Gough's denial of the existence of such books), one character insists:

You can forget the last century. And you can definitely forget the century before. Ireland as we know it – and let's thank whoever and whatever – was born some time around nineteen ninety-four. Or ninety-six? [. . .] Let the historians fight about the year. Historians like to have something to fight about. (Haverty, 2007, 112)

Though Brown's and Fogarty's arguments seem to contradict each other, they instead describe the same symptom, a fetishization of the past. Scott Brewster identifies the significant debate of the Celtic Tiger era as 'a struggle for the past and for the future' (2009, 21). And for Brewster, this manifests in two ways: the tendency to consider Ireland's past, particularly the De Valera era, as backward; and the prevalence of commemorative practices since 1990. In the cultural climate of the Celtic Tiger, a rigid distinction between Ireland's 'traditional' and 'backward' past and its 'affluent' and 'contemporary' present was valorized. Within these terms, Ireland's history is commodified and used, freezing the past in order that it serves specific purposes. Thus, within this cultural context, approaches to the past either identify moments that are read in a disapproving fashion as signalling Ireland's 'backwardness' in comparison to the 'progress' that has occurred in the years of Ireland's economic prosperity, or, Ireland's history is read reverentially and nostalgically, an attitude most prevalent in nationalistic discourse and tourist branding and advertising. As Brewster writes:

> history was being manipulated to airbrush conflict from the past for the benefit of the heritage and tourist industries, whether by recycling hoary myths and nationalist verities, or by neutralising the North as a site of political conflict and marginalising those who question the merits of economic liberalism and labour flexibility. (2009, 25)

These approaches to the past presuppose what history can do for them; the past is viewed as a self-contained object that can be used in order to satisfy pre-given narratives, fundamentally different in kind to the present moment. This commodification of the past also refuses and disavows, to use Fogarty's term, aspects of the past that do not support constructions of Ireland's prosperity and 'progressivism'. Furthermore, as Brewster points out, the emphasis on narratives of progress and intense positive social change illustrates a 'wider "chrono-politicisation" of Ireland, whereby continuity gives way to frantic acceleration, and the past is obliterated by a headlong dash for the future' (Brewster, 2009, 25). For Gerardine Meaney, 'the rapidity of change obscured the depth of continuity' (Meaney, 2010, xv). Haverty, in her novel, is astute in her analyses of these attitudes. Seoda, the character who dismisses Ireland prior to 1994, continues:

> 'I believe, Tom, that to move on the first thing you do is, you jettison the past. Bin it. Don't you think?' She sipped thoughtfully at her Château Margaux. 'You have to be convinced that progress is not only inevitable but also desirable. It's something people often don't understand.' (Haverty, 2007, 113)

Tom, the American protagonist, to whom she is speaking asks, 'We can't accommodate the past and the future, is that what you're saying?' and Seoda agrees with his interpretation, responding 'Absolutely. No way. You have to be ruthless' (Haverty, 2007, 114). That Seoda expresses these sentiments while drinking wine from an estate known for its age and heritage illustrates Haverty's sustained satirical critique of Ireland's culture of consumption throughout these years. History is to be consumed or discarded. The unwillingness of Gough, O'Toole, and Banville to consider contemporary fiction, not obviously set in the present moment, as sufficiently contemporary also alludes to an ultimate difference between past and present, undermining any connection.

Time, Memory, and the Body

Gilles Deleuze, following Henri Bergson, challenges the idea of time as a succession of moments, and conceives of the relations between temporalities as a type of coexistence (Deleuze, 1994). Alia Al-Saji describes Bergson's philosophy as follows: 'past and present are no longer located on the same line, but constitute different planes of being, related and articulated in coexistence' (Al-Saji, 2004, 208). Seeing the present as a succession of now-moments does not account adequately for the passage of time and implies that 'the past is merely a present that has passed and the future is a present which is anticipated and prefigured in the now' (Al-Saji, 2004, 205). This belies the radical difference and unknown nature of futurity as well as the intertwined and parallel nature of past-present relations. For Deleuze, the notions of past and present must be established simultaneously as each is inherently implicated in the other:

> If a new present is required for the past to be constituted as past, then the former present would never pass and the new one never arrive. No present would ever pass were it not past 'at the same time' as it is present; no past would ever be constituted unless it were first constituted 'at the same time' as it was present. (Deleuze, 1994, 81)

Thus, the past is part of the present and the present is simultaneously created as past.

Al-Saji's reading of configurations of time in Bergson and Deleuze argues that this non-linear, non-chronological relationship of coexistence between the different planes of temporality (past and present) both creates a possibility for futurity that is not prescribed or proscribed by the present and also 'permits an innovative and differentiated role for memory in the lives of subjects and in relations of intersubjectivity' (Al-Saji, 2004, 203). Al-Saji argues that memory, or how we perceive the past, is related to Bergson's analysis of representation or perception as functioning by selection; that is, when we perceive an object we are in effect selecting its boundaries and differentiating it in relation to what surrounds it, which then becomes its background (Al-Saji, 2004, 219). Al-Saji argues that this is also the case with memory and that consciousness selects the elements of the past/memory that sustain a coherent notion of self:

> consciousness attempts to impose coherence and univocity on the fluid and fragmented whole of pure memory – by closing off other histories and forms of remembering, by silencing other affective configurations of the past, that could trouble or undermine my own. (228)

If time is considered in a Deleuzian sense then the occluded elements of the past or memory can be engaged with, which will then trouble accepted presents and open up radically different and unknown futures that are not prescribed or restricted by the present. In an article concerned with the possibilities of encountering the past or of bearing witness to the past, Allan Stoekl arrives at the conclusion that Deleuze's configuration of temporality possesses the potential to disrupt to the point of undermining identity:

> Deleuze forces us to confront the question of transgression: the space of memory is [. . .] one that entails the sacrilegious and involuntary shock of a confrontation with a fragmentary, obscene past. We [. . .] are fragmentary signs, viewpoints confronting other viewpoints, shards in conflict and contiguity with other signs, other shards, other closed vessels of the past [. . .] And this contact is a shock, the force of truth that tears the interpreter from him or herself, fragmenting the intelligence even more. (Stoekl, 1998, 81)

Al-Saji notes that what governs perception for Bergson is that the selection process is made from a particular perspective and for us, this is our body. If this is the case, it could be argued that the morphology of the body inflects the way that we construct our histories and memories. Enright, McCann, and Ní Dhuibhne all challenge linear models of temporality in their fiction, highlighting complex interrelations between past and present through a privileging of memory that is material in its concerns and manifestations. Memory is shown to inhere in and through the body.

Given Haverty's incisive analysis of prevalent Celtic Tiger attitudes to history and memory in *The Free and Easy*, the novel serves as a pertinent case study as it raises many of the concerns central to this book, such as the effects of social, economic, and cultural change on attitudes towards the past, constructions of Irishness, and embodied identity. The plot concerns the arrival of American, Tom Blessman, to Ireland, sent there by his great-uncle, Prender Gast, a self-made businessman, who had left Ireland as a child, changed his name, and made his fortune in America. Gast begins to have dreams: 'He had seen a vision of the old country. The people were calling out to him. Wan, gaunt, but in spite of this strangely beautiful, they were appealing to him, beseeching him' (4). Gast is haunted by this famine-era vision, which affects his health and his ability to eat. He begins to believe that the people of Ireland are in trouble, and decides to send Tom to Ireland to remedy the situation, appealing to Tom's lack of knowledge about his dead mother: 'These are her people, Tom' (17). Tom arrives in Ireland at the height of the boom, to a Dublin that is full of opulent bars and restaurants, expensive cars, and luxurious parties, 'sleek, well nourished and happy people. Any perceptible gauntness, any trace of pallor, was clearly due not to hunger but to the low-fat regimes and gymwork of the western urban dweller' (64). It is a far remove from Gast's vision. Unable to find the starving and imploring people of this dream, Tom encounters former politician Etchen MacAnar, who believes that a spiritual hunger afflicts Celtic Tiger Ireland. Tom also befriends the Kinnane family who consist of varying types of Celtic Tiger subject and, therefore, attitudes towards history, identity, and Irishness: Eimear, for example, works in 'heritage management', concerned with 'the preservation, and when necessary the re-invention, of Old Ireland' producing 'seos' (pronounced 'shows'), one of which, central to the novel, is a re-enactment of the famine (87, 94). The famine, indeed, haunts this novel, which chronicles the heady consumption of the Celtic Tiger years. Etchen MacAnar is one of Eimear's heroes and she sees herself as 'an enabler [. . .] a conduit for the rich culture that lay buried in the psyches of the people' (95). Etchen and Eimear's positions on the past are invested in appeals to authenticity's 'value as marker of what is Irish', in Colin Graham's terms, who continues, 'Authenticity's ability to coexist with the market has not only enabled it to survive after colonisation but has allowed it to become, in some circumstances, as [Gareth] Griffiths says, a "mythologised and fetished sign"' (Graham, 2001, 144). This appeal to perceived authenticity is shown to have currency in the novel, and the notion of 'authenticity' is deconstructed by Haverty, but also by Enright, McCann, and Ní Dhuibhne, all of whose work queries assumptions of authentic Irishness and explores the mechanisms by which such 'Irishness' is produced and maintained. Indeed, such concerns are central to the work of recent Irish writer, Claire Kilroy, whose novels *All Summer* (2003), *Tenderwire* (2006), and *All Names*

Have Been Changed (2009), grapple with the relationships between authenticity, memory, and identity.

The following description of the Kinnane's Sunday dinner sums up the main positions taken by the characters towards the new Ireland:

> The very terms in which it [Sunday dinner] was referred to had divisive potential, an indication of the tensions of aspiration, culture and generation within the family. To Nina and her husband Willie [the parents], 'dinner' was any meal in which cooked protein, vegetables and preferably potatoes was the central dish. But to Dol [who embraces the affluent modernity of the Celtic Tiger] any dish eaten in the afternoon was strictly 'lunch'. And forget meat and potatoes – some ethnic combination from far-off lands consumed in a bleached-out café with plenteous white wine was Dol's idea of a good lunch. Eimear on the other hand was stern in her use of 'dinner'; not however as a gesture of solidarity with her parents as individuals but in homage to the traditions they unconsciously if haphazardly embodied. (84)

As seen here, consumption is the idiom of the novel and food is the medium through which cultural assumptions and socio-economic attitudes are expressed. Mobile phones are 'tinselly as wrapped sweets' and people look 'hungrily' at them (92, 97). Haverty parodies both the giddy consumption of the boom and the desire to retrieve some kind of authentic Irishness; this too is expressed in culinary terms and shown to be implicated in consumerism. Eimear, attempting to recreate her grandmother's jam making, imports raspberries from the southern hemisphere at enormous expense (97). Her favourite restaurant, the Braised Shamrock, modelled on a cottier's house from the early years of the twentieth century, offers authenticity on a plate, literally consumable, though Eimear is disappointed by their custard: 'The eggs are real. It's not authentic. Should be Bird's Instant' (109). Eimear's appeals to authenticity are shown to be inextricably bound up in the marketplace and her markers of the authentic are themselves a simulation. Tom and Etchen's collaborative project, PAIT, the Association for the Preservation of the Irish Traveller, is also shown to be invested in problematic assumptions. As Nainsí Houston notes, 'PAIT is based on the assumption that Traveller culture should not be allowed to evolve along with the rest of Ireland' (Houston, 2007, 15). MacAnar is later exposed as guilty of the 'misappropriation of funds [. . .] belonging to a charity [. . .] devoted to the restoration of patriotic monuments' (268). Haverty's novel highlights the dominant attitudes toward the past in Celtic Tiger Ireland, a jettisoning of the past in the name of progress as well as an obsessive commodifiction of Ireland's history. In the novel, Celtic Tiger Ireland is shown to be eating itself, ingesting consumable portions of 'Irishness' to feed its own self-image. This consumption is also shown to be gendered in the novel, for example, when Eimear explicitly connects food with the figure of the mother. I will come back to the significance of the gendering below. These dominant paradigms of commodification and/or erasure of the past are taken to task in the work of Enright, McCann, and Ní Dhuibhne, who complicate past-present relations and explore the materiality of memory that inheres in the body.

Gender and the Celtic Tiger

Although Haverty's novel, *The Free and Easy*, shows a clear engagement with the Celtic Tiger moment, the critics, Gough especially, seem to particularly ignore the output of contemporary Irish women writers in their analyses – an omission that Ní Dhuibhne was quick to point out in a letter to the *Irish Times*, incisively undermining such dismissals of contemporary Irish fiction:

> The recent spate of complaints about the reluctance of Irish fiction writers to bear witness to contemporary life in our native land prompted me to take five minutes off from my busy post-Celtic Tiger day and pay a visit to my bookshelves. There, to my great surprise, I found these recent novels, all dealing in whole or in part with modern Ireland in its various manifestations pre-Celtic Tiger, Celtic Tiger, post-Celtic Tiger: Nuala O'Faolain, *Almost There*; Mary Rose Callaghan, *Billy Come Home*; Lia Mills, *Nothing Simple*; Catherine Dunne, *Set In Stone*; Jennifer Johnston, *Truth or Fiction*; Claire Kilroy, *Only the Names Have Been Changed* [sic]. Several of my own books, which modesty prevents me from naming, could be added to the list. [. . .] Maybe that's what the fuss is about? Not enough men – famous men – have written fiction dealing with contemporary Ireland? Well then. But of course. Good fiction about contemporary Ireland does not exist. QED. (Ní Dhuibhne, 2010)

Coughlan too had earlier commented on the failure of these types of criticisms to take women's writing into account and mentions Enright, Ní Dhuibhne, Haverty, and Mary Morrissy as novelists who engage specifically with the social change of contemporary Ireland (2004, 178–80). The anxiety surrounding the state of contemporary Irish fiction highlights a sense of uneasiness with Ireland's contemporary Celtic Tiger climate, an Ireland that, for O'Toole, does not offer a 'distinctive sense of place' and also lacks 'the very notion of a national narrative' (O'Toole, 2001). Indeed, much contemporary writing by Irish women challenges exclusionary constructions of Irishness and hegemonic narratives of Irish history, both underpinned by a sense of place that is conservatively bound up with representations of the female body as land. Thus, it is not surprising that such fiction does not register for these critics.

Oppositions to the 'progressivism', which aims to locate and secure the past and force it to yield specific meanings, begin to make these conservative motivations explicit and to conceive of the relationship between the past and present in a more unstable and flexible manner. The past in much of the fiction by Enright, Ní Dhuibhne, and McCann is allowed to retain its otherness and to remain strange; in other words, it is thought of as active and fluid rather than as the frozen moments that are essential to the approaches outlined above. In such a way, the past can remain open to rethinking and revision; we can begin to conceive of the past differently allowing it to be radical to itself. Challenges to dominant paradigms of history are beginning to mount opposition to conceptions of the past as self-contained, not least in projects such as volumes four and five of *The Field Day Anthology of Irish Writing*, and the *Dictionary of Munster Women Writers 1800– 2000*, which challenge conceptions of Irish literary history and highlight genealogies of women's writing. Margaret Kelleher describes such projects as *The Field Day Anthology* volumes four and five as a 'self-conscious questioning of "received versions" of literary history, of cultural influence, and of the Irish writing tradition(s)' (Kelleher, 2003, 89). In other words, these projects aim for a rethinking of the processes by which Irish literary history is constructed, particularly in terms of histories of women's writing. As well as such retrieval projects, the relationships between past and present also need to be interrogated. Rather than conceived of as linear and successive, the relationships between temporalities need to be thought of more in terms of parallels and intertwinings. Anne Fogarty highlights Ní Dhuibhne in particular as a writer to whom the aforementioned 'historical amnesia' is anathema:

> she explores the gaps between decades of the late twentieth century that appear to be contiguous and shows how the tensions between competing timeframes and value systems are at the basis of the moral and emotional dilemmas of her characters. (2003, xii)

This interest in relations of temporality that complicate a linear paradigm is one that is also pertinent to the work of Enright and McCann, both of whom emphasize in their writing the importance of engaging with the past.

Enright, McCann, and Ní Dhuibhne produce varying configurations of the body in order to negotiate and generate questions surrounding gendered and intergenerational relations, particularly female genealogies. As previously stated, their work asks how the body and its configurations matter. The body has been a particular focus for Irish feminist critics due to the sustained historical use of the allegorical female body as a representative of the country and nation. Catherine Nash, who works in the field of Human Geography, has published numerous articles tracing this embodiment of Ireland, while also focusing on contemporary artists such as Kathy Prendergast who parody and uproot these traditional associations (Nash; 1993, 1994, 1997). Her article, 'Embodied Irishness', offers a succinct history of the various ways in which Ireland has been symbolized as female: the pre-Christian sovereignty goddess; the early-modern depiction of Ireland as a wanton, sexualized woman who must be penetrated and controlled by the colonizing British; the eighteenth-century allegorical *spéir bhean* imploring the heroic male to rescue her; the desexualized mother figure calling her sons to battle and self-sacrifice; and intersections with the cult of the Virgin Mary (Nash, 1997, 112–6). She notes that each female allegory was defined through her relationships with men and her place within the enshrined reproductive family and recent debate has reflected this: 'For more than a decade, the reproductive and sexual body has been the subject of vigorous and divisive moral and religious debate' (Nash, 1997, 116).

The body, particularly bodies different from the white male heterosexual norm, became subject to repressive ideologies that resulted from the combination of discourses deriving from Catholic attitudes towards the corporeal and a post-colonialist mindset interested in establishing and maintaining an independent nation. The latter concern with the nation resulted in emphases on borders and ideas of purity which became focused on issues relating to the corporeal, particularly in terms of the family and the reproductive body. The 1937 Constitution sanctified the institution of the family and the mother's place within it and much feminist criticism has been focused on the persistent re-inscriptions of such allegories and the implications of these ideologies and legislations on the lived experience of womanhood in Ireland.[4] As Claire Connolly notes in her introduction to *Theorizing Ireland*:

> Contemporary work by women writers, critics, painters and sculptors turns again and again to the interrelation between body and land, seeking to make sense, perhaps, of the embodied nature of citizenship and subjecthood. (Connolly, 2003a, 3)

Irish feminism, then, has been involved in a continued effort to question and subvert such traditional associations between body and woman, woman and land.

In her article 'Fetal Ireland,' Kathryn Conrad looks at abortion debates in the 1980s and 1990s in Ireland and argues that in relation to such debates '[w]omen's bodies [. . .] are battlegrounds' (Conrad, 2001, 153). She points out the similarity between the 'rhetorical construction of Ireland and the rhetorical construction of the fetus', which results in the 'discursively obscured link between the "private" choices of women and the "public" interests of the Irish Nation/State' (Conrad, 2001, 154). Debates about reproduction became inscribed with notions of nationality and Irishness, as anti-abortion rhetoric defined Ireland against the morality of Europe. Furthermore, Conrad suggests that the 'concern over "encroaching moral decadence" [from Europe] masked a concern about Ireland's seeming inability to keep its population intact and within its borders' (Conrad, 2001, 155). When the boundaries of the Irish body politic are at stake, a concomitant anxiety becomes focused on the reproductive female body. As such, the Irish Constitution firmly places women within the domestic space and uses the terms woman and mother interchangeably (Conrad, 2001; Riddick, 1990). This wording highlights the crucial space that the Irish mother occupies, subject to regulation and 'protection' in order to secure the reproduction of 'the Irish national subject' (Conrad, 2001, 158–9). Haverty, in *The Free and Easy*, also points to the mother's function to represent the traditional, the past, the 'authentically' Irish, expressed (typically for the novel) through food:

> With food, she [Eimear] went on, one has the same relationship as one has with one's mother. To adopt foreign cuisines, as the Irish had done en masse, symbolised the rejection of the mother, 'And what is the mother, symbolically speaking?' she demanded. She held up a professorial forefinger. 'All that is of value to us, our culture, our history, our traditions.' (Haverty, 2007, 108)

The mother is akin to food for the Irish people, an object to be consumed; representative of ideas of 'authenticity' the mother nourishes particular notions of Irishness. Enright also expresses this trope in *The Pleasure of Eliza Lynch*, which I will come back to in Chapter 4.

Most recently, the regulation of the mother to protect the 'ideal' Irish subject manifested in widespread xenophobia surrounding increased immigration into Ireland and the 2004 Citizenship referendum, which pivoted on the perceived threat of an influx of pregnant African women who would achieve citizenship once their children were born in Ireland. Such hysteria revealed the extent of racism prevalent in the supposedly 'multicultural' Celtic Tiger Ireland, focalized through the body of the pregnant woman, and disclosing the exclusionary conception of the Irish subject, defined along ethnic and racial terms. As Moynagh Sullivan commented, the figure of the mother in such discourse must be regulated in order to ensure the purity and integrity of the national body:

> The unborn child so vehemently protected in 1983 now finds itself in 2004 without the same champions, whose concerns are revealed as more about the quarantining of the National Body, than about the inherent value of all life. The mother who could not be trusted to deliver her child in 1983 is now under suspicion because she is *all too likely* to deliver her child and in doing so obstruct the safe delivery of a pre-1916 Irish Nation unmodified by difference. (Sullivan, 2005, 462)

Such concerns resonate throughout the work of Enright, McCann, and Ní Dhuibhne who, in different ways, all grapple with the issue of the maternal body and the relationships between mother and child, and between the mother and national space. McCann's fiction, particularly, challenges and complicates constructions of the national subject based on ethnic and racial exclusions. Enright, in *The Pleasure of Eliza Lynch*, puts a migrant pregnant woman at the centre of the narrative. In these interventions, McCann and Enright engage with an emerging group of writers who share a concern with Ireland's racial dynamics and intersections between race, ethnicity, and Irishness. Roddy Doyle was identified by Maureen Reddy in 2005 as 'the only well-known Irish writer trying to reach a broad audience with fiction that focuses on the changing Irish racial context and whose aim is to impact the developing racial discourse in Ireland' due to his short stories for *Metro Eireann*, a newspaper self-described as 'Ireland's only multicultural weekly' (Reddy, 2005, 387). Reddy is, however, also incisively critical about the ways in which his writing can, at times, reinforce white Irish dominance over representation and racial discourse. However, there are a growing number of immigrant writers tackling these issues, such as playwright and theatre-founder Bisi Adigun, who worked with Roddy Doyle on a reimagining of Synge's *Playboy of the Western World* (Adigun and Roddy Doyle, 2007), the Women Writers of the New Ireland Network, and the poets included in the recent anthology, *Landing Places: Immigrant Poets in Ireland* (2010), edited by Eva Bourke and Bórbala Faragó. Critical work has also been undertaken on the extent to which Irishness becomes a metonym for whiteness and/or authenticity in much popular culture and discourses of nationality (Chan, 2006; Meaney, 2010; Negra, 2006; 2007). Publications such as *Facing the Other: Interdisciplinary Essays on Race, Gender and Social Justice in Contemporary Ireland* (2008), edited by Bórbala Faragó and Moynagh Sullivan, provide interdisciplinary and sustained critical considerations of the 'Other' in contemporary Irish society.

These issues relating to sexuality, gender roles, the conflict between history and memory, and constructions of identity find a potent gathering point in the trope of the family and indeed, representations of the family, and the complex bonds that constitute it, are major themes that reemerge in contemporary Irish fiction. For Eve Patten and Gerardine Meaney, families in fiction by writers such as Jennifer Johnston, Colm Tóibín, John McGahern, Dermot Bolger, Mary Morrissy, and Lia Mills function as allegories of the state of the nation (Meaney, 2010; Patten, 2006). Meaney writes that, '[i]n Irish fiction [. . .] the domestic and familial are vortices of economic and political forces, philosophical and psychological intensities' (Meaney, 2010, xi). For Fogarty, it is through the 'shifting and troubled understandings of the self, of the child, of the home, of mother-daughter relations, and of transgenerational bonds' that concerns relating to economic and social change in Ireland most pointedly emerge (Fogarty, 2000, 62). One example is Lia Mills's *Another Alice* (1996), in which the protagonist is unable to develop a coherent identity due to the repressed memories of her father's sexual abuse. For Patten, this instability of self in the novel mirrors the nation's condition (2006, 268), and indeed the revelations concerning the Magdalene laundries, and the systematic institutional and clerical child abuse detailed by the Ryan Report of 2009 have illustrated the profound repressions enacted on bodies in order for the Irish state to function. Meaney likens the reactions of the public to these horrors as an uncanny return of the repressed:

> The terrible seeping sense of horror with which many in Ireland responded to the revelation of the systemic nature of the physical, emotional and sexual abuse and economic exploitation of children in 'care'

and of women unfortunate enough to be caught in the Magdalene laundry system has been deepened by the uncanny sense that this story was already known. (Meaney, 2010, xv)

Meaney continues by pointedly asking us to connect past and present and to identify the troubling lines of continuity which highlight 'what that [Irish] state and its dominant church were capable of perpetrating' (Meaney, 2010, xv). This last point is extremely important and is a framework for the types of analyses I undertake in the course of this book. The writers, Enright, McCann, and Ní Dhuibhne, all explore and question the dominant narratives that served to support the Irish state, particularly in relation to questions of genealogies and generations (maternal and otherwise), occluded histories, and the material bodies that are affected by such repressions.

The representation of mother-daughter relations, in particular, highlights the conjunction of issues relating to history, literary and otherwise, with gender politics. For Fogarty,

A predominantly patriarchal view of culture has relegated women's writing to the margins, rendering it almost invisible, and concerned itself solely with tracing lines of continuity between male artists. The cathexis of mother and daughter is, hence, in the first instance, an unwritten story in Ireland because it is largely uncharted, hidden in the obscured domain of women's fiction. (Fogarty, 2002, 85)

Sullivan argues, after Luce Irigaray, that the bodily connection to the maternal is one that is prohibited in representation: 'everyone has been carried by a womb, and this is the only experience shared universally by human beings: it is indeed the only universal that can be asserted, and is the very one that Western rationalism sought to deny' (Sullivan, 2005, 460). Irigaray argues that all knowledge production is underpinned and inherently influenced and produced by corporeality. In Western culture and philosophy the point of reference has been masculine and phallocentric, thus effacing the importance of the maternal body, resulting, in fact, in a symbolic matricide. For Irigaray, the concept of woman is the condition for and foundation upon which Western philosophy is based:

The culture, the language, the imaginary and the mythology in which we live at the moment [. . .] let's see what ground it is built on. [. . .] The substratum is the woman who reproduces the social order, who is made this order's infrastructure: the whole of our western culture is based upon the murder of the mother. (Irigaray, 1991c, 47)

Furthermore, this idea of the female is the maternal. The body of the woman is the unacknowledged ground upon which Western philosophy and formations of the subject are built. In psychoanalysis, separation from the mother's body is the condition upon which subjectivity is structured. Given the positioning of woman as foundation, combined with her lack of place within a morphologically male philosophical tradition, women meta-phorically and literally possess a fraught relationship to space: 'She is never here and now because it is she who sets up that eternal elsewhere from which the "subject" continues to draw his reserves, his re-sources, though without being able to recognize them/her' (Irigaray, 1985a, 227). The woman's positioning, which nurtures and reinforces constructions of the subject as whole, unified, and coherent, results in a need to contain and restrict female movement by confinement to the home or to a status as guarantor of the future of the nation in Irish culture. To break up such ontologies, what is required is a 'movement of revolt and refusal, a desire for/of the living mother who would be more than a reproductive body in the pay of the polis' (Irigaray, 1991c, 47).

Irigaray also argues that there is inadequate representation for the mother-daughter relationship due to the sole concentration on woman as mother. The connection between mothers and daughters is under-symbolized and therefore does not offer women the facility to negotiate this relation in positive and potential terms. Because of this lack of sym-bolization, a maternal genealogy is invisible; as Margaret Whitford argues, 'the major and most significant absence in the symbolic' is that of 'repre-sentations of a maternal line or genealogy' (Whitford, 1991, 76). This results in a 'difference in generations, or in relationship to generation' for women which also creates a troubled connection to temporality (Irigaray, 1985a, 110). As Irigaray argues, 'woman lives out the painful or impossible experience of being cut off from or in *time*' because she replaces the mother's body rather than maintaining a temporal connection with the mother (Irigaray, 2004a, 55). These erasures of the maternal body and the mother-daughter connection do not remain obscured in culture, however. As Irigaray argues, the ways in which masculine subjectivity is achieved through the separation from and complete erasure of the maternal body, entail an erasure which returns to haunt: 'once the man-god-father kills the mother so as to take power, he is assailed by ghosts and anxieties' (Irigaray, 1991c, 49).

Contemporary Irish writing, particularly that of Enright, McCann, and Ní Dhuibhne, abounds in hauntings, silences that become faintly audible, and non-linear temporalities, and I will return to this theme in the course of the book. Patten describes the predominant stylistic mode of contemporary Irish fiction as employing a 'neo-Gothic idiom' (Patten, 2006, 259). Fogarty too, in her analyses of late-twentieth-century Irish women novelists, identifies the Gothic mode as dominant, particularly pertinent for uneasy family relations, haunted domestic spaces, and unstable iterations of the self that recur throughout the fiction (Fogarty, 2002). These 'hauntings' tend to circulate around the figure of the mother in much contemporary Irish fiction, particularly in the work of Enright, Ní Dhuibhne, and McCann, highlighting the problematic place she holds in Irish culture.

Enright, Ní Dhuibhne, and McCann, who have all published around the turn of the twenty-first century, are writing through the rapid changes affecting Irish culture and economics, yet they look to complicate past-present relations in order to open up the future. Their work engages with the symbols and mechanisms through which the past is constructed and they interrogate the occlusions and silences produced by such constructions, particularly in relation to configurations of the body. As the body has traditionally been associated with 'woman' and as 'woman', it is useful to interrogate conceptions of corporeality and history in conjunction, particularly when the female body has been used to support discourses of nationalism and of Irish Studies itself (see Sullivan, 2000). Enright and Ní Dhuibhne, in their writing, explore and question historiographical practices as well as personal and cultural memory. McCann is also interesting in this context as his work provides similar interrogations of the relationships between past and present and their impact on configurations of the body. His writing focuses particularly on the male body and foregrounds corporeality as a concern for the male writer. My analyses of his novels also focus on the ways in which his narratives highlight the moments at which female corporeality becomes occluded.

Thus, this book intersects with feminist interrogations of past-present relations and constructions of particular histories to ask how conceptions of the body contribute to and are intertwined with such discourses. It explores both male and female bodies, and male and female writers, but seeks particularly to question the relationship between configurations of corporeality and historiography from a gendered perspective. These novelists explore the processes by which particular bodies and particular histories become occluded. They share a concern in their writing to rethink both the past and corporeality as no longer static, motionless, and supportive; all categories with which the feminine has been associated. They move away from paradigms that privilege wholeness and coherence as opposed to lack and chaos to refigure the relationships between past and present, between generations, and between embodied selves.

Bodies

The concept of the body often suffers from linguistic and symbolic 'representations' that configure it as coherent, whole, and possessing definite and stable boundaries. In response to an article in the *Sunday Independent* on 22 October 2000 by Mary Ellen Synon attacking the Paralympics, Terence Killeen identified this 'issue of bodily integrity – the idea of unmarred physical wholeness'. He notes that 'anything other than that wholeness is seen as threatening and dangerous' and that the body 'is the particular site for fantasies of wholeness, completion and totality' (Killeen, 2000). Diana Fuss contends in her introduction to *Inside/Out* that 'limits, margins, borders, and boundaries' form the basis of the symbolic order, and that identity, as constructed within this matrix of meaning and symbolization, 'is founded relationally, constituted in reference to an exterior or outside that defines the subject's own interior boundaries and corporeal surfaces' (Fuss, 1992, 2). The body within this symbolic order becomes an important, if not a foundational, site of the production of meaning.

Such universal notions assume the body to be white, heterosexual, and male. For example, the female body is often construed in terms of lack, as Jacques Lacan argues, or as something excessive, too fleshy, and dangerous. The legitimated body remains unmarked, yet it is this body that goes-without-saying which forms the norm against which all alternate bodies are measured. In this way these 'other' bodies are marked by their difference, written into a dialectic that erases its own construction. The white, male, heterosexual body is encoded as natural, allied with a liberal humanist concept of the subject, privileging the mind and reason. Conversely, it must be noted that the prerequisite for an alliance with reason and the mind is the possession of a particular type of body.

Lacan's account of the Mirror Stage charts a certain trajectory of human development which may account for the cultural and psychological association between the body, unity, and coherence. According to Lacan, this stage occurs between the ages of 6 to 18 months, when the child, prior to the acquisition of language, 'still stuck in his motor incapacity and nursling dependence', first encounters the mirror image of his/her own body (this does not necessarily have to be a mirror image, it may be, in fact, another child) (Lacan, 2001, 2). This exterior body image, which appears unified in contrast to the child's own lack of corporeal control, is identified with by the child and allows the illusion of mastery.

The Mirror Stage, then, is an identification with an 'Ideal-I'; the image provides a 'contrast with the turbulent movements that the subject feels are animating him' (Lacan, 2001, 3). However, it must be an illusory identification. The control anticipated by the reflection will always be delayed and 'will only rejoin the coming-into-being (*le devenir*) of the subject asymptotically, whatever the success of the dialectical syntheses by which he must resolve as *I* his discordance with his own reality' (3). This recognition indicates a dialectic which, on the one hand, mobilizes the recognition of a unified self, while simultaneously signalling 'its alienating destination', the absence that opens up between the subject and his/her 'Ideal-I' (3). This recognition, then, is always a misrecognition, 'the *méconnaissances* that constitute the ego, the illusion of autonomy to which it entrusts itself' (7). Since this misrecognition occurs at a stage in which the motor control of the human organism is at odds with the identified image, this discord produces the anxiety of the fragmented body, a fear that the autonomous image in the mirror will disintegrate. The anxiety allows for the (mis)recognition of the Mirror Stage to occur, which results, as Lacan writes, in 'the assumption of the armour of an alienating identity' (5). Thus, the human subject simultaneously encounters the alienating, though unified, image, and the fragmented body itself.

According to Lacan's Mirror Stage, the human organism misrecognizes the body as a coherent whole, as a place of fixed boundaries in contrast to the fragmented body and self-identity that forms the basis of the organism's experience. From an Althusserian perspective, culture interpellates us as embodied subjects, 'possessive' of, constitutive of, and constituted by a lived experience as a (misrecognized) coherent body, with legitimate, identifiable, and definite boundaries. However, as Lacan's mirror stage demonstrates, such a conception necessitates the erasure of possible anomalies, the smoothing over of the gaps and inconsistencies of the fragmented bodily experience. This, then, initiates anxieties concerning borders and creates taboos related to those points of the corporeal that mediate between the internal and external.

Contemporary theorists of the body draw upon such Lacanian propositions. Elizabeth Grosz's definition of the body in her article 'Bodies-Cities' bears a resemblance to the dialectic between the fragmented organism and the coherent cultural body image:

By 'body' I understand a concrete, material, animate organization of flesh, organs, nerves, and skeletal structure, which are given a unity, cohesiveness,

and form through the psychical and social inscription of the body's surface. The body is, so to speak, organically, biologically 'incomplete'; it is
indeterminate, amorphous, a series of uncoordinated potentialities that
require social triggering, ordering, and long-term 'administration'. (Grosz,
1999, 382)

According to Grosz the coherency and unity associated with the body are culturally ascribed and must be continuously re-inscribed and monitored in
order that 'the body becomes a human body, a body that coincides with the
"shape" and space of a psyche' (Grosz, 1999, 382). In the analyses of the novels
that follow, I look at the configurations of the body in conjunction with conceptions of temporal relations, as Enright, McCann, and Ní Dhuibhne often
trouble linear historiographies through a disturbance of coherent bodies.

My first chapter focuses on Éilís Ní Dhuibhne's novels, *The Bray House*
(1990) and *The Dancers Dancing* (1999). I argue that Ní Dhuibhne's fiction
represents a considered argument against attempts to disavow the past. *The
Bray House* takes traditional paradigms and methods of historiography to
task and reveals what becomes repressed in such models. *The Dancers Dancing* queries conventional constructions of Irishness and troubles linear narratives of history and Irish identity. The novels highlight the particular types
of corporeality that become occluded in these processes. Ní Dhuibhne continually stages the past's emergence into the present through corporeal
form and the body is shown to 'matter' when these paradigms of temporality are disrupted and unsettled.

My second chapter takes Colum McCann's earliest novels, *Songdogs* (1995)
and *This Side of Brightness* (1998), as its focus. These texts similarly attempt
negotiations between the past and the present through a particular attention to spatial politics and the body's relationship to landscape. *Songdogs*
stages these concerns through a narrative that explores a young man's
search for origins and a quest to understand his personal history. The disappearance of the mother forms the crux of the narrative dilemma and,
rather than offering conclusions or answers, the text instead reveals the
fraught relationship between the female body, the temporal, and the spatial. *This Side of Brightness* is also concerned with the attempts of a young
man to come to terms with his own history. This is staged in the novel
through a sustained exploration of the connections, symbolic and actual,
that are forged between the corporeal and its surroundings. The text
focuses on the relationship between the body and the New York subway,
which also becomes a potent means of linking generations, though this is
only formulated through the male line.

In contrast to this exclusion of the female from engagements with the landscape in *This Side of Brightness*, Anne Enright's fiction represents a critical exploration of the female body's connections to and relationships with the spatial. Thus, my third chapter provides readings in these terms of Enright's earliest novels, *The Wig My Father Wore* (1995) and *What Are You Like?* (2000). Both novels identify a troubled and pathological relationship to space that imbricates the reproductive body in the space of the domestic. These texts offer configurations of the body that approximate most closely the accounts of the corporeal put forward by feminist thinkers influenced by Deleuze and Irigaray. Enright privileges a transformative corporeality that is largely defined through the connections it makes with its surroundings as well as other bodies. Through such morphologies, her novels proffer productive models for negotiating maternal genealogies and interrelations that preserve otherness.

My fourth chapter continues this emphasis on the relationship between corporeal configurations in the novels and their relationship to paradigms of history and temporality. This chapter focuses on the fictionalized biographies written by McCann and Enright in the early years of the twenty-first century. *Dancer* (2003b), by McCann, concentrates on the life of the iconic Russian ballet dancer, Rudolf Nureyev, and *The Pleasure of Eliza Lynch* (2002), by Enright, explores the story of the eponymous Irish courtesan, who in the nineteenth century became consort to a Paraguayan dictator, Francisco Solano López. Both novels are interested in aspects of history that tend to be obscured in dominant narratives and both query the place of the body in historical discourses. Further, they consider the question, which types of corporeality are occluded in historical discourses? This chapter firstly explores the depiction of Nureyev's dancing body in *Dancer* and looks at the ways in which the descriptions of his corporeality encode concerns relating to alternate paradigms of temporality. Enright's focus is a more specifically feminist one. She considers the relationship between female embodiment and the creation of historical discourses. The novels foreground the materiality of the body and insist on a historiography that 'matters'.

My final chapter looks at the most recent novels by Enright and Ní Dhuibhne: Enright's Booker Prize winning novel, *The Gathering* (2007) and Ní Dhuibhne's *Fox, Swallow, Scarecrow* (2007). Both novels engage with their contemporary setting of Celtic Tiger Ireland and this chapter explores the tensions and occlusions that affect conceptions of the body, history, and memory in the contemporary moment. Both novels deal with questions of storytelling. *The Gathering* explores the relationship between memory, narrative, and the body, highlighting that, despite imperatives to discover familial pasts, any knowledge of the past is unreliable. Veronica, the narrator, uses the image of reassembling the bones of a skeleton for her acts of remembering and storytelling: 'his muscles hooked to bone and wrapped with fat' (14). For her story however, the flesh refuses to stay on the bones. The novel itself abounds in images of decaying and dead bodies and these images are quite indicative of the thrust of the novel as a whole – life, the body, memory, and this narrative refuse to boil down to clean white bones. The language of the body and the idea of touch are important concerns in the novel, particularly the implication of bodies coming together in terms of sex and desire as well as the question of who one can and cannot touch. Touch implies an intimacy and it is the means of negotiating this intimacy in the contemporary globalized world that is at stake in the novel. Similarly, *Fox, Swallow, Scarecrow* explores interpersonal relationships in the Celtic Tiger years, highlighting distance and isolation through a dominance of sleek bodies and glossy materials. The novel acerbically critiques the all-pervasive consumerist ethos of the boom years while also commenting on the denial of past and future prevalent in Celtic Tiger culture through its satirical focus on the contemporary Irish literary scene where literature becomes another commodity.

This book explores how these writers raise questions in their fiction concerning the ways in which our conceptions of corporeal morphology influence our models of temporal relations and historical narrative. The primary concerns of this book are the conjunctions between constructions of gender, configurations of the body, and the relationships between memory and history. The issue of maternal embodiment, its relative invisibility and continued disavowal, is crucial to my readings of the work of these authors. The relationship to the body of the mother is a concern that all three writers engage with on different levels and with varying results. Reconsiderations of maternal genealogies are shown to have important effects on the ways in which we configure the relationship between the past and the present.

Chapter 1

Submerged Histories:
Éilís Ní Dhuibhne's *The Bray House* and
The Dancers Dancing

Éilís Ní Dhuibhne has claimed that her writing is preoccupied with duality and ambiguity, especially in relation to questions of identity and Irishness (Ní Dhuibhne, 2003a, 105). Her novel, *The Bray House* (1990), explores these concerns through the creation of a post-apocalyptic world in which Ireland has been obliterated. An archaeological expedition to Ireland exposes the uncertainty that such questions elicit. *The Dancers Dancing* (1999), her second novel, articulates the problems inherent in a dualistic experience bifurcated between west and east, north and south, Irish and English cultural identities, and the gap between the past and the present. Her body of work as a whole displays an interest in crossing borders. In addition, Ní Dhuibhne is a bilingual writer who has published in the genres of short fiction, novels, drama, and children's fiction (under the pseudonym, Elizabeth O'Hara). Her collections of short stories, *Blood and Water* (1988), *Eating Women is not Recommended* (1991), *The Inland Ice and Other Stories* (1997), *The Pale Gold of Alaska and Other Stories* (2000b), and *Midwife to the Fairies: New and Selected Stories* (2003b), have been widely acclaimed for their postmodern engagement with Irish folk and fairytales. For example, Giovanna Tallone characterizes her writing as follows:

> In Ní Dhuibhne's post-modern rewriting of Irish fairytales the awareness of deploying contemporary writing strategies and narrative technique intertwines with conscious intertextuality and metanarrative construction. (Tallone, 2004, 204)

Ní Dhuibhne has also edited collections of poetry and folklore and is a qualified folklorist, having completed a PhD at University College Dublin on a traditional folktale narrative prevalent in both oral and literary versions such as Chaucer's 'The Friar's Tale' (Ní Dhuibhne, 1981). Her writing is lauded for its diversity, unpredictability, innovation and originality (Fogarty,

2003, ix–iv). It has often been noted that her fiction is concerned with drawing together past and present, integrating myth and modernity using structures, motifs, and influences from folklore, both from Irish sources and others, such as Scandinavian and Native-American (Fogarty, 2003; Hand, 2005). Ní Dhuibhne's writing is motivated by the complexities of the relationship between history and the present moment. As Fogarty writes:

> [T]he past, their [her heroines'] previous selves and the other Irelands that they have inhabited continue to haunt and configure their emotional and intellectual landscapes. (Fogarty, 2003, xiii)

Her fiction explores the points at which linear models of temporality become troubled and it is the gaps and occlusions in narratives of history that interest her most profoundly.

Ní Dhuibhne's writing also highlights the role that the body plays in these explorations of past and present relations. The corporeal and its associations are shown to underpin many of the instances of haunting or disturbances in the traditional patterns of temporality. The presence of the body is often connected to the positioning of actual female corporeality in the Irish cultural context in which the specificities of such embodiment have been occluded or mythologized. For instance, Ní Dhuibhne points out that her story, 'Eating Women is Not Recommended,' 'deals with menstruation taboos in contemporary Irish society' (Ní Dhuibhne, 1993, 254). In 'Blood and Water,' the narrator is repulsed by the intrusion of the past into the present, symbolized by her fear that her aunt may not have washed her hands correctly, the sight of her parents' bare feet at a holy well, and the butter-stained wall of her aunt's house, which 'becomes emblematic of her distress at the polluting otherness of this rural world' (Fogarty, 2003, xiii). The body in Ní Dhuibhne's fiction becomes a locus in which the disjunctions and complexities of history and the present moment are played out.

This chapter will focus on Ní Dhuibhne's two novels, *The Bray House* and *The Dancers Dancing*, in terms of their explorations of the relationships between history and the present. Both texts trouble straightforward linear models of temporality. *The Bray House* puts conventional Western paradigms of historiography under pressure through a futuristic setting in which our present becomes historical and has been subjected to a nuclear explosion. This chapter will explore the implications of this temporal dislocation by looking at Ní Dhuibhne's use of historiographical discourses, as well as her use of the apocalyptic event of the nuclear disaster. References to folklore and fairytales also serve to undermine traditional historiography in the novel and offer alternate narratives with which to negotiate the past. *The Dancers Dancing* uses similar strategies in terms of the folk- and fairytale and explores similar terrain; that is, the questioning of linear narratives of history. Both novels refuse ideas of the past as fixed and removed from the present. This chapter will explore Ní Dhuibhne's use of the body and corporeal references to mark disruptions in the chain of temporal progression.

The Bray House

Ní Dhuibhne's interest in the relations between past and present, myth and modernity, are made explicit in her first novel, *The Bray House*, published in 1990. The novel, which many have classified as science fiction (Meaney, 1992, 14; Hand, 2000, 104), delineates a futuristic world in which Ireland and England (and indeed most of the world) have been obliterated by an Irish nuclear explosion entitled the 'Ballylumford affair' or 'The Incident'. The explosion has occurred before the start of the narrative, on 22 April in an unspecified year at the beginning of the twenty-first century. Coincidently, the novel was written prior to the Chernobyl nuclear disaster, though Ní Dhuibhne notes that material relating to nuclear fallouts predominated in the media at the time of its composition.[1] She revised the novel following the Chernobyl disaster and stressed its ecological focus (Ní Dhuibhne, 1993, 252).

The novel begins in Sweden, from where Robin Lagerlöf, its chief narrator, leads a team of archaeologists, Karl, Jenny, and Karen, to excavate Ireland. The archaeologists' focus, in particular, is on the excavation of a house situated in what was once Bray, which becomes the eponymous 'Bray House'. The novel is divided into three sections, the second of which, chapters 12–15, is taken up with Robin's cataloguing of the contents and documents found in the house belonging to the MacHugh family as well as her report on these findings. Chapters 1–14 detail the journey to Ireland and the initial stages of the excavation, while chapters 16–24 relate the events that took place during the writing of The Bray House report as well as the journey home to Sweden. This final section reveals Robin's loss of control over her crew resulting in the disappearance of Karl and Jenny into the barren landscape of a nuclear-devastated Ireland. They return with a survivor whom they claim is a member of the MacHugh family, though later it is revealed that the woman's name is Maggie Byrne. The narration of these events forms a backdrop and counterpoint to the factual scientific language of the report and becomes 'a radical subversion of [Robin's] rational discourse' (Morris, 1996, 131). For Derek Hand, the conflict at the heart of *The Bray House* is one between competing texts, 'differing versions of Ireland' (Hand, 2000, 111). The novel is also concerned with the claims of competing histories and methods of history making. More particularly, it explores the relationship between such historiographies and the bodies they inscribe.

The novel is narrated in the first person by Robin, an unsympathetic, ruthless, and ambitious character whose main concern is the scientific and historic importance of the excursion as well as her own power, which she sees as intimately linked to the project. Her narrative voice is an inherently subjective, biased, and thus unreliable one, and her conclusions about the MacHugh family and twentieth-century Ireland remain questionable and tend toward stereotype, caricature, and overly prejudiced assumptions. The voyage to Ireland and the excavations of the MacHugh's house also parallel Robin's own recollections of her childhood and relationship with her mother, and the journey to uncover Ireland's past is also a voyage into Robin's memories. Giovanna Tallone comments that the interlacing of past, present, and future in the text, combined with the journey both in space and time, serve to create temporal gaps in which Robin's suppressed memories, particularly with regard to her relationship with her mother, are brought into focus: 'the nearly-completed process of excavation brings to the surface Robin's half-forgotten or never-confessed memories' (Tallone, 2008, 172). More traumatic for Robin, however, is the appearance of Maggie, the sole survivor of Ireland's nuclear disaster. The emergence of this body that arrives from the past serves to unsettle Robin's sense of historiography and temporality. Though her profession as archaeologist demands excursions into the past, she views personal excavation, whether her own or not, as 'embarrassing' and 'too private for general consumption', suggesting a degree of discomfort with her own relationship with her past (Ní Dhuibhne, 1990, 53–4). In the following instance, a reference to Robin's past and to her dead husband, Michael, also seems to elicit a similar response in her crew:

> Even in this ghost country, where everyone was dead, the idea of a particular dead individual frightened or disgusted them. Or was it the idea of the bereaved one, the one left behind, with the stigma of death clinging that put them off? (72)

This disgust that Robin identifies, whether felt by her crew or not, is a fear of the intrusion by history into the present which would trouble the linear break with the past that Western historiography requires. This is compounded by the fact that Michael's body is somewhere on this devastated Ireland; he was living there when the Ballylumford explosion occurred.

Ní Dhuibhne's *The Bray House* is a novel that confounds expectations, both in terms of the subject matter and style of Irish women's writing as well as the Irish novel itself. Gerardine Meaney, who in her review of the novel situates it as a politicized, eco-feminist novel, notes that:

> It is not in the realist mode, though its doomsday scenario is frighteningly convincing. It is not confessional, though it is a first-person narrative [...] This is not a novel where cozy identification with the female protagonist is possible. (Meaney, 1992, 14)

John Kenny (with a similar outlook to Gough and the other critics mentioned in the Introduction) sees the novel as radically different to the majority of Irish fiction in its concern with the future:

> In fictional terms, Ireland has practically no future. While we are replete with topical and historical novels, we are generally devoid of any consistent attempts at futuristic fiction, and Éilís Ní Dhuibhne's *The Bray House* (1990) remains the one serious exception to the commonplace that Irish writers are preoccupied with the past. (Kenny, 2003)

Nevertheless, although the novel possesses a futuristic setting, it is one that was temporally close to the time in which it was written and is now contemporary with our present moment. Rather than being concerned with past, present, or future, the novel instead explores the ways in which these temporal modalities are implicated in each other. As Elizabeth Grosz contends, the means by which we comprehend the past 'prefigure and contain corresponding conceptions about the present and future' (Grosz, 1998, 40). Thus, how we think about the relations between each of the temporal modalities impacts upon and configures our conception of the others:

> The ways in which we consider the past to be connected to and thus to live on through the present/future will have direct implications for whatever conceptions of futurity, the new, creativity, production or emergence we may want to develop. (Grosz, 1998, 40)

For Ní Dhuibhne then, engagements with the past and explorations of historiography produce an important means of reconfiguring the present and the future and, indeed, our understanding of the past. Using alternate temporalities to explore our own provides us with diverse lenses by which we may refocus the narratives that constitute our identity.

The Ireland that is represented in the narrative through Robin's memories is one in which present and past are closely aligned in a postmodern relationship that highlights the commodification of that history and of certain versions of Irishness. Michael, Robin's husband, who had lived near Dingle, felt 'like an exhibit in a folk museum for most of the year' (55). The Bray that the archaeologists excavate had been already steeped in nostalgia for Robin when she visited it prior to the nuclear explosion: 'Bray had been then a foxed mezzotint' (68). The novel highlights the complex simultaneity between past and present, the fact that the present moment coexists with a historical one. The novel also constantly brings into question the artificiality and constructed nature of any notion of Irish identity.

Ní Dhuibhne resists the science fiction classification that the novel has attracted, insisting instead that her creation of a dystopian landscape has more in common with similar writing by Doris Lessing and Margaret Atwood. It also, she contends, intertextually engages with such adventure stories as *Robinson Crusoe* (Ní Dhuibhne, 1993, 252). *Robinson Crusoe* is one of the books read and identified with by Robin on her voyage, (the link is also alluded to in her name). *The Bray House*'s futuristic setting is, in Ní Dhuibhne's words, 'a framework to look at contemporary Ireland, an imaginative way to look at Ireland the way it is today' (Ní Dhuibhne, 1993, 252). Rather than science fiction, Ní Dhuibhne views the novel as more akin to the fairy tale and to her interest in folklore:

> I would see *The Bray House* as a kind of fantasy; but even though it's a fantasy, it's about something real. I think a lot of fairy tales are like that – they're about unbelievable characters, but they have a deeper truth. Things seem to be fantastical and unreal, but, in fact, they are about very ordinary, real problems and people. (Ní Dhuibhne, 1993, 258)

Ní Dhuibhne's allusion to the fairy tale genre highlights her desire to keep these types of narratives in play because of their facility for drawing contiguities between various different temporal spaces. Although Carol Morris sees the novel as 'feminist generic fiction', instead of viewing it as a reworking of science fiction, she argues that the genre in question is 'that of the anti-utopian or critical utopian novel' (Morris, 1996, 127–8). Indeed, Christine St. Peter deems *The Bray House* to be a 'historiographic dystopia' (St. Peter, 1999, 153). The novel is simultaneously concerned with the present and possible ecological futures of Ireland and the world, yet it also preserves an interest in historiography through the narrative's archaeological focus. The close correlation between the text's present (the time of the narrative), its past (pre-Ballylumford Ireland), and our own, however, queries how we might think about history.

Histories and Temporalities

In her introduction to a collection of essays entitled, *Reading the Past: Literature and History*, Tamsin Spargo commented on a recent increase in publications concerning both the end of time and the meaning of the millennium, as well as an amplified interest in the chronologies of the past two thousand years (Spargo, 2000, 1). The marker in time that the millennium represented instigated a concern for the future which appeared to invite people to categorize the past.

The Bray House, published at the beginning of the last decade of the twentieth century, but set in the early years of the twenty-first century, can be situated within this tendency that Spargo identifies. Ní Dhuibhne's projection into the near future is a means of commenting on contemporary Ireland by relocating the present to the past. Before turning to the historiographical implications of the text, the 'catastrophic' premise of the novel is worth exploring as the disaster represents a marker in time similar to that of the millennium. Jean Baudrillard has remarked, speaking specifically about Pompeii, that 'the intellectual effect of the catastrophy [sic] is to stop things before they reach their end and to keep them in the eternal suspense of their perishing' (Baudrillard, 1991). In *The Bray House*, the Irish nuclear explosion has 'frozen' Ireland under a layer of ash.

Robin acknowledges the questionable historicity of the project undertaken by the archaeologists, while her definitions also encode a partial description of the catastrophe as an end point:

> Our excavation was of a kind relatively new to archaeology – indeed there are those who would deny that it was archaeological at all, since there was nothing archaic about it. My answer to that accusation is that the definition of what is archaic is entirely subjective, and that in any case with the disaster which brought about the conditions we were investigating the world had moved very abruptly into a new era, rendering the past, although in one sense it occurred only yesterday, a million years ago from another point of view [. . .] it is obvious to me that the pre-Ballylumford

world was more different from the world in which we now live than that itself was from, say, the Middle Ages. (108)

The typical structures of Western history are evident in this justification of the journey and project. Cultural historians, Michel De Certeau and Paul Ricoeur, both note that in order for traditional Western history to function, a rigid distinction between past and present must be established. Ricoeur argues that such a division is facilitated by the identification of a 'founding event, which is taken as beginning a new era', such as the birth of a religious divinity or the commencement of a monarch's reign (Ricoeur, 1988, 106). Ricoeur terms this idea of a new event 'the axial moment in reference to which every other event is dated'; it is axial because it is possible by reference to this particular moment to 'traverse time in two directions: from the past toward the present and from the present toward the past' (Ricoeur, 1988, 106). This moment forms the axis between two, now separate, temporal spheres. Robin's defence of the Irish project clearly identifies the Ballylumford incident as such an axial moment. What happened prior to the disaster is, for her, most definitely finished with, passed, and past.

De Certeau also notes that, in order for traditional Western history to function, a rigid demarcation between past and present must be established (De Certeau, 1988, 2). In order to facilitate such a breakage model of temporality, and for these divisions to be intelligible, a 'forgetting' must occur. However, whatever is 'forgotten' or deemed irrelevant:

> comes back, despite everything, on the edges of discourse or in its rifts and crannies: 'resistances', 'survivals', or delays discretely perturb the pretty order of a line of 'progress' or a system of interpretation. (De Certeau, 1988, 4)

In these terms, Robin's attempt to impose such rigid divisions between past and present must ultimately come under threat from the 'shards' left over from this initial fracturing. Such shards suggest the impossibility of any clean historical break. In fact, for her, the return of the repressed manifests itself in two forms, each implicated in the other: the survivor of Ireland's nuclear holocaust and her own excavations into her memory.

Modern Western history, exemplified for De Certeau by the work of the historian Jules Michelet, is a history of silences. History, as a discourse about dead bodies that can no longer speak for themselves, encrypts these dead voices in texts. The historical text gives space to these utterances in order to silence them: 'it aims at calming the dead who still haunt the present, and at offering them scriptural tombs' (De Certeau, 1988, 2). De Certeau describes such a method of historiography as follows:

> The violence of the body reaches the written page only through absence, through the intermediary of documents that the historian has been able to see on the sands from which a presence has since been washed away, and through a murmur that lets us hear – but from afar – the unknown immensity that seduces and menaces our knowledge. (De Certeau, 1988, 3)

This social body can only be represented in the text if it is silenced and absented. De Certeau also points to something that remains which cannot quite be grasped. This opacity, which is both beguiling and intimidating to our sense of what we can know, is what is important in history for De Certeau. As will be discussed later, Maggie, the survivor of Ireland's nuclear disaster, both represents and troubles this paradigm of historiography. Her appearance signals a threat to Robin's conclusions and registers the limits of her historical project. The presence of the corporeal is a powerful one in this text and represents the rupture of traditional models of temporality. The bodily metaphors that Ní Dhuibhne uses in the narrative also signal the disturbances in time that are at play in the novel.

The human body acts in the text as an important locus for Robin's negotiation of the world, revealing the underlying metaphors that propel the Western historiographic tradition. This includes a fear of and repulsion towards the embodiment of women:

> Oh, how I suspect women with fat behinds and thin birdlike legs! And what is it that I suspect? Their unconquerable feminine power, the strength of their wombs, wobbling in their capacious bodies, feeding their characters with irrationality. (47)

Robin's reaction to Karen, described above, provokes in her one of the several instances in the text of an involuntary recollection of her mother. Prior to this reaction, she had described her relationship with her mother in an unimpassioned manner, yet following her exchange with Karen, in which she dismisses her as 'probably just premenstrual', she dreams of her mother and cries out, 'Mother, mother. I'm drowning. Mother, tell me something . . . say it!' (47). These instances recur in the text, suggesting a trauma in the maternal genealogy that is possibly linked to the configuration of the female body or indeed of corporeality in general.

Robin employs the traditional method of gendering countries as female and endowing them with bodily features:

Bray Head, the Little Sugar Loaf, the Big Sugar Loaf, Lugnaquilla, Three Rock Mountain. [. . .] I picked them out, darker now, more solid, rising from a milky sea, the rounded haunches, the pointed breasts. The humps. Lumps. Tumours. (Ní Dhuibhne, 1990, 54)

England is also 'now a corpse, rotting, with no grave, even, to cover it' (40). Indications of the troubled relationship with the maternal occur once again when Robin views the 'rotting corpse' of England:

England reminded me of my mother.
I could not banish her from my thoughts, as we passed those bleak shores. Asleep or awake, she was in my mind, plaguing me. (41)

Memories of her mother haunt Robin. She will not remain in the past and Robin's language here denotes the invasion of the present by the past.

In this anthropomorphism of the landscape, the diseased bodies of Ireland and England are placed in a particular moment of the human life cycle's temporality; they are either dead or about to die. England's time is past, its body dead, though it still experiences change (either rotting or decomposition) in the present. While Ireland's metaphorical body remains living in the present tense, it is a body riddled with disease. It is either a body about to die or a decaying body, a corpse in which disease can be identified. Suspended between past and present, the body of Ireland could be viewed as existing on the boundaries of time and as occupying a liminal space in relation to temporality. Tallone argues that Ní Dhuibhne's fiction abounds in such spaces which are ' "almost" a place' (Tallone, 2004, 205).

The survivor of the nuclear explosion, Elinor/Maggie, 'unearthed' by Karl and Jenny, appears reminiscent of these temporally hyphenated bodies and is also crucially a female body.[2] Maggie belongs to Ireland's past, before the Ballylumford incident. However, she has crossed over this seemingly stable distinction between pre- and post-nuclear Ireland. She is described as 'more like a leper [. . .]. Sort of rotting' (223), linking her to the dead and diseased bodies of Ireland and England. What is also significant about these bodily representations is the sense that the corporeal boundaries are being broken down or altered, through decomposition or

abnormal growth or tumours. Representations of bodies that do not correspond to a healthy corporeal whole often encode or highlight anxieties
concerning structures that should remain stable. The disturbances to paradigms of linear history are represented through Maggie, an embodiment
of the past.

Fairies and Histories

In order to relate the circumstances surrounding the discovery of Maggie,
Jenny chooses the structures of the fairytale: '"Once upon a time," she said,
in a low intense tone, a story-teller's voice. "Two people called Karl and
Jenny were feeling very sad and dejected"' (218). This customary fairy-tale
opening signals a vague temporality, a time out of time. 'Once upon a time'
gestures towards a past that is always already past, that takes place long
before our own age, but that also exists outside the domain of the temporal.
For example, it is a temporality in which people can sleep for one hundred
years without ageing. As a narrative marker it signals that events out of the
ordinary will occur in a world or time that is not of our own. Robin, the narrator, challenges Jenny concerning this style: 'Must you use this style? It's
irritating, frankly, in my opinion'. However, for Jenny, 'It's this or nothing'
(219). Hand points out that Jenny's use of this particular narrative order
signals alternative modes of relating history; the folktale 'registers for the
reader that "truth" can be found in different narrative forms' (Hand, 2000,
114). Jenny's story is a direct defiance of Robin's authority and of the scientific discourse she uses to compile her report. It is a disputation of the paradigms of historiography with which Robin identifies. Furthermore, Maggie,
the subject of Jenny's fairytale, will represent in bodily form a profound
challenge to Robin's methods of knowledge production.

Karl and Jenny discover Maggie in 'a small, perfectly circular mound'
(220), which, upon further inspection, appears to resemble a passage tomb
(224). Jenny's description of Maggie identifies her as fairy-like:

[S]he looked totally inhuman, I fully believed she was a ghost, or some
kind of otherworld creature, the kind of thing you read about inhabiting
fairy mounds in Ireland. [. . .] Fairies, the Tuatha de Danainn, you know,
that sort of thing. A race of little people who have vanished into the
mounds. I mean she was so small, and thin, and green, and bald, she
looked like one of the more horrible kinds of gnomes we have in Swedish
tradition. Certainly not human. (222)

Here, Maggie is expressly affiliated with the fairies; she is mistaken for one due to her corporeal form: 'small, and thin, and green, and bald'. While she is not actually a fairy, she is linked to such creatures in ways other than her bodily appearance: namely, her connection to the past. As a survivor of Ireland's nuclear holocaust she is the sole living representative of this lost past.

Marina Warner's etymological exploration of the word 'fairy' highlights their association with temporality and with the past. She traces the word to the Latin word *fata*, a variant of *fatum*, meaning 'fate':

> The fairies resemble goddesses of this kind [fate], for they too know the course of fate. *Fatum*, literally, that which is spoken, the past participle of the verb *fari*, to speak, gives French *fée*, Italian *fata*, Spanish *hada*, all meaning 'fairy', and enclosing connotations of fate; fairies share with Sibyls knowledge of the future and the past, and in the stories which feature them, both types of figure foretell events to come, and give warning. (Warner, 1995, 15)

This etymological connection signals fairies' links to concepts of temporality. Fairies have access to both the past and the future, while also appearing in the present in order to speak of 'other times'. They both maintain and transgress the boundaries set in place by conventional breakage models of time. The connection to speech is important, and I shall consider this in more detail below.

Diane Purkiss identifies 'birth, and copulation, and death' as the specific dominion of the fairies (Purkiss, 2000, 52). For Purkiss, the fairytale is a means by which to encode anxieties concerning bodily health (Purkiss, 2000, 119). She also notes, in relation to the typical interdiction against eating fairy food that, 'once the boundaries of the body have been breached, magic can be done' (Purkiss, 2000, 112). If the integrity and health of the body come under threat, and if the unity of the corporeal is called into question fairies can be found, and with them a destabilizing of conventional temporalities. The representation of Ireland and England (and Maggie) as diseased and rotting bodies signals their breakdown in terms of the boundaries of the corporeal form. Alien elements such as tumours have invaded, or the entire structure has come under threat as the rotting indicates.

If fairy tales often function as a means of expressing fears about bodily health, what does Ní Dhuibhne's particular use of such structures encode? Maggie is continually referred to in terms of sickness and health. Prior to

Jenny's fairy tale narrative, Robin describes her as she first appears: 'emaciated, apparently bald, with wide crazed eyes staring from greenish skin' (216). Karl compares her to 'a leper' and describes her as 'rotting' (223). Within Jenny's narrative she describes Maggie as 'so horrible, so really horrible, like the daughter of Lazarus or something like that. You could smell death off her' (224). The reference to Lazarus here impacts upon her transgression of seemingly stable boundaries. The 'health' of history as a concept and practice also comes under threat. Its boundaries are endangered by the appearance and existence of Maggie.

Robin, as the embodiment of traditional Western historical practices, is physically affected by the appearance of Maggie. Her heart sinks even before she turns to look at the returning trio. When she examines Maggie through a pair of binoculars, she 'felt exhausted and passed my hand over my face, in a gesture quite exceptional for me' (216). Maggie is represented as a threat to the physical well-being of traditional historiography. Even Robin's gestures are altered by the encounter. Her hands passing over her face denote an attempt to block Maggie from sight as well as signalling her exhaustion and fear of defeat. The sight of Maggie provokes further involuntary reactions:

> A day, and we would have missed them. We would have sailed off, unburdened.
> Home.
> Home, which I have never had. Mother, mother! I cried as I watched the specks [Karl, Jenny and Maggie]. Mother, take me home! Mother, say it, Mother, just once. Say, say you love me! (216)

In the narrative, alongside the details of the journey and excavation, there is a parallel quest into, and excavation of, Robin's memory of her past. Maggie's appearance triggers Robin's emotional recall of her relationship with her mother, one that had previously been impassively described. The encounter brings to the fore, if only momentarily, anxieties and repressed feelings concerning the mother-daughter relationship, which hinge on dialogue and speech: 'Say, say you love me!' Robin requires a voice from the past, from beyond the grave (her mother had died of cancer three years previous to the time of the narrative), that will reassure her of the validity of this flawed relationship. This also implies a need for reconciliation between past and present. Such a quest ultimately fails as intimated by Robin's eventual suicide, which is prompted by the apathetic response of the general public to the Ireland project.

The use of fairy tale in this novel both normalizes and disorients. Therefore, mother-daughter and past-present relationships are impacted upon by seemingly contradictory impulses. In *The Bray House*, it appears that the issues of voice and speech lie at the centre of this area of tension. Fairies' speech, as noted above, both maintains and transgresses distinctions between past, present, and future. Robin implores her mother to speak at the very moment at which she is confronted with a threat to her conceptions of history and temporality.

The fairy tale, for Warner, is explicitly and implicitly related to notions of women's voices, women's speech, and women's history, and specifically stories that have been neglected by official versions of the past.[3] As discussed earlier, fairies are linked to past and future through their knowledge of both. Fairies speak in the present but talk of the past and of the future; they give warnings and predict future occurrences. Fairies act as a dialogic link to the past through speech. But Maggie does not uncomplicatedly conform to this function.

Fairy tales are also concerned with the inverse of the garrulous woman. They abound with figures of the mute silenced female, as is the case in tales such as 'The Little Mermaid' by Hans Christian Anderson and 'The Twelve Brothers' by the Brothers Grimm (Warner, 1995, 387–408). In Warner's analysis of silence in fairy tales she notes the association of sincerity and virtue with silence; Cordelia in *King Lear* is a paradigm of this type of silencing. Silence also serves a redemptive function. The sister's silence in the story of 'The Twelve Brothers' is imposed upon her by a wicked witch figure who also turned her brothers into birds. The maintenance of her silence at all costs, combined with a number of other difficult tasks, is required in order to free her brothers (Warner, 1995, 392–3). The Little Mermaid's silence is the price she must pay for fulfilling her desire. Interestingly, Robin resorts to Irish fairy tales in a vain attempt to extract speech from Maggie:

> I tried a technique I had learned from, of all unlikely places, an old Irish legend: the legend is about a mermaid who, like Elinor, refuses to speak to the human being who has captured her, and who has in fact married or raped her. In the end, by insulting her family, he manages to break her silence and, in order to protest against the calumny, she speaks. (232)

In such legends, which are not confined to Ireland, the sea maiden refuses or is unable to reveal either her origins or a particular prophesy. She is invariably linked with disaster and the emphasis on voice or lack thereof links her to the Sirens (Warner, 1995, 396–408).

As De Certeau argues, in the practice of historiography the allocation of speech and silence determine how past voices are encrypted in the historical text. Maggie took refuge and is found in an actual tomb that held her, the only representative of Ireland's future, and the ancient dead of Ireland's past. However, it is not long before she is once again 'entombed', in the Gothenburg Old Folk's Home where no one is interested in her story. Jenny's fairy tale insists on Maggie's silence. And it is a silence that is threatening to Robin. Her anxiety concerning Maggie's muteness is bound up with notions of power and knowledge:

> I was sure that Elinor was not dumb. Moreover, I was convinced that she had already given quantities of information to Karl and Jenny. I knew that they had silenced her, by what threats, bribes, falsehoods, I did not know. But they had done it, to keep valuable data from me. They wanted my enterprise to fail, they wanted to steal the most important facts. Ruthless, selfish, blindly ambitious, is what they were. I would not succumb to their power. (229)

Furthermore, Maggie's silence, in which Karl and Jenny are complicit, emerges as a way to challenge Robin, who is herself ruthless,[4] selfish, and blindly ambitious. Warner has noted the power silence possesses in fairy tales: 'fairy tales give women a place from which to speak, but they sometimes speak of speechlessness as a weapon of last resort'. Silence can then be 'another stratagem of influence' (Warner, 1995, xxi).

When Maggie does eventually speak, we as readers have access to her story only through Robin's narration, which renders it almost irrelevant: 'Apart from her story, which was of course fascinating in its way, I did not record very much from Maggie at this point' (247). Maggie's tale proves of little interest to her as it cannot definitively prove that Robin is 'the world's most perceptive archaeo-anthropologist!' (248). Jenny notices that Robin's own version of history is more important to her than any living proof would have been. In fact, Robin believes that her methodology will generate historical 'truth', regardless of what may have actually happened: 'The story I'll write is the true story of the MacHughs. Even if a MacHugh came along and suggested otherwise, I would believe that. The MacHugh would be wrong' (248). Morris compares Robin's desire to enforce Maggie's speech to that of colonization: 'appropriation of the story and the language is a necessary colonising act' (Morris, 1996, 138). Yet, Maggie's presence highlights the limitations of such a colonization and raises questions concerning the extent to which one can 'know' the past. In an exchange with Robin in which she claims importance for their project because 'when there's nobody telling the story . . . that's when archaeologists need to step in', Jenny recognizes the uncertainty of ever ascertaining the truth: 'That seems to mean that nobody ever knows whether what they discover is worth a fig or not' (249). Robin is forced to agree. For the reader, these questions are brought into focus through the juxtaposition of Robin's report, her conclusions, and a familiarity with present-day Ireland.[5]

Apocalypse

It is significant that such questions are raised in a novel concerning a post-apocalyptic Ireland. The term 'apocalypse' originates from the Greek translation of the Hebrew 'gala', which denotes 'unveiling' (Jay, 1993b, 84). For Derrida, this is specifically connected to ideas of truth: '[a]pocalypse means Revelation, of Truth, *Un-veiling*' (Derrida, 1984, 24). But, the apocalypse in much nuclear-centred theory is also posited as something that cannot be known or represented. In *The Bray House*, the nuclear explosion serves to cover Ireland in a layer of ash and Ireland has been, in Baudrillard's words, kept 'in the eternal suspense of [its] perishing' (Baudrillard, 1991). Hand has noted that when excavated and catalogued by Robin, the 'Bray House' becomes representative of this buried Ireland, and Robin's conclusions merely serve to reproduce 'various stereotypes and caricatures of Ireland and Irishness' (Hand, 2000, 111). An unproblematized access to the past through texts is negated by Robin's conjectural and absurd conclusions. The 'unveiling' and 'uncovering' of Ireland's past (and indeed present) is rendered complex. According to De Certeau, historians must always be aware of a historical sublime, something that eludes representation, 'the 'other' that moves and misleads' (De Certeau, 1988, 14).

Maggie's appearance, initial silence, and discounted story query the practices of history, as well as formulating concerns regarding any fixed conceptualization of Ireland and Irishness. The novel asks us to remain aware that any attempt to represent the past, or to insist on unchanging categories, will involve something 'forgotten' that will inevitably return to haunt. For Robin, this revenant from the past is embodied in the figure of Maggie. What is shown to be at stake in the disturbance that she elicits in Robin's scientific methodology is the revelation of an erasure of the mother. The type of Western historiography that Robin represents is shown to rely on such a suppression of the maternal. She has succeeded in her field through a dis-identification with her mother and her past. Ní Dhuibhne, in *The Bray House*, places in clear

focus the trauma that underlies such paradigms of history. The novel complicates our notions of the relationship between past and present in ways that
open them out for reinterpretation and refiguration. *The Bray House* asks us
to remain aware of our approaches to questions of history and to the particular bodies that may be inscribed and/or occluded by particular ways of talking about the past. For Ní Dhuibhne the bodies that may be obscured by
certain narratives of history inevitably return to haunt the present or future.
Ní Dhuibhne's second novel, *The Dancers Dancing*, engages with similar concerns of history and temporality, particularly in relation to the 'shards' of the
past that haunt the present and that trouble lines of progress.

The Dancers Dancing

The Dancers Dancing, published in 1999 at the cusp of a new millennium,
concerns a group of girls at a transitional stage of their lives and their
experience of Irish College in Donegal. Questions of identity and Irishness
lie at the heart of the narrative and indeed, Claire Connolly uses the opening section of the novel to begin a discussion of Irish Studies and the place
of cultural theory within it in her introduction to *Theorizing Ireland*. Connolly has also cogently pointed out that the layering of perspectives in the
initial section of the novel serves to raise such pertinent questions as 'What
does Ireland look like? [. . .] Where do you need to be in order to get a
clear view?' (Connolly, 2003a, 2). The two major terms through which the
novel addresses such concerns are time and space, specifically history and
landscape configured through the trope of mapping. Both are significant
to the protagonist Orla's attempts to negotiate questions of identity and her
relation to the dual aspects of her life:

> Two sides to the Crilly coin: the good and the bad, the tourist west and
> the dull east, the rare Irish and the common English, the heathery rocky
> lovely and the bricky breezeblock ugly, the desirable rural idyll and the
> unchosen urban reality. Holiday and work. Past and present. (6)

The novel resists such binaries and constantly problematizes associations that
view the West as authentic and Irish.[6] As an articulation of movement between
conceptual dichotomies, *The Dancers Dancing* shows a concern with liminal
spaces and times. The liminal is defined by the *Oxford English Dictionary* as 'of
or pertaining to the threshold or initial stage of a process'. The sense of movement is important here and I want to consider the idea of the liminal as a

productive space rather than the conceptual holding ground that it can easily become. I will begin with an engagement with the questions of both mapping and temporality and move on to trace their implications in the novel.

The novel, set in 1972, charts the experiences of several teenage girls from both Dublin and Derry as they enter Irish College in the Donegal Gaeltacht. It is an experience that is familiar to the majority of Irish people, yet, as Ní Dhuibhne points out, one that has rarely, if ever, been dealt with in literature (Ní Dhuibhne, 2000a). The novel, developed from her short story 'Blood and Water', concerns the embarrassment and disgust that a young Dublin girl feels towards her aunt in Donegal. *The Dancers Dancing* expands this premise and explores the relationships between the protagonist Orla, her Donegal aunt, and her peers in Irish college. The novel is structured around a series of short episodes, predominately in the present tense. These are narrated in the third person and largely focalized through Orla, though the point of view shifts at times to other characters in the novel. The last chapter, set several years after the Irish College experience, is narrated in the first person by Orla and is the only occasion on which 'the point of view of the historical present of retrospection shift[s] to the present time' (Tallone, 2008, 181). The episodic, fragmented nature of the short chapters serves to 'undermine the creation of an extended, uninterrupted and whole story' (Hand, 2005, 224).

The novel operates additionally within the *Bildungsroman* genre, a narrative mode intimately concerned with identity and usually focused on the transitional stage of life between childhood and adulthood. José Santiago Fernández Vázquez has commented on the colonialist underpinnings of the genre, which require the concept of the child/primitive in order to chart the progression to a civilized adult state. He has also suggested, however, that the use of the genre provides a post-colonialist means of resistance in order to refigure questions of identity (Fernández Vázquez, 2002, 86–7). The protagonists of *The Dancers Dancing*, pre-pubescent girls on the threshold of adulthood, reflect the preoccupations of the *Bildungsroman*. Their experience of Irish College marks one of the first occasions the girls spend any sustained period away from home and thus the events of the narrative possess the potential to represent life-altering and significant changes. However, the narrative denies such a teleological impulse and resists closure. As Hand notes:

> What Ní Dhuibhne does is attempt to create a fiction that engages with the possibility and potentiality of the past and childhood: to open it up to interpretation and investigation, rather than close it down by 'fixing' an end point toward which it moves. (Hand, 2001).

This positioning of the past and childhood as liminal, in the sense outlined above, insists upon a productive engagement, and the eschewing of closure permits rearticulations of the past to proliferate. This dynamic sense is expressed in the narrative both spatially and temporally; the novel focuses on various 'spaces' that can be considered as liminal, most importantly the burn, but also the metaphorical body. Mapping, a sustained and significant metaphor in the novel, links the concerns of space and time and demonstrates the instabilities inherent in any attempt to represent or control landscape or history. These disjunctions then allow the liminal to function in a productive manner in order to initiate rearticulations of personal and public history and memory.

Mapping

Maps can function as a guide in various ways, as the narrator of *The Dancers Dancing* tells us, as well as to document, control, and render a landscape knowledgeable and readable. Gerry Smyth points out that the process of mapping is interconnected with that of naming, and he argues that space that has been neither named nor mapped becomes 'chaotic and dangerous' (Smyth, 2001, 40–2). While maps have undoubtedly possessed imperialist and colonial implications, Connolly has suggested the potency and potentiality of engaging with cartographic representations: 'maps can provide enabling escape routes as well as confining images', due perhaps to Ireland's ambiguous historical relationship to mapping (Connolly, 2003b, 27). She argues that mapping possesses the promise and possibility of reconfiguring connections between oneself and one's 'social space'. This same possibility can be seen in *The Dancers Dancing*.

The novel begins with an emphasis on mapping; the first chapter is entitled 'The Map' and it opens with a familiar analogy – land as body:

> Imagine you are in an airplane, flying at twenty thousand feet. The landscape spreads beneath like a chequered tablecloth thrown across a languid body. From this vantage point, no curve is apparent. It is flat earth – pan flat, platter flat to the edges, its green and gold patches stained at intervals by lumps of mountain, brownish purple clots of varicose vein in the smooth skin of the land. (Ní Dhuibhne, 1999, 1)

Our vantage point in relation to the land differs from that in *The Bray House*. The elevated perspective, from which we as readers view this corporeal landscape, is compared to that of early cartographers. What we are looking at here is akin to their maps which present the viewer with the previously unseen: 'this is what it [the earth] looks like really! See you! Look!' (1). The map speaks to the spectators, offering them a reflection of themselves in their landscape. These maps also transgress the boundary between reality and fantasy; the mapmakers submit to their 'desire to decorate', including unicorns and griffins alongside pictures of wolves and bears. The narrator describes these cartographers as 'licentious', since they include elements that one would not expect to find in the 'real' world. Their decoration is in excess of what we consider 'normal'. These maps, according to the narrator, 'are the best, the truest maps: at once guide and picture' (2). However, all maps have limitations. People's faces cannot be seen, for instance, nor their names heard: 'Inside is what you can't see, maker of maps. Behind or below, before or after' (2). One can only see the here and now; the truth and the story lie 'in-between,' in the 'chthonic puddle and muddle' and the story can only be 'clear as muddy old mud' (2–3). This initial description emphasizes the liminal space of the 'in-between' and problematizes it as a means by which to achieve comprehension.

In Ní Dhuibhne's text, land and body converge. The landscape is at once a 'chequered tablecloth thrown across a languid body', thus joining the two, while also exhibiting corporeal afflictions – 'varicose vein[s] in the smooth skin of the land' (1). Varicose veins mark something in excess of the 'normal' boundaries of the body. According to the *Oxford English Dictionary*, varicose veins are 'abnormal'; they 'enlarge' otherwise healthy bodily structures. As Connolly notes in her analysis, the map we are shown continuously threatens to spill out of its frame (Connolly, 2003a, 1). Maps continuously remain unstable in this novel, since conceptions of mapped space refuse to remain firmly in place. For instance, the border to the North of Ireland, or the six counties, must be crossed twice in order to reach Donegal, which is technically part of the South or the Republic. The power of mapping to control and delineate space is undermined in the text and forms an element in Orla's acceptance of the various types of difference that she both encompasses and encounters. At the beginning of the novel, Orla holds two maps in her head, that of Dublin and that of Tubber (6), but towards the end of the narrative she embraces spaces that resist mapped representation, such as the burn and the sea. As Patricia Coughlan writes, 'once Orla has overcome her fear of passing her aunt's house, she immerses herself joyfully in the boundless, fluid element of the sea' (Coughlan, 2004, 191).

Temporality

The varicose veins of the land are echoed later in the narrative when Orla is asked to bring her Auntie Annie elastic stockings to provide support for her varicose veins. This request elicits countless hours of shame and embarrassment on her part, since Annie is, in Orla's eyes, the epitome of abnormality. For Orla, the problem with her aunt encompasses a general misalignment. Auntie Annie is 'out of kilter, not plumb with the world' (138). Her bodily appearance is described as 'crooked', her walk is 'awkward' and her voice similarly bears out this unevenness. Indeed, for Orla, normality is allied to evenness and symmetricality:

> Normal people are people who are more or less identical to everyone else, and *who fit, tongue and groove, foot and slipper, into their time and place.* Normal people are in tune, and the most normal people of all are those who hear the latest air *split seconds before the majority* and set the tone, beginning to sing in time to it, *split seconds ahead of the posse.* (139, my emphasis)

Here normality is about fitting in, being correctly connected to both time and place, and is constructed in terms that are predominantly corporeal. Auntie Annie is 'positioned at an oblique angle' to her hometown, Tubber (139). She is also anachronistic in her clothing and appearance. To fit is to correspond bodily as well as to appear even and symmetrical; tongue and foot must fit into one's time and place. However, to be normal, to fit perfectly into one's milieu, is to be slightly out of time, ahead of time. Thus, even when one achieves 'normality' and evenness, one can still to be out of sync with most people's temporality. 'Normal' people must constantly look forward in order to fit into the present and inhabit the future in order to inhabit the present. Thus, although Annie exhibits excesses and dislocations in terms of spatiality and temporality, Orla's definition of normality unconsciously acknowledges that it is based on similar disjunctions, at least in relation to time.

Temporality is also subject to a mapping impulse in the novel. Headmaster Joe, the principal of the Irish college, conceives of the students' activities as a virtual map:

> It is all mapped out and at all times a copy of the map is in his head, every pupil carefully spotted on it. But of course there are intervals, interstices,

crevices in the edifice he has constructed that he can't afford to know about. Creases of time, worn patches and tiny holes that in the beginning seem too insignificant to be worth thinking about, but which are gradually expanding as the summer wears on. Slowly his map is cracking, and through the cracks the insects start to creep. (67)

The map is represented as a tangible, material entity, which can crease and whose charted surface can be damaged. This map fails to remain flattened and smooth in a similar manner to the landscape encountered at the beginning of the novel. Headmaster Joe's map contains folds, fissures, cracks, and '[c]reases of time'. These cracks allow alien presences, such as insects, to invade the map's surface, akin to the movement of the first map's river or burn which transgresses the boundaries attempting to frame the landscape.

These disjunctions in time can be related to Derrida's *Specters of Marx* and in particular his analysis of Hamlet's phrase, 'The time is out of joint'. Derrida queries how time, or a time, can be thought to be 'out of joint', dislocated from itself. This arises through a consideration of the temporality of the spectre, specifically the ghost of Hamlet's father and Marx's spectre of communism that haunts Europe in the first line of *The Communist Manifesto*. The time of the ghost, of haunting, complicates a linear view of temporality. Derrida plays with the French term for ghost, *revenant*, which literally means 'that which comes back' (Derrida, 1994, 177n). The ghost, then, is occupied in a returning action. Does this imply a return from the past? Or does the ghost come back from a future time? From whence does the ghost return? Marx's spectre of communism haunts from the future, because the ideal of communism that haunts and terrifies contemporaneous Europe has not yet arrived, rather it returns from this virtual future to inhabit the present. As Derrida writes:

Haunting is historical, to be sure, but it is not *dated*, it is never docilely given a date in the chain of presents, day after day, according to the instituted order of a calendar. (Derrida, 1994, 4)

The time of the spectre is always already disjointed from itself. To think the ghost is to acknowledge the 'non-contemporaneity of present time with itself (Derrida, 1994, 25). To think about the present is also to consider the time of the spectre; the present occupies a transitory place between what has happened and what will happen, '*between* what *goes* and what *comes*, in the middle of what leaves and what arrives, at the articulation between what absents itself and what presents itself' (Derrida, 1994, 25). Thus, the present marks a juncture between two absences, but a juncture that, by its very nature, is always out of joint with itself due to its articulation of 'two directions of absence, at the articulation of what is no longer and what is not yet' (Derrida, 1994, 25). The movement of *différance* is discernible in this conceptualization of the present; the present is both differed from itself spatially and is infinitely deferred temporally. Importantly, Derrida uses the word 'dis-location' when speaking of the temporality of the spectre. In *The Dancers Dancing*, the character of Auntie Annie appears to be the living embodiment of this disjuncture and double sense of space and time, as discussed above, but it is the burn that represents the space most conducive to such dislocations of time.

The Burn

The burn, or river, occupies a significant position concerning temporality in the narrative of the novel. We first meet the protagonists as they wash their clothes in its waters and its importance is marked from the beginning by its presence on the initial map presented to us in the first chapter: 'The burn. A narrow bold blue-black line meandering in the nervous way of mapped rivers from one edge – the brown triangle of hills – to the mono-blue sea' (2). This cartography of the land asserts a particular perspective in relation to temporality, insisting firmly on a sense of a present. What you cannot see is 'behind or below, before or after' (2). The past and the future are not representable on this map, which is rigidly two-dimensional and synchronic. However, the river occupies an odd position in this depiction: 'endlessly beginning and endlessly ending, endlessly moving and endlessly unchanging' (2). It marks an alternate temporality in the map; its beginning and end are infinitely deferred.

While washing their clothes in the burn in the second chapter of the novel the girls sing a song concerned with their future, 'Che sera sera'. The narrator reminds us: 'The future, even of the song, is not theirs to see. But by now their future is their past, an open book, a closed chapter, water under the bridge' (5). Several temporal ambiguities can be identified at this point in the narrative. The future is presented as a possession, a visual possession, which cannot be accessed. Furthermore, past and future are correlated; the narrator's voice speaks from a present that relegates the girls' future to the past. It is also a temporality that is textual, in book form and both open and closed. An open book asks to be read, it is still current,

whereas a closed chapter implies something that is finished. The river metaphor also belies a similar ambiguity. 'Water under the bridge' denotes a
past event, something forgotten, yet fluidity in relation to time is also
implied.

For Orla, the burn is a location that combines privacy, excitement, and
danger; the latter of which are connected to a fear of otherworldly presences, namely fairies. It is fairies that she is worried about during her first
visit to the burn, rather than, as the narrator points out, the fact that if she
slipped she would possibly never be found. Interestingly, one of Pauline's
first reactions to the burn is to quote from 'Snow White': 'Mirror, mirror on
the wall who is the fairest of them all?' (115). The reference to fairytales is
not coincidental due to their corporeal and temporal connotations, discussed above. Fairies are also specifically connected with the liminal and
Purkiss points to many of the traditional folkloric associations that link
them with such a sphere. They infringe on a community from its outside,
they prey on people in transitional stages: 'young men, women in childbirth, and babies and children' (Purkiss, 2000, 48). She writes:

> Fairies both are and are not; they exceed the terms of what is likely or
> acceptable or sayable in the everyday. They are encountered on boundar-
> ies either in space – between town and wilderness – or in time – at mid-
> day, at midnight, at the change of the year, on the eve of a feast, [. . .]
> They could also be encountered at moments of social or physical transi-
> tion: birth, copulation and death, adolescence, betrothal, defloration,
> and of course death and burial. (Purkiss, 2000, 86).

Thus Orla's fear of otherworldly presences in the burn is not unjustified
and, despite the lack of actual fairies, the attention drawn to their possibility signals the potential for disruptions and for the articulation of what
could otherwise not be voiced or engaged with.

Orla's discovery of a dozen baby skulls in the burn becomes significant
here. Their discovery can be related to De Certeau's notion of the 'resistances', 'survivals', or 'delays' that complicate the linear progression of history. This unearthing of possible evidence for practices of infanticide
represents a return of the repressed, articulating buried historical trauma.
The burn, the locus for fairy presences, operates as a type of chora for alternate histories to be realized. Curiously, before unearthing the skulls, Orla
already knows what they are. She has access to some kind of past knowledge
of which she is unaware. For instance, she dreams about circumstances surrounding the presence of the skulls and conjures up a newspaper article

with which she seems to be already familiar, concerning a woman, presumably an ancestor of hers, Nuala Crilly, who kills her baby by throwing him into the burn.

Importantly, the narrative signals that these circumstances may not be the actual historical events that account for the presence of the skulls:

> Can you dream what you do not know? Usually the stories that unfold in Orla's head while she sleeps are mixed-up images that she recognises from the life she lives during the day, from stories she has read or heard or seen. (210)

The implication remains that the Nuala Crilly story is an amalgam of various texts, and the ambiguity concerning the historicity of this dream is allowed to linger. Orla's dream engages with the unacknowledged history of possible infanticide without attempting to explain it away. The sustaining of the ambiguity allows the presence of the skulls to remain haunting to us as readers. In *Specters of Marx*, Derrida speaks of mourning, in particular the impulse to name, identify, and localize bodily remains in order that they remain there: 'one *has to know* who is buried where – and *it is necessary* (to know – to make certain) that, in what remains of him, he remain there' (Derrida, 1994, 9). The uncertainty that the narrative allows in relation to a need to name in order to enact closure permits a movement of the past through the present. It allows the past to inhabit the present and facilitates Orla's acceptance of her Auntie Annie, which occurs when she realizes that Annie's ability to tell stories is valued by her Irish college teacher, Killer Jack, who records them. History and the past are allowed to transgress their normal boundaries; they are permitted to be in excess of themselves in the location of the burn and in Orla's oblique relation to Auntie Annie.

The sociologist Zygmunt Bauman's conceptualization of 'liquid modernity' rather than postmodernity might prove useful here. The metaphor of liquid or fluid is particularly applicable to the current state of modernity which privileges lightness, speed, and mobility. Bauman points out a 'time sensitivity' of liquids in opposition to the tendency of solids to 'neutralize the impact' of time: 'In a sense, solids cancel time; for liquids, on the contrary, it is mostly time that matters' (Bauman, 2000, 2). Rather than the rigid break between past and present on which linear views of history rely, the metaphor of the burn in *The Dancers Dancing* signals a fluidity which allows past and present to bleed into each other. Throughout the novel then, the resistances of landscape and time to attempts at mapping and containment mirror the concomitant challenge to the trajectory of historical progress that suppresses certain histories, such as the forgotten history of the baby skulls.

The transgression of boundaries also extends to the corporeal. Orla's reactions to her transformation experienced at the burn are generally described in physical terms. For instance, her body reacts in a profound way to the discovery of the skulls in the burn; she begins to menstruate. The moment before she discovers the skulls 'she begins to feel tired, and the damp greenness of the burn seems to be seeping into her stomach, pressing upon it' (201–2). Shortly after this liminal experience at the burn, Orla's meeting with Micheál, the Banatee's son whose acceptance of Auntie Annie acts as a significant factor in Orla's reconciliation with her, also instigates a bodily reaction:

> It's as if she were going under ether, as in the dentist's chair, but the ether is not smelly or frightening. Not at all. It's as if she were going under-water, under glaucous, clear water. Under water, but breathing deeply and calmly of the freshest air. (217)

Furthermore, when Orla visits Auntie Annie, accompanied by Aisling and Micheál, she 'feels something break inside her head, like the shell of an egg. Her big secret is disintegrating' (221). These reactions share a sense of bodily boundaries being broken down, and are connected with Orla's transformation at the burn. This breaching and dismantling of boundaries allow Orla's acceptance of her aunt, and this reconciliation is an acknowledgement of spatiality and history as different from themselves while concurrently facilitating an acceptance of the other.

As in *The Bray House*, *The Dancers Dancing* draws attention to the fear that the female body elicits. The narrative makes explicit the repressions to which this corporeality is subject, particularly in terms of a maternal genealogy:

> Women in Dublin don't want to acknowledge the existence of breasts: they haven't got them, and if they have, those protuberances certainly don't contain anything as messy, as repulsive, as animal, as *wet*, as milk. I ask you! Milk comes from bottles and Cow and Gate cans, thank you very much indeed! Bosoms are dry pointy pincushions, tucked away in brassieres. And there they stay. (56)

The culture of the 1970s refuses to acknowledge the connection established when a mother breastfeeds her child. This denial is also connected to a fear of the leakiness that women's bodies are seen to possess. Orla's anxiety in

Irish College that some disaster will befall her mother is fuelled by this occlusion of an intergenerational relationship:

> Orla has to write so often. She has to keep in touch, keep Elizabeth informed that she is here, alive, that she cares, that she needs her. She has to receive messages back from Elizabeth to assure her that she [Elizabeth] is not ill, that her kidneys and her back and her head and all the rest of her substantial but absurdly delicate body is all right. (60)

Like Robin in *The Bray House*, Orla yearns for communication with her mother which is unforthcoming. Her unease concerning her mother's health reflects the positioning of the maternal body in the Irish cultural imaginary that resists recognition of a connection with this corporeality. Orla's need to 'receive messages' from Elizabeth becomes linked to the engagement with the past that *The Dancers Dancing* encourages.

The uncertainty surrounding the origin of the skulls accommodates the ghosts that haunt the text, but there is no attempt to pin them down, or name them in order to exorcize them. The narrative facilitates this ambiguity, this awareness of the historical sublime in De Certeau's terms, by allowing alternate histories and spatialities to complicate each other and 'other' themselves by their fluidity and non-containment. The conclusion to the novel is markedly open-ended. Entitled 'Now', the last chapter is set several years after Orla's experience in the Irish College. She is now an adult with her own children, on holidays in a Gaeltacht complete with 'a heritage centre, vast as a cathedral' and noticeably different from the former Tubber (239). It is here, at the water's edge, that she glimpses a man who may or may not be Micheál. It is merely a glimpse, however, and despite Orla's desire to 'speak to him and find out everything. Learn his story' (241), she does not encounter him again. The novel ends with Orla's words: 'Since then, I have not seen him' (242).

The absence of a conclusive ending and the failure to impose a definite shape on the events of the novel or on Orla's discovery of the skulls emphasize that the past and its ghosts remain haunting presences that cannot be explained away. In other words, *The Dancers Dancing* eschews containment of spatiality, temporality, and history, and instead permits a productive engagement with the 'other'. The narrative enunciates fluidity, an excess of boundaries, like the burn 'endlessly ending and endlessly beginning'.

Conclusion

The Bray House and *The Dancers Dancing* are set in the future and the past respectively but are more concerned with the relationships between various temporal modalities and the present. Each text refuses to consider the past as a fixed entity and resists linear, progressive paradigms of historiography and temporality. For Ní Dhuibhne, engagements with the past are productive if they allow an openness to, and acknowledgement of, the possibility of knowledges that are other than those that traditional narratives of history privilege. The relations between temporalities in Ní Dhuibhne's fiction advocate a reconfiguration of the way we think about time in the manner outlined by Grosz: 'The past endures, not in itself, but in its capacity to become something other' (Grosz, 2000, 1018–9). The babies' skulls in *The Dancers Dancing* and the appearance of Maggie in *The Bray House* attest to this potential of the past to become new.

Ní Dhuibhne's novels bring into focus the implications of certain types of historiographies for particular bodies. Robin's embodiment of a linear, causal paradigm of history and its methodologies in *The Bray House* involves a repression of a relationship with the maternal body, a fear of female corporeality, and discomfort with the disintegration of bodily boundaries. *The Dancers Dancing* also illustrates disruptions in linear conceptions of temporality. The narrative displays a playful attitude to configurations of time. Past and present are shown to be contiguous and to relate in complex ways that resist paradigms of progression and causation. The alternate relationships that the novel creates between temporalities allow the emergence of bodies and histories that had previously been invisible or occluded in dominant narratives. Ní Dhuibhne's fiction demonstrates Grosz's contention that the body is the repressed and the unacknowledged condition of the production of knowledge systems. In her novels, explorations of the processes of historiography and conceptions of temporality reveal the types of bodies that underpin these particular ways of assessing former eras. For Ní Dhuibhne, the emergence of the past into the present is predominately figured in bodily form; the corporeal is implicated in disruptions of linear time, thus drawing attention to the body's role as the unacknowledged condition of historical and temporal knowledges.

Chapter 2

Corporeal Genealogies:
Colum McCann's *Songdogs* and
This Side of Brightness

Colum McCann's textual concerns and locations reflect his peripatetic life. Born in 1965 in Dublin, he graduated from the College of Journalism in Rathmines and left Ireland to undertake a journey by bicycle across North America, from Massachusetts to San Francisco, at the age of 21. He completed a degree in English and History at the University of Texas in Austin. He has lived in Ireland, Japan, and North America, and now resides in New York. In 1990, he was named Young Journalist of the Year in Dublin; this distinction coincided with his winning of the Hennessey Award for Irish Writing for his short story 'Tresses', published in *The Sunday Tribune*. These two awards reflect his skills in documenting social reality as well as his interest in narrative and the importance of storytelling. John Kenny notes McCann's 'increasingly successful splicing of aesthetic seriousness with social concern' in a review of his collection of short stories, *Everything in This Country Must* (Kenny, 2000b). As a journalist, McCann has contributed to publications such as *The New York Times*, *The Irish Times*, *The Guardian*, *The New Yorker*, *Atlantic Monthly*, and *GQ*.

McCann has published two collections of short stories, *Fishing the Sloe-Black River* (1994a), which won the Rooney Prize for Irish Literature, and *Everything in This Country Must* (2000) composed of two short stories and a novella, all set in Northern Ireland. *Fishing the Sloe-Black River* introduces concerns that are sustained throughout McCann's fiction, those of exile and displacement His characters are often wanderers and nomads, either 'seek[ing] a way 'home' or a way to escape home' (Hunt Mahony, 1998, 261). The stories also foreground the body, observing the effects of emigration and diaspora, and focusing on the violence that is visited on the corporeal due to such traumas as anorexia, AIDS, boxing, Hiroshima, murder, and self-immolation. His novels, *Songdogs* (1995), *This Side of Brightness* (1998), *Dancer* (2003b), *Zoli* (2006), and *Let the Great World Spin* (2009), explore such issues through narratives that centre on journeying and dislocation, though this book will focus on his earlier three novels. *Songdogs* details a son's retracing of his father's travels through Mexico and North America before a reconciliation in Mayo. *This Side of Brightness*, which was nominated for the Booker Prize, focuses on both the homeless who inhabit New York's subway and the immigrant sandhogs who dug and built the tunnels. *Dancer* is a fictionalized account of dancer and Russian exile, Rudolf Nureyev, as he defects West. This chapter will focus on McCann's two earliest novels, *Songdogs* and *This Side of Brightness*; they are juxtaposed because of their similar structures that alternate between past and present, and their exploration of the relationships that can be forged between temporalities.

McCann is interested in notions of Irishness as transgressive of the boundaries that traditionally define a nation. His characters reflect this attention to the nomadic and the transnational and his writing bears important similarities to the theories of the nomadic subject outlined by feminist critic Rosi Braidotti. Braidotti's concept of nomadic subjectivity denotes a type of critical thinking that permits one 'to think through and move across established categories and levels of experience: blurring boundaries without burning bridges' (Braidotti, 1994, 4). Based on Deleuze's concept of deterritorialization, Braidotti argues that what is at stake is 'a total dissolution of the notion of a center and consequently of originary sites or authentic identities of *any* kind' (Braidotti, 1994, 5). McCann's fiction aims to complicate such notions of authenticity but does not deny the importance of making connections between generations. Braidotti's emphasis on 'blurring boundaries without burning bridges' is an important distinction to make in terms of McCann's fiction. While his writing resists privileging authenticity in terms of nationality or identity, his novels, particularly *Songdogs* and *This Side of Brightness*, continually stage attempts to engage with the past, ideas of history, and conceptions of genealogy. These efforts at negotiation do not represent a search for lost origins but rather display the value that acknowledgements of the past can possess for the present and the future.

McCann's foregrounding of the corporeal, begun in *Fishing the Sloe-Black River*, becomes an important means for this traffic between the past and the present in his later works. Imaginative engagements with the body's morphology permit his various characters to formulate connections to the landscapes and cityscapes in which they live as well as to construe links to their own specific histories and genealogies. For Braidotti, reconceptualization of the body and its relationship to subjectivity is an important foundation of the 'project of nomadism':

The body, or the embodiment of the subject is to be understood as neither a biological nor a sociological category but rather as a point of over-
lapping between the physical, the symbolic, and the sociological.
(Braidotti, 1994, 4)

In McCann's fiction it is these overlaps that provide the productive means
of connecting and engaging with both spatial and temporal concerns.

This chapter will explore McCann's novels, *Songdogs* and *This Side of Brightness*, which both stage attempts by young men to come to terms with the
history of their families as well as their own lives. I will look at how McCann
formulates relationships between the body and its surroundings as a means
of negotiating the past.

Songdogs

Colum McCann's first novel, *Songdogs*, published in 1995, traces the relationship between estranged father Michael Lyons and his son Conor, mediated by the latter's endeavours to negotiate his parents' past. The narrative
of *Songdogs* centres around Conor's week-long visit to his ageing father in
Mayo while waiting for his American Green Card. Conor has been travelling around Mexico and North America vainly in search of his Mexican
mother, Juanita, who had left the family home following the father's publication of photographs in which she is featured naked. He has retraced the
steps of his parents, or more specifically those of his father, from Mayo to
Mexico and then to San Francisco and Wyoming before returning to Mayo,
where the narrative of *Songdogs* begins. His attempts to narrativize the past
are initiated and punctuated by the photographs his father, Michael, has
taken throughout his life. The novel is narrated in the first person by Conor
and moves structurally between past and present; it shifts between his present trip to Mayo, his reminiscences of his journey in his father's footsteps,
and his retelling of his father and mother's life. John Tague, in his review of
the novel, argues that it is 'obsessed [. . .] with the questions of parentage,
origins, and belonging' (Tague, 1995a). These concerns form the backbone
of the narrative but the answers to these questions are shown to be elusive.
For instance, Conor's father Michael is unaware of his own parentage, his
mother also left him, and even his name lacks authenticity. Abandoned on
a clifftop and raised by two Protestant ladies who christen him Gordon
Peters, he renames himself to fit in with the local community. Following the
death of his guardians, and with all his ties to Mayo severed, he embarks on

a journey that will take him from the Spanish Civil War in Madrid to Mexico where he meets his future wife; he travels through San Francisco, Wyoming, New York, and finally to Mayo where Conor is born. These flashbacks to the life of Michael and Juanita are voiced through Conor and thus are subject to his reinvention. Conor's attempt to find meaning in the events that led to his mother's departure, as well as his search for her present whereabouts, drive his narrative. Both are frustrated in the novel.

The narrative predominately focuses on issues relating to memory as well as the effort to formulate meaningful relationships with the past. These concerns are epitomized by the opening epigraph taken from F. Scott Fitzgerald's *The Great Gatsby*: 'So we beat on, boats against the current, borne ceaselessly into the past'. The quotation highlights a physical struggle with time that is figured as fluid, unidirectional, and irresistible. The preface of *Songdogs* points to the unattractive implications that encounters with the past may possess. Conor recalls his first sighting of coyotes prior to his return home. These coyotes, the 'songdogs' of the title, 'aren't as foolish as us – they don't trespass where the dead have been' due to their instinctive avoidance of fields in which dead coyotes have been hung as a deterrent:

> An eruption of brown fur against a field of melting snow, their [the dead coyotes] bodies hanging upside-down, tied to the post with orange twine. Two neat bullet holes had pierced their flanks where brown merged white. They were foot-dry and rotten with stench. (1)

Journeys into the past in the epigraph and opening paragraph are configured as unavoidably magnetic as well as imprudent; they involve trespassing and encounters with the rotten bodies of the dead. These caveats against engaging with the past prefigure the underlying pattern of such actions on the part of Conor. The explicitly physical nature of the coyotes' bodies set up as a deterrent also highlights the central role that the body plays in such negotiations of the past. Nonetheless, however imprudent an excursion into the realms of the dead might be, the past is still configured in the novel as exciting and imbued with potential:

> But the past is a place that is full of energy and imagination. In remembering, we can distil the memory down. We can manage our universe by stuffing it into the original quark, the point of burstingness. It's the lethargy of the present that terrifies us all. (73)

The warning presented by the dead bodies of the coyotes fails to act as a deterrent for Conor, who 'cannot help this wandering backwards. It is my own peculiar curse' (143).

The titular 'songdogs' refers to a myth Conor has heard in America from Navajo Indians who believe that coyotes sang the world into existence with their voices: 'The universe was etched with their howls, sound merging into sound, the beginning of all other songs' (72). Conor applies this title to his mother and father, they are his own songdogs due to the stories they tell him about their past. Their stories create him and bring him into being. The evocation of this myth signals an alternative to the warning represented by the dead coyote bodies of the preface. Conor's re-appropriation of his parents' stories becomes a means for him to narrate the past in order to come to terms with it. Their stories inaugurate his interaction with the past.

Landscape and the Body

The emphasis on travelling and exile in *Songdogs* is highlighted by Eamonn Wall in his article on the novel: 'In terms of the Irish diaspora, *Songdogs* is both relevant and prophetic' (Wall, 2000, 281). The novel explores emigration from an Irish perspective, but also, and more importantly, it focuses on the experience of the immigrant to Ireland, Juanita, whose corporeality is affected by her move from Mexico. She experiences intense nausea when travelling away from Mexico to San Francisco and again on the journey to Wyoming. The first time that she looks at herself after leaving Mexico, she sees herself as fragmentary and disjointed:

Combing her hair in a broken mirror, she must have been amazed at what the cracks did to her face, fracturing her eyes down to her nose, sending cheekbones into a landslide, displacing one ear upwards so that it almost floated above her head. Maybe she ran her brown fingers over the broken sections, reached to take the ear, watched it float away again, her body not belonging to her anymore, the rhythms of the boat journey still moving within it. (80–1)

In New York she begins to lose weight and suffers a miscarriage. Juanita is continuously figured in McCann's narrative as connected to the landscape; she names the winds in Mexico and is particularly delighted when a wind from the Sahara carries red sand to Mayo: 'She didn't wash the windows for weeks, enthralled by the revisit of red dust to her life' (168). The enclosed landscape of Mayo is represented in the novel as one that fails to sustain Juanita; as Conor notes 'it's confined here, the land, the space' (94). While Michael yearns to travel and is represented as being at ease when moving through space: 'I loved him for the gigantic way he walked – shoulders swinging, everything in a loop around him' (173), Juanita becomes more insubstantial and withdrawn the further she moves away from her homeland. As in the broken mirror, her body becomes displaced and distorted once she moves beyond the borders of Mexico and is finally taken from her in the publication of the photographs. Indeed, Wall reads the publication 'as an act of colonization by an Irish photographer', and argues that the disintegration in Michael and Juanita's marriage is contributed to by her alienation from the natural world with which she is familiar (Wall, 2000, 285). Wall's reading of the text views Juanita quite firmly as connected to her mother country. Although the narrative of *Songdogs* represents quite a traditional association of the female body with the landscape, the text displays the negative effects of this association through Juanita's physical reactions to travelling. The symbolic attempts to appropriate the female body and to make it a national icon have actual effects on individual female existences. Juanita's displacement and eventual disappearance in the novel may be explicated by Irigaray's argument that, within the dominant cultural imaginary, woman is positioned as the unacknowledged ground that supports the Western philosophical order: 'Woman is still the place, the whole of the place in which she cannot take possession of herself as such' (Irigaray, 1985a, 227).

The narrative, at times, undermines straightforward connections between corporeality and geography. Conor, while looking at a photograph of Juanita in New York, attempts to imagine her thoughts:

> Maybe she's wondering what she's doing here. Wondering what has led her to this. Wondering if life is manufactured by a sense of place, if happiness is dependent on soil, if it is an accident of circumstance that a woman is born in a certain country, and that the weather that gives birth to the soil also gives birth to the unfathomable intricacies of the heart. (138)

The combination of Conor's imaginative suggestions with the questioning nature of Juanita's supposed thoughts serves to undermine simplistic ideas of nationality and home. Conor cannot sustain his analysis of the photograph, pointing out immediately afterwards that 'maybe Mam isn't thinking this way at all' (138). While on his journey to find her, he fails to locate her at all, least of all in Mexico.

Juanita is never entirely comfortable in Mayo. Wall argues that the novel is the first of its kind in its exploration of Ireland as '*frontera*, constantly crossed and recrossed, [rather] than a fixed nation' (Wall, 2000, 284). However, the novel draws attention to the precarious positioning of the mother in negotiations of nationality, identity, and home. In *Songdogs*, Juanita herself is continuously described as positioned on the edges, at the boundaries of designated spaces. Conor's first memory of her in the novel is the image of her standing by the riverbank watching as he and his father struggle against the river's current (4). The river in *Songdogs* is connected both with time and with the double movement towards the past and the future. In this instance, Juanita is positioned apart from, and at the edges of, concerns with time and memory. Later in Mexico, Michael finds Juanita 'at the edge of town, hysterical, with fists flailing at the sky' following his disappearance for a number of days (57). Michael also occupies some of these liminal positions though he is accorded an agency that is never afforded to Juanita. He is born 'on a clifftop overlooking the Atlantic' (5), and as a child spits into the ocean from the cliff: 'At the time he didn't realise that his spit was aimed westward – at Mexico, at San Francisco, at Wyoming, at New York – where in later years it would truly land' (7). Michael can project elements of his corporeality forward in time and space, highlighting the difference between male and female bodies in the text in terms of their relation to space and landscape. Where Michael is afforded mobility, Juanita is trapped. Juanita's hobby of constructing a stone wall from their house in Mayo to the main road to make 'some sort of crease in her boredom' (159), also becomes a means for her to mark this alien land-scape with her presence and to disrupt it: 'it broke the land in a splendid way' (157).

Conor's journey backwards into the past is also an attempt to locate and secure his mother. Aidan Arrowsmith views Conor as Zygmunt Bauman's 'typical "liquid modern" subject', caught between a rootless lifestyle and a desire to form connections with his past: 'On the one hand is freedom via the rejection of nationalism's roots fetish. On the other is a growing need for connectedness and identity amidst the fragmentation of the contemporary postmodern' (Arrowsmith, 2005, 312). His engagements with the past are mediated through photographic images of Juanita, which for Arrowsmith, reveal that 'the tactile point of connection to ori-gin, now signif[ies] only loss and emptiness for Conor' (Arrowsmith, 2005, 313).

Photography

Conor's first glimpse of his father upon returning home is of Michael fishing in a now polluted river. The river is slow now, mirroring the movements of Michael. Conor watches him unobserved: 'I sat on my backpack, behind the hedge, where the old man couldn't see me, and watched the slowness of the river and him' (3). Conor's positioning as undetected observer introduces the dominance of the scopic field that is played out in this narrative. Power is accorded to those who wield the gaze. Conor's view also instigates a memory of childhood, of his father teaching him to swim against the current, to resist the powerful flow of the river. Finally, when tired, Conor and his father would allow the current to carry them along: 'The old man would give a nod to the river. It was the law of water, he told me. It was bound to move things on' (5). Memories are prompted by visual cues, and more specifically in the novel, by photographs.

Photography has been central to Michael's life; a camera 'woke' him from the lethargy he experienced following the death of his guardians, the Protestant ladies, when he was 16. The camera is found in the dust, and already belongs to the past when Michael discovers its presence: 'It was an old model with a dickybird hood' (9). The power that the camera affords him is linked to the temporal and to the ability to arrest the movement of time through the image: 'He didn't know it then, but the camera would burst him out on to the world, give him something to cling to, fulminate a belief in him in the power of light, the necessity of image, the possibility of freezing time' (9). This power associated with the camera, and with his positioning as observer, also appears to affect his corporeality and being in the world: 'It was a world that had seldom seen a lens of any sort, and my father moved around it, taller now, his body filling out, sleeves rolled up, drama in the exhibition of himself' (10). Although positioned behind the lens of the camera, Michael himself appears to inhabit the realm of the visual; he becomes an image, an exhibition. Furthermore, Michael's actual body seems influenced and altered by his use of the camera. The power associated with the ability to capture images is enacted on his physical body. Photographs also provide Conor with a means to gain access to events that took place long before his birth. It is through photographs that he achieves contact with the past and through them can reconstruct the histories of his father and mother.

Roland Barthes's final publication, *Camera Lucida*, is explicitly concerned with the relationship between photography and memory, precipitated by a photograph of his mother. Barthes attempts, in this extended meditation on the medium, to discover and delineate what he terms the *noeme*, or the particular essence, of photography. For him, photography has a specific and unique relationship to the real; what it represents has actually been there at the moment it is photographed. This profound affiliation with the actual contributes to what Barthes terms the *spectrum* of the photograph 'because this word retains, through its root, a relation to 'spectacle' and adds to it that rather terrible thing which is there in every photograph: the return of the dead' (Barthes, 1993, 9). The *noeme* of photography is 'that-has-been'; the photograph attests to a reality, a moment, an event that has now departed and that can only partially be grasped by the image itself. As Derrida writes in his eulogy to Barthes:

> Although it [the referent] is no longer *there* (present, living, real, etc.), its *having-been-there* is now part of the referential structure of my relationship to the photogramme, the return of the referent indeed takes the form of a haunting. (Derrida, 1988, 281–2)

The photograph haunts in its unique relationship to the past, to the dead, and to what-has-been. Furthermore, photography's *noeme* is the fact that the operator (photographer) 'has seen the referent (even if it is a matter of objects) *in flesh and blood*, or again *in person*' (Barthes, 1993, 79). Here, Barthes points to the important relationship between material bodily presence and photography, both in terms of the presence of the photographer and the subject photographed (if the focus of the photograph is a person): 'Photography[. . .] began, historically, as an art of the Person: of identity, of civil status, of what we might call, in all senses of the term, the body's *formality*' (79). Photography as an art form, then, is culturally and historically linked with ideas of subjectivity, with identity, and with the body. It requires material bodily presence. This presence, however, is one that remains hauntingly absent to the viewer: 'it has been here, and yet immediately separated; it has been absolutely, irrefutably present, and yet already deferred' (77). The moment is always already in the past and hence photography's intimate link with death and memory. The image is, for Barthes, immobile and mortified in comparison to one's experience of self, which is continuously dispersed and in movement. The photograph transforms the subject into an object, into a 'Total-Image, which is to say, Death in person' (14). However, Barthes stresses that a photograph is not, nor can be, a memory:

> The Photograph does not call up the past [. . .]. The effect it produces upon me not to restore what has been abolished (by time, by distance) but to attest that what I see has indeed existed. (42)

Photography can usurp memory; the power of the visual image captured in the photograph often becomes the source of particular memories.

Photography in *Songdogs* acts as both a mnemonic aid and a hijacker of particular memories and events, the latter tendency exhibited by Michael's relationship with certain images that he produces (see Michael's photograph of Manley discussed below). Conor's memory, or more specifically, his ability to narrate his parents' past, is heavily reliant on a photographic punctuation. When Conor travels to Mexico in order to search for his mother he brings a photograph album with him and later describes a habitual need to continually refer to the photographs. His narrative is ordered around specific images on which he can embroider and to which he can attach both the stories his parents had told him and his own imaginings. (The phrases 'I imagine', 'I can imagine', or 'I can picture' prefigure a number of the 'reminiscences' in the novel). His mother's friend Cici, whom he meets in San Francisco, seems to give him the permission he needs for these acts of invention:

'You know what I think?' she [Cici] said. 'I think memory is three-quarters imagination.' [...]
'And the rest is pure lies,' she said. (112)

If memory itself is fabricated, then Conor's interventions need not disturb the fabric with which it is woven. The narrative reveals the difficulty of accessing the 'truth' of the past. The reader only has access to the lives of Conor's parents through his recreations. The only reliable prop for him seems to be the images presented in his father's photographs, though these are not unproblematic.

Although I use the term 'memory', the photographs instead aid Conor's engagement with his parents' recollections of a past he neither occupied nor experienced. Marianne Hirsch, in her study of the relationship between photographs, the family, and memory, describes this particular use of memory as 'postmemory'. Although she signals her wariness of the implications that the prefix 'post' has, namely 'that we are beyond memory', she delineates post-memory as:

distinguished from memory by generational distance and from history by deep personal connection. Postmemory is a powerful and very particular form of memory precisely because its connection to its object or source is mediated not through recollection but through an imaginative investment and creation. This is not to say that memory itself is unmediated, but that it is more directly connected to the past. (Hirsch, 1997, 22)

Post-memory is associated with the experience of those for whom narratives of events prior to their birth have possessed substantial influence, sometimes to the extent that their own memories must be mediated through the stories of a previous generation. For Hirsch, the concept of post-memory has emerged specifically in relation to the children of Holocaust survivors, though she does allow its applicability to 'other second-generation memories of cultural or collective traumatic events and experiences' (22). For Conor, the understanding of his traumatic experience of maternal loss must be mediated through the narratives of his parents, which he then embellishes with his own speculations.

Interestingly, the connection that Hirsch posits between 'first- and second-generation remembrance, memory and postmemory' is the medium of photography and she describes the link, after Barthes, as 'umbilical' (23). Barthes uses the metaphor of the umbilical cord in *Camera Lucida* to elaborate the intimate relationship between the subject of the photograph and the spectator:

> From a real body, which was there, proceed radiations which ultimately touch me, who am here [. . .] A sort of umbilical cord links the body of the photographed thing to my gaze: light, though impalpable, is here a carnal medium, a skin I share with anyone who has been photographed. (Barthes, 1993, 80–1)

Hirsch comments that Barthes's metaphor configures photography as 'inherently familial and material, akin to the very processes of life and death' (Hirsch, 1997, 5). Even more apparent is the explicit corporeality described here and, furthermore, the invocation of the maternal. Before turning to the maternal implications of the photographic process I will explore the explicit connections with the body.

The Photographed Body

Descriptions of bodies often function in *Songdogs* as visual signatures for particular characters, forming part of their initial depiction. When introducing characters, McCann attributes recognizable physical characteristics to them; Cici, for example, is 'pockmarked' and 'thin as a rib' (81, 83). Delhart, her former boyfriend, has a face 'not unlike the shovels of the ditch diggers – long and brown and weathered and too well used' (105). These bodies exist, for McCann, in the visual register. They exist to be looked at. Michael's photographs are of people, not landscapes. What, then, is the relationship between photography and the body? What kind of corporeality does the photographic image configure?

In William A. Ewing's introduction to an exhibition entitled *The Century of the Body*, he poses the question as to why the twentieth century displayed a change in the way that the human body was conceptualized. His reasons include medical breakthroughs, the rise of feminism, and the threat to the physical body due to increased automation, but he also notes the importance of the camera (Ewing, 2000, 13). The twentieth century is the century of the camera and with the production of hand-held cameras, the general public can, for the first time, document themselves in images. John Pultz, in his book *Photography and the Body*, claims that photography 'has done more that any other medium to shape our notions of the body in modern times' (Pultz, 1995, 7). What impact, then, does this visual medium have on our perceptions of the corporeal? Pultz offers some associations that photography has accumulated, namely the connections between photography and modernism, industrialization, and the Enlightenment. The medium of photography, Pultz argues, has appeared particularly amenable to Enlightenment empiricist philosophy, which claims that knowledge is obtained from experience through the five senses:

> Photography seemed the perfect Enlightenment tool, functioning like human sight to offer empirical knowledge mechanically, objectively, without thought or emotion. The existence of photography also buttressed the Enlightenment account of the coherent individual, or subject. A whole series of relationships within the photographic process – camera to subject, lens to film, observer to photograph – reproduce the position of a privileged, unique Enlightenment subject: the observer apart, freely viewing some object or scene. (9)

In this account, then, the act of photography and the photographed image operate in the same manner as the misrecognition of Lacan's mirror stage, offering a unified whole subject or body image with which to identify. Indeed, Michael's use of the photograph's relationship to memory in *Songdogs* seems to compound this misrecognition. Michael finds his friend Manley in Madrid without one leg, his neck covered in boils. However, following Manley's disappearance, the photographs Michael had taken of him become the dominant memory:

The photos that they had taken years before in Mayo, with Manley in his outrageous suits, became my father's most vibrant memory of his friend. When the old man talked of Manley he remembered him as sixteen-year-old with a lustful glint in his eye, rather than as a legless soldier who reeks of piss at night. It was something the old man often did – if a moment existed in a photograph, it was held in that particular stasis for ever. It was as if by taking a photo he could, at any moment, reinhabit an older life – one where a body didn't droop, or hair didn't fall out, or a future didn't have to exist. Time was held in the centre of his fist. He either crumpled it or let it fly off. [. . .] it was his own particular ordering of the universe, a pattern that moved from past to present, with the ease of a sheet dropped into a chemical bath. (23)

The photograph recuperates and reassembles Manley's body into a more desirable one. Both the photograph, and the memories that rely on such images, permit misrecognitions on various levels; Manley's body is re-imagined as whole, and the image gives access to a past in which the body remains static, unchanging, youthful, and whole. The specular order allows this retention of wholeness to take place; it permits a privileging of the coherent and the unified, specifically at the level of the corporeal and its place within memory.[1] The photograph gives power over temporality to the photographer, in this case, Michael.

As noted, Conor's position at the beginning of *Songdogs* as invisible observer sets a precedent for the ways in which the act of seeing is configured in the novel. Conor continuously watches people from distant vantage points, whether observing his father making flies from the roof of the shed, to his use of his father's camera lens to spy on people from afar. From Conor's vantage point his father appears old and fragile, and possesses an ageing body: 'I was shocked to see the lineament of his body – as thin as the reeds I used to make holy crosses with during February winters' (4). Their initial conversation concerns how each one is 'looking':

'would ya look at the cut of ya.'
'You're looking well yourself' (14).

However, Conor is positioned (or has positioned himself) as the privileged spectator. It is his gaze to which we are privy; the gaze of his father is mediated through his narrative and his relationship to the photographs. Michael's vision is no longer the dominant one; his eyesight is failing and he requires the additional aid of glasses in order to recognize his son: 'Cocking his head sideways like a curious animal, he closed his right eye, fumbled in his coat for his glasses' (13). Michael must adjust his body in order to see correctly. His gaze and his body no longer operate in a complementary manner. At times, he fails to see Conor:

> I gave him a wave but he didn't respond, even with the glasses back on. Perhaps the light was glinting on the window, but I was sure he couldn't see me – most likely his eyes are on their way, too. Bodies fall like rain at that age – drops collide into one another. (41)

Conor, as possessor of the privileged gaze, looks at his father with a clinical eye (the eye that sees everything) and sums up his body as ageing, decrepit, and fragile. Interestingly, in this quotation, the fact that Michael's access to vision is deteriorating is immediately followed by Conor's observation that his body is declining. Occupying the position of the spectator is represented in the novel as coterminous to the possession of a healthy, whole, and unified corporeality. This is demonstrated by the change in Michael's body following his acquisition of the camera, 'taller now, his body filling out' (10). Michael's body is continually referred to as distasteful, as old, and as failing once Conor has returned to Mayo. The power inherent in the act of seeing is again configured in favour of Conor when, later in the narrative, he walks in on his father examining himself in a hand mirror:

> he was squatted down, by the dressing table, naked, bent over a handheld mirror, examining something on his backside. His legs came down, spindle-like. There was a small chain of blood on the inside of his buttocks, dried there. (123)

Michael appears vulnerable here, awkwardly posed in order to catch a glimpse of himself, in order to ascertain the extent of his illness. His body becomes the object of the gaze on all levels, removing power and agency and causing intense embarrassment.

Photography is figured in an Oedipal relationship of power; it binds father to son, and also creates connections between them:

> Years later, when I went through boxes in our attic, there were shots of women naked in lamplight, women parading in front of his [Michael's] camera [. . .] I was a teenager when I discovered them. I'd sit, perched on a slat of wood in the attic, thumping away at my body, in the beginning

of its articulation. I became the camera, became the cameraman, and all the time hated my father for being privy to these visions. I walked into the photos, parted the canvas doors of the tents, stood, bemused at first, talked to the women. The women smiled at my curious appearance, beckoned me backwards to the 1930s, asked me sly questions. [. . .] the women would move around in the photographs for me, come behind the camera, take me by the hand and lead me somewhere no lens could watch, let me touch them, open my shirt buttons with a flick of their fingers, let me wander, sleep beside them. (22)

The photographs in this extract provide a portal both to the past and to Conor's sexual fantasies. The photographs are no longer stable flat images; they invite the viewer to enter the frame, to journey into the past. Conor can walk *into* the photos, can talk *to* the women, and can even *touch* them. The women depicted in the photographs can move around within them and can even leave the frame to join Conor behind the camera. The sexual power of the image, or the photograph, is signalled here. Conor hates his father's actual presence at the time of the photograph, of his position behind the lens, and the power that this confers. Looking at the photographs permits Conor to occupy the same position as his father once had as the cameraman. However, a different physical reaction is produced when Conor finds photographs of his mother:

When I first saw them – years ago now – they made me sick to the stomach. I hardly even realised it was her at first, and unlike the ones of the women in Spain, I never again looked at them in the attic, never found myself part of them. (59)

Conor acknowledges, however, that these are 'the greatest pictures' taken by his father and describes his mother's figure in them: 'She almost seemed to leaf her way into the lens, a brooding silence of body, an acceptance of danger, an ability to become anything that he wanted her to become' (60). Juanita seems to embody the potential danger of the photographs, yet in an almost desirous way. She gestures towards the future destinations of the photograph, at least in Conor's description. In a prefiguration of the eventual problems that come to be associated with the photographs, the prints are stolen and distributed around Juanita's native Mexican town, triggering the departure of Michael and Juanita. This double exposure of Juanita's body, once in Mexico and finally in Michael's published books of photographs, raises questions concerning whose body and subjectivity possesses power in the scopic realm. Juanita seems doomed to be configured as the object of the gaze.

The predominance of ocularcentrism, which is expressed in the narrative of *Songdogs*, has been explored and critiqued by Irigaray. Her philosophical project in her early work returns to two main concerns: first, the dominant scopic economy or ocularcentrism of Western culture, which is allied to and constitutive of, phallogocentrism, and second, the schizophrenic split in this culture between the sensible and the intelligible, a split that is underpinned by the demoting of the role of the corporeal, which is associated with women in the symbolic order. As Grosz writes, Irigaray advocates 'returning the male body to its products' which would reveal the masculine corporeal morphology that structures philosophy (Grosz, 1999, 209). Conor's disgust for his father's ailing body registers just such a resistance to engagements with male corporeality.

Irigaray argues that the Western philosophical tradition is built upon an erasure of the mother and maternal origin. The reliance on ocularcentrism that is inherent in this philosophical tradition since Plato's use of metaphors of the sun to denote creativity permits a fantasy of self-birthing. In her critique of Plato's myth of the cave in *Speculum of the Other Woman*, Irigaray argues that it elides the material and maternal. As Martin Jay writes, Irigaray reads the myth as:

> a kind of phantasmic primal scene in which the role of the mother in engendering culture is elided in favor of the father, the solar origin of Ideas, the specular fount of sameness. The painful birth process is forgotten, repressed, in the service of a male myth of autogenesis. (Jay, 1993a, 537)

Hirsch, in *Family Frames*, points out the relationship between photography and reproduction, reinforced by Barthes's image of the umbilical cord which connects the gaze of the viewer to the object photographed. Hirsch comments on a double anxiety related to the maternal connotations of the act of photography. The anxiety concerns both the medium's ability to create as well as its 'distance, alienation, disembodiedness, objectivity, instrumentality – its ability to kill' (Hirsch, 1997, 170). Barthes's insistence on the capacity of photography to '"resurrect" the object represented' (Hirsch, 1997, 170), his continued reference to the 'return of the dead' enacted in the photograph signals a type of monstrous birth (Barthes, 1993, 9). Hirsch writes:

> When he [Barthes] finds the winter-garden image of his mother as a little girl, he is, in fact, able to resurrect her, to 'give birth' to her, thus actually displacing her own maternity. [. . .] Usurping the maternal function,

Barthes's camera technologizes and instrumentalizes the function of giving life, shaping a masculine maternity or a paternal form of generativity,
a techno-birth. (170–1)

Hirsch, in a chapter concerning the relationship between the mother and
the photographic gaze, notes the importance of the maternal gaze in psychoanalytic theory to subject formation: 'We need only remember Roland
Barthes's evocation of the clarity of his mother's eyes and his fantasy
of being seen and recognized, reflected in those eyes' (155). She cites
Winnicot's re-evaluation of Lacan's mirror stage which replaces the mirror
with the mother. What happens when, as in *Songdogs*, the mother's gaze is
no longer accessible and she is reduced to an image?

The reliance on photography and the visual in *Songdogs* becomes a symptom of and a means to alleviate and control the loss of the maternal. As
Juanita's disappearance is bound up with the publication of photographs
that should have remained private and the unveiling of her body as private
object, the focus on the ocular in the novel is not accidental. Neither, I
would argue, is Michael's role as photographer and Juanita's position as the
ambivalent subject of his gaze. The maternal body and its display as sexual
body seem to be important issues here, particularly for Conor.

Laura Mulvey, in her landmark essay 'Visual Pleasure and Narrative Cinema', discusses how women within cinema, and culture in general, are coded
as occupying the place of the image, as 'connot[ing a] *to-be-looked-at-ness*'
(Mulvey, 2000, 487). Mulvey identifies two strands in how pleasure in looking is constituted: first, scopophilia, 'pleasure in using another person as an
object of sexual stimulation', and secondly, an identificatory impulse with
the image seen, as delineated by Lacan's mirror stage and thus linked to the
formation of the ego (487). Throughout *Songdogs*, Juanita is constantly ush-
ered into a position as object of a male gaze. She poses for Michael when he
first encounters her in Mexico, although her performance is for Michael
himself rather than for the camera. Neither the camera, nor the photographic images, are of concern to her. However, after the photographs of
her are publicized in Mayo, she becomes increasingly self-conscious and
aware of her location within the dynamics of the gaze. Due to her sense of
displacement from the Irish landscape, Juanita eventually rejects her codification as an object to be looked at and displayed, by a double act of invisibility. She burns the books in which the photographs are published as well as
Michael's dark room and photographic equipment, before literally disappearing herself. It is this conflagration that marks the turning point in the
lives of Michael, Conor, and Juanita, the moment that Conor is trying to

recuperate and render meaningful. Juanita succeeds in wresting control of her image, though it is at the expense of erasing herself. She can no longer be grasped by narrative, memory, or photograph. Conor cannot find her, literally or metaphorically. Her history following the destruction of the dark room remains unknown, though the novel insinuates that she has drowned herself in the river, particularly when Michael finally permits himself to discuss the matter with his son. Although the exchange is brief, Michael raises the possibility of her suicide in the river. It seems somewhat appropriate that it could be to the river, associated with time and the pull of the past, which she has finally returned.

Textual descriptions of her within the photographs themselves never seem to remain stable. She is never quite captured and controlled. Her body is depicted as on the verge of slipping away: 'Her body sweeps away from her in the photograph, along the *chaise-longue*, a sheet of paper flying in the breeze' (144). It is this particular pose that Conor's father relishes, 'he is enjoying the capture of it', though it is clear that even within the final image her corporeality continues to 'sweep away from her' (144). Her body never seems quite coherent in either the photographs or in Conor's 'memories' of her. What the photograph 'captures' is merely the elusiveness of any attempt to render the body in a coherent, unified sense. It is significant that it is Juanita's physicality that registers the difficulty of capture; it is her body that finally eludes the attempts of Michael, Conor, and the reader to locate and make sense of her disappearance. Her final destination remains unknowable.

The photographs that Michael eventually publishes of Juanita deprive her of a sense of control over herself in time or over her physical existence: 'Instead of Mam's own body breaking itself down in the slow natural entropy of motherhood and age, it became something else altogether – destroyed for her in a strange sort of way' (170). The power of the photographic image is such that it halts the movement of time. Michael intends it as a memorial, and interestingly, the photographs and the incidents that they precipitate force Conor's continuous attempt to engage with memory and narrative, and result in Michael's desire to forget:

'Why did ya let that happen?' I said. 'With the photos.'
'Ah, Jaysus, is that what this is all about?'
'I'm just asking. Why did ya…?'
'Can't a man forget?'
'Don't think so'. (191)

The question, 'Why did you let that happen?', is never answered though a tentative kind of reconciliation between father and son is initiated, which is furthered by Conor's assistance in bathing his father. The mother is used here as a ground (to use Irigaray's terminology) upon which the father-son genealogy can be repaired. This is not entirely successful within the novel and McCann's narrative seems to make explicit the limitations of this appropriation of the maternal. The mother has been doubly silenced and neither Conor nor Michael can locate her or bring her back. As Aidan Arrowsmith suggests, 'The connection he [Conor] seeks eludes him' (Arrowsmith, 2005, 313).

Conor seems to physically enter photographs taken in New York in an attempt to communicate with his mother: 'I stand in front of her and ask: Are ya happy, Mam? She doesn't reply' (139). When, in the second photograph, he does finally talk to her, she merely says, 'When are you going to get rid of that stupid earring, Conor?' (142). Conor gives it to her, thus passing on an object which had been offered to him by one of the searchers for his mother when she disappeared. The implication is that the earring belonged to his mother; it is all that remains. By surrendering the object to her in an invented 'memory', Conor begins an acceptance of past events. The fact that he no longer wears the earring is one of the first things noticed by his father when he returns home.

What then of issues relating to memory and the past? Memory, in *Songdogs*, is constructed in visual terms; photographs provide the thresholds and the means by which to imagine a past one never occupied. The photographs appear to confer a power to the viewer, that is, Conor, in terms of the construction of a narrative to encapsulate the past; yet they also deny him absolute mastery over bygone events or over what he sees. He cannot remain a detached observer but is drawn into the photograph. Conor's engagement with the past initiates an intertwining between photograph, his parents' narratives, and his own inventions. Conor looks to the photographic image to enact the return of the departed, to recall his mother, though this can never fully be realized.

In Wyoming, Conor had helped his Native American friends, Eliza and her son Kutch (his parents had known Eliza in the past and had been present at Kutch's birth) to remove dead coyotes from a fence. Eliza makes bracelets from their teeth and later she and Kutch bury the bodies. The removal of the coyotes represents the rescinding of a bodily warning against journeying among the dead and travelling into the past. Immediately after the burial, Conor returns to his photograph album. In a similar manner to his relationship with the photographs of the Spanish women, he describes walking into the photographs and entering the past in a physical way. These are the New York photographs. In the first photograph Conor describes, it is only by 'walking into the photographs, going beyond the rim and up very close' that one can distinguish the faces of the people that populate the scene and recognize that they are Irish immigrants (136). The dynamic interaction between viewer and photograph that he describes is interesting. His portrayal of his act of viewing as a physical motion illustrates his attempts both to see all and to communicate with the dead, or those that are gone. He attempts to revitalize those that populate the photograph, although 'for time immemorial, that boy will be leaping. And I will never know if the ball is caught' (141). The photographs are continuously resistant.

Conor's experience of post-memory remains complicated. The reliance on the visual and the investment in the power of the gaze permit, yet impede, access to his parents' lives and to his understanding of past events. The photographs serve both to revive his mother while simultaneously signalling her continuous departure, silence, and invisibility. She is on the verge of disappearance in most images and she can never quite be grasped. The ending of the novel seems to gesture towards Conor's acceptance of both the limitations of the visual order as well as the necessity for invention and imagination.

Interspersed throughout the novel are Michael's vain attempts to catch an imaginary salmon in the now polluted river which bring to mind the mythic salmon of knowledge. Michael believes in the existence of this 'giant pink salmon' despite Conor's scepticism. As the novel concludes, he is again 'on the riverbank, clapping his hands together and laughing and shouting at the magnificence of his fish'. When asked 'Did ya see it, son?', Conor replies, 'Yeah, I saw it', in recognition of his father's need to maintain the fiction (212). The visual order is revealed here as a location for invention, imagination, and reconciliation between father and son, which however necessitates the occlusion of the mother and the maternal.

This Side of Brightness

McCann's second novel, *This Side of Brightness*, was published in 1998. It is his first sustained narrative set entirely in the United States, extending on the American episodes of his short story collection, *Fishing the Sloe-Black River* published in 1994, and his first novel, *Songdogs*. It is, he claims 'consciously non-Irish', though the novel contains significant Irish characters (Battersby, 1998). McCann argues that 'it is possible to write an Irish novel without writing a word about Ireland [. . .] [*This Side of Brightness*] wasn't on the surface an Irish novel but the opening scene begins in 1916 and there is a sort of resurrection scene' (McCann, 1994b). The novel tells the story of three generations of the multi-racial Walker family in New York City from 1916 to the early 1990s. McCann extensively researched his story, documenting his progress in journalistic reports (McCann, 1996; 1997).

The narrative, at the beginning, centres on the character Treefrog, who lives in the tunnels of the New York subway. Interspersed with Treefrog's narrative is that of Nathan Walker, a young black man from Georgia, who works as a sandhog in the tunnels in 1916. Walker is involved in an accident in the tunnels in which he and his friends are blown upwards through the Hudson River. All survive except one, Con O'Leary, an Irishman, who remains buried in the tunnel walls. Walker marries Con's daughter, Eleanor, with whom he has three children, two girls and a boy named Clarence. Clarence fights in the Korean War where he meets Louisa, a Native American, with whom he has a son, Clarence Nathan. Eleanor is later killed in a car accident and Clarence murders both the driver and a policeman before escaping to Georgia to see the swamps and cranes (birds) that Walker often reminisced about. Here he is beaten and killed and in the subsequent years Louisa becomes an alcoholic and heroin addict before finally overdosing. A profound relationship develops between Walker and his grandson, who is gifted with perfect balance. Clarence Nathan eventually gets a job in skyscraper construction due to his aptitude for height; he marries a girl named Dancesca and has a daughter, Lenora. On one occasion when he accompanies his grandfather to the tunnels to visit Con O'Leary's body, Clarence Nathan fails to save Walker from an oncoming train. Following Walker's death Clarence Nathan begins to injure himself and also starts to touch his daughter inappropriately. His wife and daughter leave him and he moves into the tunnels becoming Treefrog, a nickname given to him by his colleagues on the skyscraper. Here he lives in a 'nest' only reached by a precarious negotiation of catwalks until he encounters Angela, a fellow tunnel dweller, to whom he is attracted.

The relationship between these parallel narratives only becomes clear towards the end of the novel. Retrospectively, the narratives can be seen to operate as a Möbius strip, one beginning as the other concludes, though they are positioned side-by-side throughout the novel. The circularity of events twists the narrative back upon itself to reveal the interwoven nature of both stories. Nathan's grandson, Clarence Nathan, becomes the tunnel-dwelling Treefrog, inhabiting the subway tunnels dug out by his grandfather although the connections do not become apparent until late in the text. Treefrog's narrative also contains his reminiscences about his former life with his wife and child. Links between the two major, seemingly separate, stories are also signalled aesthetically in the novel. Each section subtly references its predecessor; the river mentioned at the end of Chapter Four becomes an icicle hanging near Treefrog's nest in the following chapter, representing his frozen life.

The Subway

This Side of Brightness tells the story of the Walker family but it also recounts the history of the New York subway in its various incarnations from its inception to its subsequent decay. According to McCann, 'There are 800 miles of tunnels in New York. They were built by Irishmen, Italians and African-Americans, many of whom lost their lives in the construction [. . .] There are between 2,000 to 5,000 living underground in Manhattan. A good 75 per cent of them are African-American males' (McCann, 1997).[2] Michael W. Brooks, in his history of the subway, argues that it operates for this city, more so than any other, as a symbol of New York as a whole and has been continuously evoked as a type of infernal space. However, at its inception, it signalled a new conception of the city in terms of its spatial awareness. The rapid transport promised by a working subway would expand the confines of the city, alleviate the overcrowded slums by linking undeveloped land with the urban working centre, and also enable early New Yorkers to 'define a new kind of metropolis' (Brooks, 1997, 3). This utopian vision of the subway and the city it served did not survive the subway's completion due to overcrowding and delays in creating sufficient functional lines. The subway's fate as a negative symbol of urban life was thus cemented.

Brooks notes that, for many of the writers and artists who chose to focus on the subway and skyscraper from the 1920s, these architectural features become 'emblems of the city's moral condition' and these two opposing but ultimately related structures became representative of the 'complex opposition between upward and downward, aspiration and confinement, freedom and compulsion, and, ultimately, life and death' (Brooks, 1997, 122–3). *This Side of Brightness* plays out these relationships, staging an obsessive desire for balance that must ultimately be forsaken.

The subway's main function is connection, yet this aspect of underground transport is invisible in the novel. The tunnels are, instead, represented as self-contained spaces, differentiated from the outside. Although the subway is identified as a public space in most of the literature concerning it, the tunnel in the novel is associated with the Walker family on a more private level. It is interwoven into the narrative of the family, particularly on the level of Walker's personality. The subway comes to represent a space of escape from the public arena and a space associated with memory, symbolized by the 'fossilisation' of Con O'Leary in the tunnel. While its function as a means of physically linking places is of little concern to the narrative of *This Side of Brightness*, the subway works to connect on a more abstract level. It operates as an important intermediary in the early stages of the relationship between Walker and Eleanor and also forms the most powerful element in the bond between Walker and his grandson. In McCann's novel, the mythology of the subway becomes the mythology of the Walker family. The family is deeply imbricated in the physicality of the city. The city's architectural development has had profound implications for their life. The story takes us from tunnel digging to subway train riding to dwelling in the tunnels themselves. The life cycle of the subway is represented in the novel as well as the story of the Walker family.[3]

The history of the subway, as outlined by Brooks, represents its development as explicitly and implicitly connected to the utopian imaginings of the city itself. Initially promised as a means to remedy the problems of urban life, the subway became instead a symbol of its dissolution. The utopian image of the subway was imbricated in a conception of the city as an organized, working system, not unlike certain discourses of the human body. In such rhetoric, the subway becomes the veins and arteries that supply the city with life. Although it was imagined at its inception as a means of uniting the city, it became a way of highlighting its divisions and hierarchies (Brooks, 1997, 53–4) Clarence Nathan's impression of Harlem corresponds with this view. Harlem is,

> so alive that its own heart could burst from the accumulated grief. As if it all might fulminate under the gravity of living. As if the city itself has given birth to the intricacies of the human heart. Veins and arteries – like his grandfather's tunnels – tumbling with blood. And millions of men and women sloshing that blood along the streets. (McCann, 1998, 185)

The subway seems to be consistently associated with corporeality. As its cultural value decreases, the rhetoric either involves comparisons to 'lower' bodily regions, such as the bowels, or it is linked to a kind of menacing and consuming womb. Jim Dwyer, author of *Subway Lives*, refers to the subways as the 'midwifery and mortuary to the city' (Dwyer, 1991, 10), while Garrett Ziegler terms it 'the black womb of the tunnels' (Ziegler, 2004, 285). In *This*

Side of Brightness, Walker relates a story concerning the beginnings of the tunnel in the 1860s when they dug the underground in secret. The foreman of the tunnel is christened 'The Tapeworm' due to the fact that 'he once cut a digger's stomach with a knife after the digger told the secret that they was building a tunnel' (47). The appellation is also presumably due to a cultural awareness of the underground's metaphorical inscription as intestinal.

The subway also becomes the subconscious of the city. McCann, in his article entitled 'The Mole People', confirms this view. He writes that 'the tunnels are the subconscious mind of the city. Everything that the city wants to forget about – its filth, its ruin, its violence, its dispossessed – ends up in the darkness, all of it waiting to get out again, as if in some vivid dream or nightmare' (1997). However, in his novel, the repressed erupts from the depths of the underground, symbolized in the incident of the tunnel blowout.[4]

The blowout itself is figured in particularly corporeal terms, beginning with McCann's description of the hole: 'At first the weak spot is the size of a fist, then a heart, then a head.' Furthermore, due to the intense air pressure Walker's own body occupies the space of a plug:

> Walker's feet can't grip the soil. He slides towards the widening hole and is sucked into it, shovel first, then his outstretched arms, followed by his head, right up to his shoulders, where his body stops, a cork in the tunnel. His upper torso belongs to the soil, his legs to the tunnel. (11)

He is propelled upwards through the riverbed by the pressurized air as it is released through the hole. He rises, it seems, through a brutal history of the Hudson River:

> Still conscious, he rises through the riverbed. Past what? Dutch ships sunk centuries before? Animal carcasses? Arrowheads? Scalps with hair still growing? Men with concrete blocks attached to their feet? The dead from slave ships, bleached down to the bone? All the time the air cushions Walker against the tremendous weight of soil and sand and silt. He is an embryo in a sac, sheltered as he is slammed upwards, five feet, ten feet, through the riverbed, the air pocket cutting a path through the dirt, keeping him safe. (15)

Walker is birthed from the darkness of the tunnel into the 'pure blackness, water blackness' of the river; he shoots from the earth to the water before a second birthing into the air above the river's surface. Walker is followed by his fellow sandhoggers, Power and Vannucci. Their ascension through the river to emerge on the surface of the East River is figured in particularly traumatic somatic terms: they experience,

> the shock of water, struggling for breath, chest heaving, the panic of being surrounded by water, convinced they will drown, they will all drown, pike and trout and dirt and pebbles will make a home in their bloated bellies, barges will scour the water for their bodies, seashells will nestle in their eyeballs'. (15)

The sandhoggers are particularly aware of their bodies and of their materiality which can be easily destroyed due to the nature of their work. They are attuned to how bodies become elements of historical landscapes and how their corporeality might become a component in the river's material existence. The birthing metaphor allows their experience to be figured in terms of a resurrection, it accords them power, 'they have been blown upwards like gods' (16). Con O'Leary remains the exception and his body is caught between tunnel and riverbed as canvas and clay are spread over the river bottom to seal the hole. His wife, Maura, understands the fate of his body, telling her neighbours that 'her husband has already become a fossil' (20).

Ziegler points out that the subway is also often imagined as inorganic and technological. During the interwar era when 'subway use was at its peak', passengers experienced alienation:

> The sheer lack of individual control occasioned by the subway left its passengers completely at the mercy of the mysterious powers of planned technology. (Ziegler, 2004, 290)

Rosalind Williams also comments on this point of view in her book, *Notes on the Underground*, remarking that representations of subterranean space often denote 'the displacement of the natural environment by a technological one' (Williams, 1990, 4). In *This Side of Brightness*, however, the representation of the subway and its tunnels instead explores the relationship between the city and the body and the inextricable links between urban landscape and corporeality. Technology and 'nature' remain interwoven. The body and city rely on each other and feed off each other for metaphors and for memories.

The relationship that the novel explores is akin to Grosz's attempts to theorize alternative conceptions to the existing models that link corporeality and architecture. The first such model views the city as 'a reflection, projection, or product of bodies', whereas the second correlates the two resulting in ideas of the body politic (Grosz, 1999, 382–3). Grosz instead calls for conceptualizations that move beyond these two paradigms, 'a model of the relations between bodies and cities that sees them, not as megalithic total entities, but as assemblages or collections of parts' (385). The city acts as an element in the social, cultural, and biological configurations of the corporeal and is also the locus for 'the body's cultural saturation, its takeover and transformation by images, representational systems, the mass media, and the arts' (386). Concurrently, the body also impacts upon the landscape, altering it to suit its own needs.

The representation of the subway in the novel highlights these connections between the urban landscape and the human body. McCann distinguishes the sandhogs by their corporeal appearance: 'Some have tattoos, others have jiggling bellies, a few are emaciated, most are sinewy' (5–6). Indeed, in much of the art that appeared in the 1920s and 1930s, which focused on the subway builders, it is the explicit physicality of their bodies that is portrayed.[5] The sandhogs' bodies are affected on a profound physical level by their actions in the tunnels. Above all, their profession exerts an influence over their health:

> If they could reach down into their throats they could chisel out diseases from their lungs. The tar and the filth could come away in their fingertips. They could hold a piece of flue-coloured tissue and say: This is what the tunnels have done to me. (6)

The continued presence of the tunnels is expressed somatically. Their bodies have been inscribed and altered by the materiality of the tunnels. Bodies are revealed as fragile, yet also resistant and enduring.

Flesh and its desires are evoked by the 'muckers' as they progress deeper into the darkness of the tunnel in order to alleviate the sense of danger and potential death that are associated with their profession:

> 'Hotter than a whore's kitchen today,' says Power.
> 'Ain't that the truth?'
> 'Ever been in a whore's kitchen?'
> 'Only for breakfast,' says Walker. 'Grits and eggs over easy.'
> 'I swear! Listen to the youngster!'
> 'And a little sizzling bacon.'
> 'Whooeee, I like that.'

'Backside bacon. With a little on the rind.'
'Now we're talking'. (5–6)

Evoking both sexual desire and appetite for food, the muckers reaffirm
their corporeality in the face of 'the belly of blackness' (5). McCann's metaphor also draws attention to a figuration of the tunnels as capable of consuming its workers in an obliterating darkness which thus requires them to
become aware of their own somatic presence. In a superstitious gesture to
ensure good luck they touch the planks which hold the tunnel in place,
verifying both their own existence and the wood which keeps them from
being swallowed up by the mud of the riverbed. Indeed, Brooks recalls the
words of the artist George Tooker, which confirm this attitude towards the
subway tunnel; the subway for the latter 'represented "a denial of the senses
and a negation of life itself"' (Brooks, 1997, 169).

Walker's corporeality is noted by the other tunnel workers. He is 'tall and
muscular' and is the most proficient of the sandhogs. They 'envy his fluidity,
the way the shovel seems to meld into his whole torso, the quiet mastery of
his burrowing' (8). He appears comfortable in the subterranean tunnel,
smearing the mud from the river onto his body to keep himself cool and
refusing to succumb to the fear of being injured that is a constant in a sandhogger's life:

He knows that at any moment an avalanche of muck and water could
sweep the men backwards. They could drown with the East River going
down their throats, strange fish and odd rocks in their bellies [. . .] Or
escaping air could suck them against the wall, whosh them through space,
shatter their spines against a breast board [. . .] Or the bends – the
dreaded bends – could send nitrogen bubbles racing to their knees or
shoulders or brains. Walker has seen men collapse in the tunnel, grasping
at their joints, their bodies ribboned in sudden agony – it's a sandhog's
disease, there is not a thing anyone can do about it, and the afflicted are
taken back to the manlock where their bodies are decompressed as slowly
as possible.
    But these things don't scare Walker – he is alive and in yellowy
darkness he uses every ounce of his body to shove the river tunnel
along. (9)

Walker's salvation seems to be his command of his body. His corporeality
is represented as strong and resistant to the tunnel. It is with his body

that he is capable of altering the terrain of the underground and thus he remains immune to the fear of that landscape's power over him. Interestingly, the darkness here is depicted as lightened and yellowy; it is no longer an all-consuming blackness thus according with Walker's attitude.

The novel explicitly links issues of race to the representation of the subway in a manner that parallels the tunnels' connection to the corporeal. Brooks notes that for many writers and artists who dealt with the subway, particularly with ideas of the crowd that inhabited its trains and spaces, the issues of race and gender proved problematic: 'observers of the subway crowd could not help seeing that the distinct historical experience of women and African-Americans in the city as a whole were reflected in their experience underground' (Brooks, 1997, 159).[6] Indeed, he highlights the racial tensions implicit in the subway. While the space offers a means for the different races to 'mingle easily', the subway also replicates the 'separations and tensions of the larger society [. . .] in covert, unacknowledged forms. The subway became a place of repressed resentments' (Brooks, 1997, 183).[7] Such an assessment suggests the underground as a type of subconscious.

Brooks notes that African-American writers and artists viewed the subway as both symbolic of New York and, more particularly, as deeply connected to Harlem. It is fitting that Nathan settles in Harlem and refuses to leave. Harlem was the area of the city focused on by subway developers as the part of New York that would most obviously benefit from the reality of rapid transport. A typical promise ran as follows: 'You have no idea of the happiness, comfort, and prosperity which quick transit will bring you here in Harlem. Your vacant lots will be built upon, your vacant houses filled' (qtd. in Brooks, 1997, 23). Harlem's fate becomes fundamentally linked to how the subway develops and in time it represents topside's equivalent of the subway. Certain writers have, as Brooks contends, specifically linked the creation of this section of New York as a predominantly black community with the development of the subway (183–9).

Representations of the subway were also used 'to almost simultaneously assert and deny the importance of racial difference' (Brooks, 1997, 185). This tension is observed in McCann's novel through the attitudes of the sandhogs while digging the tunnels:

> He [Nathan Walker] knows there is a democracy beneath the river. In the darkness every man's blood runs the same colour – a dago the same as a nigger the same as a polack the same as a mick. (5)

The use of racist terms maintains the inequalities that are upheld on the surface; however, Nathan identifies the space of the tunnel as a haven of equality that is not available to him anywhere else:

> It strikes Walker that it's only in the tunnels that he feels any equality of darkness. The sandhogs were the first integrated union in the country and he knows that it is only underground that colour is negated, that men become men.
> Not even in the gloom of the cinema can he slip like a snake through his own skin. (37)

This is borne out by the prevaricatory appellations used for Nathan: 'He ain't a nigger, son, he's a sandhog' (41). It is only outside the tunnel that the individual features of the men can be distinguished. The darkness of the underground obliterates these somatic signifiers: 'For the first time all day they can see the cleft in Con O'Leary's chin, the scars around Nathan Walker's eyes, the rude bumps in Sean Power's nose and Rhubarb Vannucci's sleek brown skin' (11).

The equalizing darkness of the tunnels is mirrored in the relationship of Nathan and Eleanor; it is in the darkness of cinemas as well as on empty streets, that is, public spaces not visible to the general public, that they can express their love. There is danger in the communal gaze. Eleanor observes that the disapproving glances of the public possess a very real implication for the safety of their bodies: 'When you walk past and you feel like they've just sliced you? Like they've got these razor blades in their eyes' (85).

In the novel, the subway, and more specifically its tunnels, represent what is amiss with New York urban life as well as delineating a space that the multi-racial Walker family (albeit only the male members, and specifically Walker himself) can think of as somehow connected with them. Very few, if any, of the instances of race-oriented violence that occur in the novel actually take place in the tunnels despite the dominant cultural assumptions that hold the underground space of the subway to be a locus for race-focused violence.[8]

The life of the Walker family seems to mirror the public perception of the subway as delineated by Brooks in *Subway City*. Walker's largely positive relationship with the tunnels occurs contemporaneously with the utopian visions of the space. Treefrog's descent into the tunnels corresponds historically with the period in which the subway's symbolic value was at its lowest. This occurred because hysteria concerning violence on the subway became widespread and mostly directed towards African-Americans and Hispanics. Treefrog's emergence at the conclusion of the novel also reflects Brooks's perception that the semiotic function of the subways is shifting to include its conception as 'a place to celebrate the urban experience' (224). Interestingly *Subway City* and *This Side of Brightness* were published within a year of each other and perhaps reflect the new cultural attitudes towards this architectural feature in the late nineties.

Walker's body is continually represented as consistent, strong, and defiant of the tunnel: 'Walker's body remains constant, the big arms, the tough ribcage, the ripple of muscle' (45). McCann uses Walker's corporeality as a point of reference, a fulcrum around which the story can be built. Although it is initially noted that his body does not alter much as time passes, incidents such as a new scar provide opportunities to expand upon the narrative. Later in the tale, however, Walker's body begins to deteriorate due to rheumatism, a souvenir from his career as a digger. Although the pain forces Walker to take notice of his body, he also begins to retreat into memory in order to distance himself from the pain:

> It's almost as if he doesn't inhabit his body, but hovers somewhere beyond it, a wheel of energy watching himself beginning to break down [. . .] Standing by the stove, again removed, again hovering. Walker watches himself as a boy, guiding a canoe through the black swamps. (110)

The body itself serves as a repository for memory. It will not let you forget, as Clarence Walker, Nathan's son, observes: 'We forget we have blood 'till it comes out from us' (143).

Memories of Con O'Leary seem explicitly connected to the corporeal for other characters. Walker recalls his assistance in a fight and also relates to Maura, Con's trick of holding a bullet in his stomach while digging for the entire day. Con's memory becomes embedded in and embodied by the tunnel; Walker greets him in the soil every morning and in later life he and his friends often travel the subway to speak to him and to read him baseball scores. An excursion of this kind, on foot within the tunnel rather than by train, becomes the occasion of Walker's death. Maura's dreams depict the slow decay of his body in the tunnel:

> the dreams that she has of her husband's watch – it is there, ticking away in his ribs, his bones are knotted together with suspenders and the second hand is counting the dripaway of his flesh. (35)

She also continuously imagines his 'resurrection', his ascent through the riverbed. The story becomes an important element in the courtship of Nathan and Eleanor, Maura's daughter.

Memory, or the past, in the novel can resurface in the present:

The remainder [of a silence remembering the dead in the tunnels] is like the silence of having forgotten something very important, then remembering it and re-living it all at once. (42)

Memory seems to manifest itself somatically. Treefrog, for example, while reliving the memory of his daughter on the swing 'feels the familiar huge hollowness in his body and [he] pulls away, wincing at the vision' (33).

Within the tunnels memory resides in specific spaces: 'That's where the foreman with the glass eye sat [. . .] And the welder went on fire here' (40). The memories all concern physical damage due to the nature of the sandhogger's work. Bodies are irretrievably altered by the tunnel experience. Time's progression is also felt in terms of the tunnel's effect on the corporeal: 'Walker notes the passing of years by the way the tunnel dust settles down in his lungs; by the wrinkles that appear at Maura O'Leary's eyes' (47). As in *Songdogs*, memory is represented as a creative process: 'And so Walker tells her [Eleanor] things that help her sleep, things he invents and remembers and, by remembering, invents' (82).

Body Image

In her analysis of various theories of corporeality in *Volatile Bodies*, Grosz notes the existence of the body image or 'imaginary anatomy', which functions as an intermediary between the physiological and the psychological but illustrates their interconnectivity and interdependence (Grosz, 1994, 79). Her account is based on the work of both Lacan and the neurophysiologist, Paul Schilder. The body image is composed, not only of one's anatomy, but also of psychological processes and sociohistorical situations. It is 'an internalized image or map of the meaning that the body has for the subject, for others in its social world, and for the symbolic order conceived in its generality (that is, for a culture as a whole)' (Grosz, 1994, 39–40).

A distinction between the mind and the body is never clearly delineated in *This Side of Brightness*. 'For a moment suicide scratches the side of his brain. He lets it rest there and gouge a ditch into his thoughts' (226–7). Mental processes are described in a physical manner. The body is imagined by certain characters in the novel as a location in which trauma can be played out. Clarence, while on the run following his murder of Hoover McCauliffe (who had knocked down and killed his mother, Eleanor) and a policeman, conceptualizes what might happen to his own body:

> He could fall right now, land on the tracks and lie there, snakelike, and wait for the segmentation of his body, let the wheels chop him into the tiniest of pieces, let his head travel a mile from his feet, slice his heart into two pumping pieces, scatter his toes to the different winds. (144–5)

The image of the body is, for Clarence, a means of enacting and expressing psychological pain. His grief and guilt are imbricated in the destruction he wreaks on his abstract corporeality. In Georgia, Clarence continues to inflict pain on an imaginary body:

> The razor feels cool against his throat. He imagines it going deeper and deeper into his neck, right down to the tendons and the veins and beyond – when the veins are open and deep, his baby boy will swim down into his bloodstream, his groin, his brain, his heart. (146)

Walker's idea of his own corporeality is also affected following the deaths of both Eleanor and Clarence. His body becomes 'a dark room of nothingness' and his reaction is also to imagine a process of fragmentation and disintegration:

> He might let his body melt into the cushions and stay there forgotten, like one of his dropped coins. He might reach down for the decayed parts of himself and throw them out of the window to the ghost of Clarence below on the stoop, bits of arms, legs, fingers and an eyeball as currency for the gone. (150)

He is only reconciled to his life in any way when viewing Louisa's performance of a crane's dance; the sight of a body synchronized in movement is soothing.

Thus, the body image can also be employed to initiate a healing process. Papa Love, another of the tunnel dwellers, uses a representation of his corporeality to express his grief following the death of his lover:

> He began walking after his lover died, walked the length and breadth of the city, slept on the steps of a church, and then one summer he decided

to strap his heart to a cardboard box [. . .] and he strapped his aorta on one side, and he strapped his pulmonary on the other, and he tied them both very neatly together, and he strapped all his veins longways down the cardboard, and he strapped all his arteries in the opposite direction, and he weaved them together with a muscle of his heart and he felt as if all his blood was exploding and he lay down on the brown sprawl and looked down the length of the dark tunnel. (135)

For Papa Love, as for the other characters, projecting an image of one's body outside oneself and taking control over its morphology allows participation in processes of grief. His painting of his sorrow gives him both his tunnel name and precipitates his move into the underground space. Treefrog imagines Angela standing on his painful liver in the stance of a sandhog. She digs the diseased flesh away:

Angela scrapes all the residue from him and when a spot is clean she leans across and kisses it and it sends a shiver through the rest of his body. All the filth comes away at her feet and she buckets it out of his liver and, when he is cured, they dance around his liver together in an ecstatic twirl, their eyes closed, round and round and round, Angela with her colourful beads bobbing in her hair, and then there is a sucking sound and they are blown upwards through his body and out his mouth and she stands in front of him, smiling, all the bile gone.(71)[9]

In Treefrog's use of the body image, not only does he envisage a healing process that will take place later in the novel, but he identifies his body with both the physical space of the tunnel and with his grandfather's experience in it. The forthcoming process of psychological reconciliation for Treefrog is prefigured here by an imaginative engagement with his corporeal space and with his body image.

The body image attests to the interconnectedness of the psychical and the biological. In the novel, the use of this 'imaginary anatomy' by the characters reveals the ways in which psychological processes are dealt with by their alterations of the imagined body's morphology. Treefrog's dream excavation of his diseased liver also introduces another important vector in the network of relationships that create the body image; that of one's surroundings and more specifically here, the subway tunnels. As mentioned, Treefrog configures his body in this dream as synonymous with the tunnel and its blowout. More precisely, he identifies his liver with the tunnel. The tunnel here becomes a space linked with disease and with the lower regions of the body.

Mapping and Touch

Brooks, in his detailed history of the New York subways, only briefly mentions the homeless who dwell in the tunnels, referencing Jennifer Toth's earlier account entitled *The Mole People* (1993). Brooks reads her text and the general cultural reception of these people as an example of 'myth overwhelm[ing] mundane reality' (Brooks, 1997, 220). The tunnel dwellers are represented as 'the unsettling phenomenon of human beings who have been completely subsumed within a mythic identity' (Brooks, 1997, 221). Brooks does not elaborate on the specificities of the myth; they are, however, explored in more detail by David L. Pike in his article 'Urban Nightmares and Future Visions'. He comments on a dominance of references to infernal descents. Pike identifies various narratives that surround the 'mole people'. These tend to focus on the physical attributes of the people such as stories describing webbed feet. He also notes the 'allegorical resonance of social and racial alienation' that permeates much of the fiction dealing with subterranean life (Pike, 1998, 20). Pike concludes that depictions of New York's underground continue to engage with issues of poverty and violence, issues which are connected to the use of subterranean space as a potent site in which the fears of society can be articulated, as well as its desires. Treefrog's narrative serves, in *This Side of Brightness*, as a means in which these fears and desires can be both identified and played out. The body, in this context, also acts as an important locus for the expression of these tensions.

Following the description of the 1916 blowout, the third chapter opens with Treefrog's uncertainty concerning his continued consciousness: 'There is a moment upon waking when he thinks he might not wake forever. Treefrog touches his liver to make sure he is still alive and remembers the crane he found frozen yesterday in the Hudson' (22). Upon waking and in order to assert his existence, Treefrog needs to touch his own body, to pinch it and to hold his hands over a candle flame long enough for them to experience pain. The experience of corporeality and of one's own tangibility is vital in the darkness of the underground; it is here that the issue of touch becomes important.

This Side of Brightness consistently focuses on the materiality of the body. Corporeality drives the narrative forward as time is marked by alterations on the flesh of the characters. The bodies of the characters are deeply influenced by their surroundings; they are inextricably connected to place, whether it is the physically detrimental effects of the tunnels, the danger implicit in the public eye for the Walkers, or the harsh reality of tunnel

dwelling for the moles. For Treefrog, as the apex of the generational triangle that is explored in the novel, touch, arguably the most physical of the
senses, becomes integral to his sense of self as evidenced in his need to
haptically map the places and people he is familiar with.[10]

Furthermore, it is an inappropriate use of touch in relation to his daughter that forced his relocation from topside to the tunnels:

> his hands are at her armpits and he wishes he could lift his history out of
> her, his daughter, he is touching her and he will touch her again and he
> will be found out and he will come down the tunnel and he will try to
> murder his hands in shame. (105)

For Treefrog, this act is connected to his grandfather's death. It specifically
encodes his failure to lift his grandfather from the tunnels before the next
train arrived, following a walk to visit the site of the 'resurrection' and Con
O'Leary's body, though for his family the touch is far more troubling and
abusive. Clarence Nathan dreams that he is 'chopping his hands off and
sucking out the marrow in his bones until there is a hollow corridor along
which he walks, as high with despair as Manhattan' (222). The body becomes
the city; his veins become the subway tunnels in which he will live. From this
moment Clarence begins to 'murder his hands', inflict wounds and stub
out cigarettes on them to counteract the pain of losing his grandfather. It is
also then that his desire to touch everything twice begins; balance and symmetry become inextricably linked with the memory of his grandfather, and
touch becomes connected with the trauma of his death. Clarence Nathan
continues to scar his body, burning himself with heated paperclips:

> His heart doesn't feel in any way involved, only his body. The sensation of
> it. The deliciousness. He welcomes it, greets it. The body as his form, the
> pain as its content. His skin looks like a desertscape of these imprinted
> patterns, equally scorched on both sides of his body, burnt on with the
> curiosity of an onlooker. (225)

While the sandhoggers revelled in their physicality and exalted their materiality in order to survive in the consuming darkness of the tunnels, Clarence
Nathan inflicts pain on his body in order to limit his feeling to the physical.
This incessant and violent focus on the material also serves to reiterate his
existence in a negative version of the sandhogs' superstitious touching of
the tunnel walls and constant invocation of the flesh and its desires. Clarence Nathan has taken this superstition to an extreme, touching everything

with his hands twice, as well as insisting on symmetry and balance in every action.

Touch is also connected with blindness in the novel. Treefrog creates his maps with the sense of touch alone, with his eyes shut: 'He knows that to be blind means that everything is abrupt, that nothing announces its approach except memory. All true light recedes with the memory of light' (247). For the inhabitants of the subway tunnels vision ceases to be the primary sense. Treefrog moves around his 'nest' without using sight. He 'feels the darkness, smells it, belongs to it' (23). His morning ritual involves touching the walls of his cave before committing what he has felt to paper in the form of a haptic map, a cartography of what he has touched:

> Circling the small cave, he trails his hand against the wall as he goes, feeling the crevices and coldness. With each change in the landscape he opens his eyes and marks an increment on the graph paper. He returns and feels the same place with his other hand, caresses the rock, and lets the cold seep through his leather gloves. (23)

Treefrog knows his surroundings underground without looking at them. In the darkness, his sense of touch keeps him anchored to familiarity: 'Every hollow and crinkle of mud is recognised from the way it touches his feet' (24). Treefrog's daily ritual of mapping the haptic experience of his cave is his means of securing the space surrounding him and of registering his presence:

> He draws a quick profile of where he has walked. This is his most important ritual, he cannot start his day without it. He exaggerates the features to ten times their map size, so that, on paper, the nest looks like a rumple of huge valleys and mountains and plains. Even the tiniest nicks in the wall become huge hollows. Later he will transfer them to a larger map he has been working on for the past four years, a map of where he lives, hand-drawn, intricate, secretive, with hills, rivers, ox-bow lakes, curved creeks, shadows, the cartography of darkness. (24–5)

The maps are Treefrog's means of expanding the limited spaces of the subway tunnel, of re-drawing the landscape that he inhabits.

Mapping in the novel appears to be a means of marking presence, of delineating and affirming one's existence. Treefrog conceptualizes his feelings through the medium of mapping. He first detects Angela from the shadows of the tunnel: 'If, at that time, [he] had made a map of the beats of his heart, the contours would have been so close together that the lines would almost have touched one another in the steepest and finest of gradations' (60–1). His explanation for his need to make maps is so that God can find him, 'can follow the contours all the way back here' (210). Treefrog also conceptualizes language in terms of cartography:

> Back down under the earth where you belong. Each letter like a perfect mirror of the one that has gone before, his handwriting tiny and crisp and replicate. He could make a map of those words, beginning at the B and ending at the g – where all beginning begins and ends – and they would make the strangest of upground and belowground topographies. (139)

Treefrog maps Angela's face deploying the same method he uses for his nest. By touching her face he transforms it into a landscape which he then can alter. He doctors her face as it is laid out on the graph paper, her imaginary anatomy, by erasing a bruise on her cheek. His desire to chart language, his nest, and people to whom he feels connected articulates his need to remain linked materially to the world.

The ritual of mapping contributes to Treefrog's continued craving for repeated actions and for balance. This is associated with his corporeality and his need to keep his body balanced, which is reflected in another of his recurrent habits, playing handball:

> He slaps the ball first with his right hand, then with his left – there are laws to this game: he must maintain the balance of his body, keep the equilibrium, never hit out of sequence. If he hits twice with the left hand he must hit twice with his right. When he slams with the centre of the right palm he must slam with the centre of the left. (26)

His longing for symmetry has, in the past, been etched on his body; his body is literally scarred from a yearning for equilibrium. Having stabbed a man in the belly, Treefrog inflicts a corresponding wound to his own body. Later, in his cave, he considers whether he should complete the symmetry by stabbing himself on the opposite side of his body, though thumb pressure and the thought of the knife pressing through his skin suffice. A favourite trick of his in the past had been to balance on one foot on a parking meter. Now, he can balance perfectly on the catwalks which lead to his nest above the ground of the tunnel.

The idea of balance and of symmetry remains important to the novel and is centred around the motif of the cranes and of dancing. Nathan dances like a crane the morning after his wedding and it is Louisa, his daughter-in-law, who wakes him from his misery following his son's death with an imitation of the cranes:

> Walker, embarrassed, turns his head slightly, but then returns the gaze as Louisa dances, hands outstretched, arms in a whirl, feet back and forth, the most primitive of movements, dissolving beyond the boundaries of her body. (154–5)

John F. Healy, in his article on the novel, discusses the mythologies associated with the crane that may have influenced McCann's choice of the bird: 'the exotic and mysterious crane consistently has symbolized grace, longevity, pureness, loftiness, auspiciousness, and immortality' (Healy, 2000, 110–1). The crane dance becomes a symbol of happiness and of balance. It is the crane dance that Treefrog performs at the end of the novel to signify his new-found happiness.[11]

Louisa's balance begins to deteriorate as she continues to drink. Losing her initial fluidity, she is prescribed pills for dizziness. Balance in the novel becomes associated with well-being. Balance is also Clarence Nathan's 'inheritance' (170). His ability to run along and perform handstands on a wall seventy feet above ground level is linked to a certain physical stability: 'His heart is steady anywhere. The blood flows equally to each part of his body' (170). His skill for balance attracts his future wife Dancesca to him, her name also signalling the important role dancing has in the novel.

Nathan's body acts as an important symbol for Treefrog's idea of his own personality and actions. His ultimate logic for touching his daughter stems from a desire to lift Nathan out of her and to recreate Nathan's death to ease the hollowness of his own body. It is Nathan's body that has been instrumental in forming the subway tunnels in which Treefrog now lives. In turn, Nathan's rheumatic pain derived from this tunnel work is now recreated in Treefrog's body.

Following his narration of his past to Angela, Treefrog notes that '[h]e has emptied himself of history and everything Clarence Nathan Walker has ever known in his life stands between here and a tunnel' (240). However, the act of narration has returned him to himself, completed the symmetry that he has been striving for:

> Yet he moves with a strange fluidity, a sureness, balancing on the edge of a track as he goes. Clarence Nathan has revisited himself, arrived full

circle, each shadow of himself leading to the next, which is just another shadow in the funhouse darkness. (241)

He returns as Clarence Walker and encounters his other self, Treefrog, in the tunnels. In that moment 'all inheritance moves through him' and he recalls incidents in his grandfather's life. This new certainty of himself is reflected in his corporeality:

> His body is assured, each move comes around to the same move, he could walk these columns and beams endlessly. Ten feet in the air, he knows that – even if he wanted to fall – there would be a difficulty in it, his arms would fight against memory and the limbs would catch and hold and he would be dead but his body might still be alive. (243)

The hollowness he has previously felt in his body since the death of Nathan dissipates following his destruction of his cave. Clarence Nathan juxtaposes his 'resurrection', from the tunnels and from his identity as Treefrog, with his grandfather's much more dramatic eruption from the riverbed on a geyser of water. At the conclusion of the novel, Treefrog permits 'a word rest upon his tongue, just once, a thing of imbalance', the word 'resurrection' (247).

The depiction of the subway and its tunnels in *This Side of Brightness* occupies a spectrum of meaning from the positive to the dystopian. McCann never seems willing to allow any one level of symbolism to dominate; the underground space in this novel is one that can be positively altered by one's own corporeality, but its relationship to the body remains a problematic one. Ultimately, in the text, one must emerge from the depths in order to gain access to a more fulfilling life. Treefrog's ascent from the tunnel at the conclusion of the narrative echoes similar texts. Pike points out that in Richard Wright's novella 'The Man Who Lived Underground' (1969), and in Ralph Ellison's *Invisible Man* (1952), the protagonists eventually return to the world above the tunnels despite their previous invisibility there: 'The undeniable materiality of life underground serves to embody the experience of invisibility above ground' (Pike, 1998, 23). Pike concludes that, in these texts, the underground serves as 'a potent symbol because of its visual concreteness and familiarity, but by that very token it can never be a locus for social change' (23). Nathan's violent ascension from the riverbed prefigures Clarence Nathan's abandonment of his underground identity, Treefrog, though he humorously points out the differences in terms of a decline between the two emergences: 'Our resurrections aren't what they used to be' (244). The final word of the novel is uttered by Clarence Nathan as he leaves the tunnel: 'resurrection'. Resurrection implies a lightness, an absence of weight, and a rising. Indeed, as Treefrog walks out of the tunnel he feels 'a great lightness to his body, not a single shadow cast in the tunnel' (248). Weight in the novel has been largely associated with negative emotions, especially guilt,[12] yet the positive weight that remains at the end of the text is the image of Treefrog 'hefting the weight of the word upon his tongue, all its possibility, all its beauty, all its hope, a single word, resurrection' (248). Language is here seen as the key to escape from the frozen life of the tunnel. Treefrog continuously writes his real name in the snow in order to remember it, and his oral account of his misdemeanour initiates his surfacing from the tunnel. Significantly this occurs outside of the tunnel, on a beach, thus beside a moving body of water as opposed to the predominant images of frozen water that dominate Treefrog's narrative. At the beginning of the novel a similar phrase is used in relation to Treefrog's grandfather following Con O'Leary's death: 'Walker wipes the tears from his eyes, and hefts the weight of another word upon his tongue: Fossil' (21). Treefrog's choice of word implies a movement upwards and outwards in opposition to the static implications of fossil, a word that is consigned to the past as 'resurrection' is to the future.

Conclusion

McCann's novels *Songdogs* and *This Side of Brightness* both stage attempts to come to terms with the past on the part of young men. Similar in their structures which alternate between past and present throughout the novels display endeavours to find meaning in traumatic events. However, McCann reveals that searches for authenticity and meaning are not always successful. The endings to these novels are ambiguous. Conor, in *Songdogs*, has failed not only to discover the whereabouts of his mother, but also to ascertain if she is still alive. He has attempted a partial reconciliation with his father but is on the brink of returning to America at the conclusion of the novel. It is unclear whether he will ever revisit Mayo or keep in contact with his father. A similar uncertainty presides at the ending to *This Side of Brightness*. Although the novel ends on a hopeful note, the reader is left to wonder whether Treefrog will leave his home in the tunnels to begin a new life and find his wife and daughter, or whether he will simply remain in his 'nest'.

This ambiguity is important, however, for the questioning of ideas of home and nationality that the novels undertake. Conceptions of home are shown to be fluid and transitory; Treefrog's virtual interment in the subway tunnels may suggest the dangers of attaching oneself too rigidly to place. However, the connections that are drawn between the body and space in both novels reveal important considerations. The narrative of *Songdogs* plays on associations between female corporeality and landscape, particularly in relation to Juanita's relationship to Mexico, North America, and Ireland. The novel displays the effects of such associations on actual bodies and the attempts made to anchor her corporeality through photography by Michael and storytelling by Conor, which ultimately result in her disappearance. Michael and Conor can initiate reconciliation but it takes place at the expense of the female and maternal body. Juanita remains missing, silenced, and invisible at the end of the novel.

This Side of Brightness foregrounds the metaphorical and actual connections made between body and landscape specifically in terms of the New York subway. The subway tunnels become a means of linking the generations of the Walker family, though only for its male members. Imaginative engagements with both space and corporeality offer the characters a means of initiating processes of healing, such as Treefrog's haptic maps and his image of Angela excavating his liver.

While McCann's two novels focus on the connections between corporeality, landscape, and generations, these are figured solely from a male perspective. Anne Enright's first two novels, *The Wig My Father Wore* and *What Are You Like?*, take on these concerns, specifically in terms of the mother-daughter relationship. The novels also probe in a more exacting way the pathological relationship between the female body and conceptions of space that *Songdogs* touches on through Juanita.

Chapter 3

Doubles and Dislocations:
Anne Enright's *The Wig My Father Wore* and *What Are You Like?*

Enright remarks at the beginning of her recent collection of essays, *Making Babies: Stumbling into Motherhood*, that she has 'always paid close attention to what the body is and what it actually does', combining an ontological curiosity with an approach that is oriented around potentiality (Enright, 2004, 2). Furthermore, in her writing, Enright continuously refuses to configure the corporeal as a stable entity. Dorothea Olkowski notes that the concept '"Body" is too easily taken to be a thing, final, finished and fully formed' and that the work of Deleuze, including his publications with Guattari, may facilitate ways of thinking about the body outside of these terms and of enabling it to be conceptualized in terms of potentialities and becomings (Olkowski, 1994, 120). Rather than ontological or epistemological explanations of the body, Deleuze is more concerned with a dynamic corporeality and with the linkages and connections that it can make and the assemblages that it forms. Grosz describes Deleuze's idea of the body as 'a discontinuous, nontotalizable series of processes, organs, flows, energies, corporeal substances and incorporeal events, speeds and durations' (Grosz, 1994, 164). Deleuze's work, then, is particularly useful for considering Anne Enright's configurations of the corporeal in her fiction.

Enright, who was born in 1962, is of a similar generation to McCann, but rather than emigrating, chose to remain in Ireland, though she has lived in England and Vancouver. She completed a B.A. in Modern English and Philosophy at Trinity College Dublin in 1985, which she followed with an M.A in Creative Writing at the University of East Anglia under Malcolm Bradbury and Angela Carter. She has worked in theatre and television, most notably as a producer/director for RTÉ's *Nighthawks* from 1986 to 1993. During this time she published her short story collection, *The Portable Virgin* (1991), the success of which, including winning the 1991 Rooney Prize, encouraged her to become a full-time writer. Her novels include *The Wig My Father Wore* (1995), *What Are You Like?* (2000a), *The Pleasure of Eliza Lynch* (2002b), and *The Gathering* (2007), which won the Man Booker Prize in 2007. She has also published the aforementioned memoir on pregnancy, childbirth, and motherhood, as well as two further short story collections, *Taking Pictures* (2008b) and *Yesterday's Weather* (2008c),[1] and regularly contributes to *The Irish Times*, *The Guardian*, and *The London Review of Books*.

Enright's writing style is fragmentary, episodic, and postmodern in its emphasis on parody, intertextuality, and narrative incoherence. She is continually lauded for her wit and humour,[2] and has been compared to such writers as Laurence Sterne for her flouting of narrative conventions and Jonathan Swift for her marked focus on the bodily: 'what is Anne Enright like? Flann O'Brien, yes, Tristram Shandy, a little, or Jonathan Swift meeting Kurt Vonnegut on speed?' (Foster, 2000). For Colm Tóibín, she 'has taken up and refined the legacy of Sterne and Flann O'Brien and placed it in a Dublin which, for the first time in its long life in fiction, has become post-Freudian and post-feminist and [. . .] post-nationalist' (Tóibín, 1999, xxxiii). Enright, however, argues against the prefix 'post', which to her 'means redundancy-afterward', in favour of equivalent words in other languages: 'the Spanish can say '*supaire*' – modern, meaning even more modern – or '*epaire*,' hyperrealism' (Enright, 2003, 64). Indeed Enright's eschewal of a classic-realist style or form, 'her deliberate suppression of explicit connections between elements of a text' highlights, for Patricia Coughlan, her affinity to 'modernist and some postmodernist representations' (Coughlan, 2004, 184).

Enright's work engages with the changes and transformations in the country prior to, and during, its newfound prosperity and economic success. For Coughlan, *The Wig My Father Wore* is 'as much concerned with the effects of this shift as it is with gender roles and relations among the young media elite in the Dublin of the early 1990s' (2004, 178). Coughlan also points out that the 'games with language' in this novel, 'play an important role in generating a coruscating account of 1990s Irish postmodernity at the moment before the economic boom' (Coughlan, 2005, 349). Enright's fiction investigates what happens to the body – to the maternal body in particular – at this moment of cultural change.

The short stories in her collection, *The Portable Virgin*, continuously reiterate a sense of instability. They describe bodies that trouble any sense of totality and coherence as well as exploding any notion of 'stillness' such as that proposed by Cheryl Herr, who observed that 'in traditional as well as colonial and postcolonial Ireland, the body has frequently been associated representatively with danger and has been scrutinized with an intensity that *stills* (photographically)' (Herr, 1990, 6–7). Rather than this photographic immobility, Enright identifies the influence of television on her writing in relation to her novel *The Wig My Father Wore*.

> The way people structure their books has been changed by television. Things happen faster; it's a three-minute culture. You want to move on; you don't trust the reader not to become bored; you have to get in there fast. Some of the book feels as though it is happening in rewind, and the reader might find it disjointed, though you can't write about television without fast cutting. The book literally does go into rewind at the end, with the frantic studio section. (Enright, 2003, 63–4)

Bodies in her writing are reflective of this influence. What are implied in such experiences of embodiment are the ideas of movement, process, and becoming, which are most often connected to the themes of sexuality and desire. For example, in the short story '(She Owns) Everything', the protagonist's experience of sex 'seemed to scatter and gather her at the same time' (Enright, 1991, 6). There is no attempt to secure or cohere her body. Some characters experience this incoherent corporeality in a negative fashion such as the narrator of the story 'Revenge': 'My head, you see, is a balloon on a string, my insides are elastic. I have to keep the tension between what is outside and what is in, if I am not to deflate or explode' (Enright, 1991, 39). Despite her own lightness and insubstantiality she comments that limbs are 'heavy things' when contemplating her husband's body and the bodies of the couple that they are to sleep with. Her troubled relationship to 'leaky bodies' seems compounded by her recollection of wetting the bed as a child.

However, rather than an experience of the corporeal as exceeding or transgressing boundaries, the bodies that Enright inscribes resist such ideas and emphasize the link to notions of process. In 'The House of the Architect's Love Story', bodies and houses bleed into each other and become almost interchangeable:

> The place rose like an exhalation. The foundations were dug, the bones set, and a skin of brick grew around the rest. It was wired and plastered and plumbed. Much like myself, the first time I slept with the architect. (Enright, 1991, 61)

Again it is an experience of sexuality that facilitates the body to be conceptualized in these productive terms. Enright claims that the short stories in *The Portable Virgin* represent this idea of process: 'They are trying, by accumulation, to become "themselves"' (Enright, 2003, 58). In her fiction it is the process of making connections that is important rather than a teleological conclusion.

In this chapter, I will focus on Enright's earliest novels, *The Wig My Father Wore* and *What Are You Like?*. Both share similar concerns in their interest in the types of relationships that are forged between twins and doubles, and between mothers and daughters. Like McCann's fiction, explored in the previous chapter, these novels explore interconnections between the body and its surroundings, but in Enright's texts, this is focused more specifically on female corporeality and domestic space. The configurations of the body in these novels offer alternate ways of negotiating these various relationships and posit new paradigms for engagements between generations and between the self and the other.

The Wig My Father Wore

Enright's first novel, *The Wig My Father Wore*, published in 1995, begins with the arrival of Stephen, an angel, to the door of Grace, the narrator. The rationale of the angel is signalled from the outset: angels are 'ordinary men who killed themselves once when times were bad. Now they had to walk everywhere, setting despair to rights, growing their wings' (1). The specific sources of Grace's despair are never explicitly stated, though the novel begins with her confession that 'By that time I needed anything I could get, apart from money, sex and power which were easy but hurt a lot' (1). Stephen's purpose in saving Grace from her despair is, in Enright's words, a reversal of 'Victorian male writing about a female "angel" of domesticity, virtue, and grace, who saves the man' (Enright, 2003, 60). Enright also compares the novel to 'a *bildungsroman*, in reverse, where the main character becomes more innocent as the book progresses' (Enright, 2003, 59). The initial plot is also reminiscent of the visitation by the angel Gabriel to the Virgin Mary.

The novel revolves around Grace's relationships with Stephen, her family, and the television show for which she works, entitled *The Love Quiz*. Her relationship with her mother is a particularly fraught one. Stephen touches this nerve with his initial question: '"And how's your mother?" he said. Which I thought was a little low, since she is fairly happy now, considering' (2). Grace's bewigged father of the title has suffered from two strokes and subsequently 'lives on the wrong side of the mirror' (51). He provides a surreal source of humour in the novel through his *Alice Through the Looking Glass* use of language.

The Wig My Father Wore is narrated in the first person by Grace, and the main text is interspersed with reproductions of filming schedules for *The Love Quiz*; credits for the show which become phallic-shaped on the page; live action sequences of Grace as producer, a television guide; fragments of recipes, theatre bills, poetry, and information about a miraculous medal, as well as various lists. The novel is constructed in a deliberately fragmented and episodic manner leading some critics, such as John Kenny, to dismiss it as 'typographically tricksy' (Kenny, 2000a). Other reviewers commended Enright for her 'taut, scornful one-liners' and 'epigrammatic style' (Kellaway, 1995; Patterson, 1995). Coughlan recognizes that the narrative and language games that Enright plays are productive rather than merely playful: 'A certain deliberate excess of linguistic effect over fictional cause creatively disturbs the surfaces of her previous works set in quotidian Dublin' (Coughlan, 2005, 349). Coughlan also points out that Enright's methods of 'collage and montage', which serve to frustrate narrative coherence, and highlight and undermine 'the false order constructed by the authorities and regulators of Grace's social world' (Coughlan, 2004, 184). The narrative, then, with its resistance to coherence, mirrors the configurations of the corporeal within the text. Enright's representations of the body stress process and transformation and facilitate engagements with the past and also, more particularly, highlight negotiations with a female genealogy. Enright mediates these concerns through the actual transformation of the narrator's body combined with the motif of doubles and twins.

Twins and Doubles: or, 'The Difference Between One and Two'

The Wig My Father Wore introduces concerns that are carried through to, and elaborated on, in her second novel, *What Are You Like?*. The most apparent of these continuities is the motif of twins and doubles, which becomes of central importance to Enright's second novel. Grace, in *The Wig My Father Wore*, is continually connected in the narrative to the motif of the double or twin. When asked to read Grace's horoscope, Stephen automatically associates her with the sign of twins, Gemini, despite Grace's protestations that she is not in fact this star-sign (90). Grace has, however, already marked herself as double due to her possession of two names. She has detached herself from her childhood and has split herself in two by changing her name from Grainne to Grace, 'Grainne is my childhood name' (37).[3] Marcus, a colleague on *The Love Quiz*, accuses her of disassociation: 'We were all virgins. Even you had a childhood and lost it'

(45). Grace is adamant that her body has always been as it is now: 'The first fact, fuck it, is that I never was a virgin, never had a hymen, never knew the difference between loss and gain' (45–6).[4] The denial of ever possessing a virginity or hymen is concomitantly a refusal to have ever considered her body in terms of a closed vessel or space that has never been perforated. Such refusal permits her to enact the split between Grace and Grainne.

Furthermore, an ambiguous reference to a dead twin is hinted at: 'And holding on to my heel, says Stephen, as Esau held onto Jacob, was my twin brother, whom I dragged out behind me, dead' (170). Grace refuses to believe Stephen's version of her birth, claiming that it is 'Too easy [. . .] Too like original sin' (170). She instead insists that her twin is the tumour her mother had removed when they were children:[5]

> But I know my twin, who also had hair, who also had a tooth. I know how he stayed where he was, even as she let me go. I know how she hoarded him without knowing, how he grew in the dark until they dug him out and put him in a jar. The size of a heart. (170–1)

Grace links her 'twin', the tumour, to her father's wig. Indeed, for her, the wig has actually fathered the tumour:

> I knew where she got it. I knew what had put the hairy thing in her tummy. It was not my father at all, but the thing on his head. That was why it hurt her. Why it was not a baby. We were right to be afraid. (149–50)

Her attitudes towards her father seem to circulate around and fixate on his wig. Enright notes that the wig represents 'a very sexual object – this big mysterious thing her father has. It might be the equivalent of not mentioning sex' (Enright, 2003, 60). Indeed, due to the arrival of the wig Grace observes that 'My parents' bedroom became even more secret' (29). This link with the sexual is also reflected in the choice of a name for the wig made by Grace's sister: 'Brenda, the youngest, said 'Rat', which is also a word for penis' (27). Marina Warner devotes two chapters of her study on folk and fairytales, *From the Beast to the Blonde*, to the symbolic connotation of hair, observing its links to the sexual. Hairiness is often associated with the animalistic, with the bestial, and thus with lust. The wig becomes representative of everything that remains repressed and unmentionable in relation to the body; as Coughlan contends, the 'concealed baldness stands in a metonymic relation to the whole hidden life of the body, its joys, its odours, and its innocent ungainliness' (Coughlan, 2004, 183).

Grace attributes a personality to the wig: 'It rode around on his head like an animal. It was a vigorous brown. I was very fond of it as a child. I thought that it liked me back' (25). For Warner, hair is symbolically constituent of our sense of self: 'the dressing of hair in itself constitutes a mark of the human' (Warner, 1995, 371). Hair also maintains a paradoxical duality in symbolization; linked to the animalistic and sexual and thus to life, yet somehow not quite part of the body itself. It continues to grow after death and is itself made up of dead cells. Warner notes that:

> hair is the part of our flesh nearest in kind to a carapace [. . .] hair is also the least fleshy production of the flesh. In its suspended corruptibility, it seems to transcend the mortal condition, to be in full possession of the principle of vitality itself. (Warner, 1995, 372–3)

Enright's wig seems to encompass these symbolic associations to excess. Animalistic, with a personality and vitality of its own, it is also a dead thing. The wig of Grace's father becomes, like his hairbrush, 'a sacred, filthy thing' (27).

The wig also becomes a type of other self, which is both part of her father and separate from him. Grace's father becomes linked with the motif of doubling, through an association with mirrors: 'My father in the mirror was even stranger than my father in the room' (99). This is made even more explicit later in the narrative:

> Spot the difference between my father and my father. Between him and himself. Between his hair and his head [. . .] My father hated cameras but he put a mirror in every room, because they forget you when you walk away. (109)

References to mirrors recur throughout *The Wig My Father Wore*. Mirrors in literature are conventionally associated with the motif of the double and with divisions of the self.[6] Indeed Lacan's mirror stage charts the emergence of duality at the level of subjectivity; the fragmented embodied identity that is the organism's experience which is at odds with the image of the coherent self of the mirror image. Associated as it is with the other side of the mirror, the wig's relationship with the tumour, in Grace's eyes, positions the tumour in the space of her reflection. It belongs with the wig in 'the place behind the mirror' (110).

Stephen is insistent about both the idea of twins and Grace's misremembered childhood, both of which are connected to Enright's configuration of the body in this text. Stephen himself also acts as a kind of double to

Grace. He invites a little girl into the house, prefiguring Grace's own bodily regression into childhood, and recounts fairytales concerning twins. He stresses that 'the space between [twins] does not really exist' and his stories highlight the interdependency of a geminate relationship:

> He tells her the story of two fat twins, who wished for the same thing only differently. The elder twin wished that she would always be slim no matter what she ate, and the younger wished that she would always be eight and a half stone. As the years went by the younger twin got fatter and fatter until finally she was so huge she couldn't see over her stomach to read the scales – which always, but always, told her that she was eight and a half stone. The elder thought this was great and stuffed her face to her heart's content until one day she fell through the floorboards and when they finally hauled her out, discovered that she was a very, very small two tons. The difference in their relative density forced the twins to hold on to each other at all times, in case the older should sink or the younger float away. (107–8)

Juliana De Nooy, in her study of twins in literature and culture, notes that imbricated in stories concerning twins is a difficulty concerning ways of thinking about such a pair: 'at stake is the question of the viability of a certain understanding of coupledom, a coupledom not defined by dialectical opposition' (De Nooy, 2002, 75). Stephen's stories articulate this difficulty; his twins cannot be characterized as wholly same or wholly different. De Nooy points out that literary representations of twins most often depict separated twins or resolve the above-mentioned dilemma by dispatching either one or both halves of the duo. The couple is commonly figured in terms of a dualistic opposition: the good twin versus the bad twin. Difference and otherness are either negated in order to stress ultimate sameness or are 'magnified into opposition' (76). She suggests that the reason for these common narrative trajectories in stories concerning twins is that 'twins threaten our notions of discrete bodies and indivisible individuals [. . .] they disturb the opposition between same and different, and between self and other' (76). For her, the appearance of the twin represents 'any kind of difference, any figure of the Other [. . .] and any duality' (De Nooy, 2005, 4).

Although the question missing from Stephen's list is never explicitly recovered it seems that this issue, the relationship between same and different, the 'difference between one and two', is crucial to the novel (56). Enright's text may appear to conform to conventional narratives of twinship.

There is a strong suggestion that Grace is the surviving half of twins, yet this is merely an implication. Grace herself refuses this explanation of her origins. However, while she may not actually possess a dead twin brother, she does explicitly connect herself with ideas of the twin, splitting herself in two and linking herself to her mother's tumour. This latter 'twin' proves complicated as the tumour is 'birthed' much later than Grace's own birth. The narrative sustains the ambiguity concerning twinship, refusing to resolve this relationship.

De Nooy notes that images of wholeness often proliferate in twin narratives. In Patrick White's *The Solid Mandala*, a marble becomes a symbol of the desired unity. In Michel Tournier's *Les météores*, a glass bulb and an egg represent wholeness (De Nooy, 2002, 79). Bruce Chatwin, in his novel *On the Black Hill*, uses the image of the egg to denote unity and to explore the intricacies of the relationship both between the twins themselves, and their negotiations with outsiders. For De Nooy, Chatwin's use of ovular imagery in the novel suggests that 'you cannot make a relationship, any more than an omelette, without breaking eggs' (De Nooy, 2002, 84). The recurrent references to broken eggs in Chatwin's novel advocate a move away from the boundaries that preserve sameness in order to open the relationship to the possibility of difference.

Enright's imagery follows similar patterns. Stephen's first alteration of Grace's house is to remove all the glass light bulbs from their sockets: 'The whole house is swimming, empty and electric, as the open sockets leak into the evening light' (22). Without the containing spaces of the bulbs the house becomes open to the flow of electricity; the leaking electricity also feeds into the references to waves and currents of both water and electricity that are repeated throughout the novel.[7] However, it is Grace's body that provides the novel with a means to work through ideas of wholeness, unity, and their opposites. Margrit Shildrick's justification for a poststructuralist ethics that 'demonstrates the inescapability of the leaks and flows across all such bodies of knowledge and bodies of matter' seems applicable here (Shildrick, 1997, 4). The configurations of Grace's body, and those that surround her, move between enclosed, smooth, egg-like spaces and those not easily confinable by the terms in which we conventionally think about the space of the corporeal.

'It wasn't easy,' Grace claims when referring to an experience of being in love, 'this difference between one and two' (56). This 'difference' becomes connected to ideas of love and relationships, the distinction between being alone and considering another person. The novel explores the contrast between two different types of love or desire: a 'spiritual/ascetic male idea of love' connected to Catholicism, and a desire that Enright associates with the female. It 'includes pregnancy and children as well as sex' and, in her eyes, remains under-symbolized in narrative and culture (Enright, 2003, 59). The contrast Enright identifies between these two types of desire also corresponds to the traditional distinction between gendered bodies which she draws upon in her depictions of Stephen and Grace. Stephen as an angel represents man as acorporeal, while Grace is associated from the beginning with her body by Stephen: 'He revealed himself on the threshold with broad comments about my fertility. Who needs it?' (1). As the novel progresses, Stephen gradually transforms both Grace's house and, more importantly, her body. However, the binary opposition between male/female, acorporeal/corporeal is continuously undermined.

Stephen is disassociated from corporeality yet situated in a body which bears the marks of his former life and death; his smile is 'of celestial beauty which spread over most of him, but missed the marks on his neck' (2). He does not make a dent on the sheets when he lies down, though his hands are cold and 'his shit smells like shit and then some' (38). What Stephen primarily misses in his angelic existence is 'the passage of time, he missed his body, more than he missed the body of his wife' (7). As the story unfolds, Stephen becomes more fleshy and corporeal:

He is getting thicker. The edges are flattening out of his face and the marks on his neck have faded to a porcelain blue. In a year's time, he says, I will be naked and chubby and carrying garlands for you. I do not want a child, I tell him, let alone a cherub. (38)

Further on in the novel, he develops the ability to bleed (102).

In contrast to Stephen's burgeoning fleshiness, Grace's body begins to lose its normal functions: 'I realise that whatever he is feeding me, it is two weeks since I have been to the toilet and I kind of miss it' (124–5). Stephen's presence and influence begin to alter her corporeality:

So I look at myself and everything seems changed under the broken angle of the water – paler, new. My front no longer breaks the surface to look at me like a quiet brown frog. My nipples have faded and there is something wrong with my stomach. For one thing, it doesn't seem appropriate to call it a stomach anymore. It is a smooth white belly with obscure functions and an iridescent perfect glow. (125)

The conventional language used to describe the body no longer seems appropriate for the corporeality she is now acquiring. Her body grows younger; it moves from 'pubescent' through the disappearance of pubic hair (126, 137). Grace describes it as 'the childhood body' and 'my new girl's body' (163). This corporeality that Stephen has given her is explicitly connected with her own childhood and past: 'I will cover my body like the memory it is' (138). However, it is not a body that remains detached in the past (as one could argue her 'twin' does, as representative of her childhood), rather it mingles with her various pasts as well as her present:

> The body that looks back at me is nine years old, or fourteen mixed with nine, or my own, mixed with all the bodies I used to have. I wonder if I am a virgin again. (137)

Stephen's manipulation of her body connects her materially to her past. Although appearing as a smooth, intact, virginal body, this corporeality is continuously altering itself, constantly refiguring its boundaries and morphology to the point at which it 'is a blur' (146). The configuration of her body-self as transformative and suggestive of her childhood permits a reconnection with her own detached past and, indeed, with the temporality that Stephen misses as angel: 'I piss myself, with my new child's bladder, urgently, easily, back into the flow of time' (166). Zygmunt Bauman, in his analysis of the liquidity of late modernity, argues that for liquids it is 'the flow of time that counts', in contrast to solids: 'when describing solids, one may ignore time altogether' (Bauman, 2000, 2). Thus, along with the abundance of waves and flows in the narrative, the development of Grace's body into a more transformative 'liquid' one contributes to a reconnection with temporality.

These waves and flows are not only liquid, but also refer to the technological airwaves and signals of the television and Grace's job as producer of these flows. Television in the novel is continuously linked to ideas of time; to the fast-paced life of the studio; and particularly to the past of childhood and how it is remembered. The gaps in Grace's childhood memories are revealed through the medium of television, or rather through a television guide that Stephen has found detailing her first night's viewing: 'It is the night of the orbit, not by Apollo 8 as I had thought, but by Apollo 11, the mission that put the first men on the moon. These tricks of memory do not distress me' (31). Her childhood becomes a type of television broadcast that she can alter: 'Now my childhood rearranges itself, the phantom Apollo 8 is regulated to a kind of misalignment of the pixels, the shadow of another channel breaking through' (31). Enright reproduces the layout of the television guide on the page; the programme descriptions replaced by Grace's memories create an odd juxtaposition of present, past, and future. The facsimile of the television guide in which Grace's present reminiscences appear is labelled 'T.V. Tomorrow' so that in the past Grace's memory has not yet occurred. These disjunctions in temporality and memory remain with Grace, 'I'm still trying to remember the films I wasn't allowed to stay up to watch' (33). Her mother claims that 'they were at the seaside in the summer of 1969 and weren't anywhere near a television, so when it came to the moon-landing we listened to it on the radio and looked out the window at the moon' (36).

Television seems to allow the characters a means of readjusting and rein-venting their own pasts: 'Marcus [one of Grace's colleagues] invents his childhood by watching old movies. He remembers films that never made it to Bumfuck, Co. Leitrim, which is his home town' (33). Marcus also accuses Grace of remodelling her past and by implication, herself:

> 'I have to admire you,' says Marcus, 'You make yourself up as you go along.' [...]
> 'How do you remember *The Herbs?*' he says. 'You didn't even have a telly until 1969.' [...]
> 'I hate to break it to you Grace, but *The Herbs* was BBC [...] You had to invent some fucking Protestant childhood with *Bill and Ben the* fucking *Flowerpot Men.*' (34–5)

For Grace, the act of remembering and of looking at the past is fraught, not only in terms of what is surveyed but because the act has implications for one's sense of self as mediated through the body: 'I told him about looking back. How you lose what you look at. How you turn to salt' (40). Recalling the past not only displaces it but also dissolves the subject. The development of Grace's 'childhood body' also forces her to reassess her memories of her past and childhood, particularly in relation to her mother:

> 'It's not my fault,' she [Grace's mother] says. 'You only remember the bad things.'
> I look at the photograph. My mother is beautiful. She is in love. She looks like the sort of mother you are supposed to remember [...] I cannot fit it inside my head. (171)

However, the embodied self she has constructed for herself has no space for this reassessment.

Maternal Genealogies

Enright's novels stage a continued negotiation with the issues of mother-hood made explicit in her memoir, *Making Babies*. In *The Wig My Father Wore* and *What Are You Like?* she also specifically explores the mother-daughter relationship. For Irigaray, this relationship is one that lacks adequate sym-bolization in Western culture. It hinges on the single symbolic position available to women, thus creating intergenerational antagonism for that status. The importance of the mother-daughter relationship in *The Wig My Father Wore* is indicated early in the narrative: Stephen's third question to Grace is 'And how's your mother?' (2). Grace's response is indicative of the troubled relationship the two women share: 'there are things between every mother and child best forgotten' (2–3). This insistence on an erasure of the past that mother and daughter share accounts for Grace's fractured mem-ory of her childhood. Grace has deliberately erased any positive connection to her mother. Their telephone conversation attests to this failure of con-nection and communication:

> 'It's Saturday,' I said. 'How are you?'
> 'I'm fine,' she said, because we both lie the same way. 'Any news?'
> 'Nothing much,' I said (there is an angel in the kitchen, breaking the toaster). (5)

Stephen, on the other hand, 'seemed to get on fine' with Grace's mother (7). His job, it seems, is to discover the question that is missing from the list of questions he asks Grace when he arrives. Following his first encoun-ter with Grace's mother 'He announced that he had half an answer at least' (8).

Stephen's alteration of Grace's body initiates a concern about the impli-cations of this new morphology. The development of her body into that of a child, while connecting her with her past, also erases its traces and inscriptions:

> I said 'I want my body back. I want my hands back and my cellulite and my stupid-looking feet.' It surprised me as I said it, but I missed the lines and the markings and the moles ticking away like timebombs. I missed my mother's knees and my Granny's hammer toes. I missed the subcutaneous ridges and drifts and all the mongrel contours mapping the history of this poor body and what it has been through – which is not enough. (126–7)

Grace's nipple disappears when Stephen touches her breast yet as his hand moves down her body Grace objects to the removal of her belly button:[8]

> I am resolved that no matter what he did to my breast, he isn't going to touch my belly button . . . I think of what it had been tied to – a dead piece of my mother and me they hadn't bothered to bury.
> 'It's mine,' I said. (129–30)

Connections between mother and daughter are marked physically on the body. Despite feelings of ambivalence about or even dislike for her mother, Grace cannot be parted from the bodily signifier that marks her as human, in contrast to Stephen who, as angel, does not possess a belly button. The navel signals the physical connection, the fleshy link of umbilical cord between mother and daughter and it is the disappearance of a female genealogy that Grace resents in her new child's body. Stephen's attempt to 'whitewash' her body, as he has done her house, results in a realization of what is at stake in an erasure of the maternal: namely, an integral part of the self.

Domestic Spaces and the Body

Enright continually associates domestic spaces with the body, particularly the female body: 'I look like something in the room is faintly rotting, when my mother looks freshly re-upholstered' (74). This cross-connection is also proposed, more specifically, in terms of the pregnant or fertile body. Grace's house, especially the wallpaper, become important images for attempts to recover genealogical links with the past, epitomized in the figure of Mrs. O'Dwyer, the former occupant of the house. Enright explains her motivation in an interview:

> Well, it's [women's lost history] buried under the wallpaper. We are living in it; it's in bits, it's half-mad, the wallpaper and all the historical bits and scraps which are all real things. That's a menstrual image – we have to rip at the lining of this for something new to happen. In this next book [*What Are You Like?*], the mother finally speaks in it, as the nearly last thing, and so another woman's story is finally uncovered. (Enright, 2003, 64)

Grace's house in the novel is figured as a physical locus for the uncovering of women's histories and for the specific connections between women and domestic spaces. Grace's mother articulates this last point: "'A house needs children," said my mother. She wanted to say that only a baby understands a carpet, that walls need to be written on, to keep them in their place' (85). For Grace, the house refuses to remain stable and becomes active in its revelation of its 'hidden histories':

> Over the last month or so, the paper has started to come away from the wall. It is covered in big fat bubbles, like something surfacing in slow motion. When I first moved in I painted everything magnolia, because I said you can't make decisions just like that – a house has to grow on you. So it heard me and did. (84)

The wallpaper presents itself like 'a button undone, or a scab waiting to be picked', suggesting both the removing of a layer of clothing and a freshly healed wound. Grace is compelled to peel off the wallpaper accompanied by her mother's 'reproductive glee' and the sounds of Oprah Winfrey's television show in which surprise births are being discussed (84–5). This section of the novel is strongly reminiscent of Charlotte Perkins Gillman's short story 'The Yellow Wallpaper' in which the protagonist tears the wallpaper from the room in which she is recovering in order to release the woman she imagines trapped behind the pattern of the wallpaper (Perkins Gilman, 1892). References to the story are also included in the texts that are uncovered. One such text reads: 'I know who The Woman Next Door is. Just in case you read this with your yellow eyes' (89).

In Enright's fiction the domestic space and women's reproductive bodies are always somehow inextricably linked, feeding off each other for metaphors as in her short story 'The House of the Architect's Love Story': 'This baby is a gothic masterpiece. I can feel the arches rising up under my ribs, the glorious and complicated space' (Enright, 1991, 62). The act of removing layers of wallpaper yields up 'the very odour and idiom of murdered wives, of misery, the axe in the head and a corpse bricked into the wall' (Enright, 1995, 85). This hidden history then becomes a dead body that speaks back in *What Are You Like?*

The violence of this imagery of murdered wives is carried forward into the fragments of text that are uncovered in the process of peeling away the layers of wallpaper in Grace's house, including a bill from a butcher's shop smeared in blood upon which is inscribed 'in a female hand [. . .] a list "Chop. Chop. Chop. Chop. Cutlet."' (86). The 'women's lost history' that is buried under the wallpaper becomes fragments of texts, including a passage concerning Our Lady of the Scapular, a personal letter, random words, a poem 'by a lunatic', and a recipe which on initial reading appears to suggest instructions for cooking people: '*4 persons.* Wash well in salt and water [. . .] If there are any clots of blood, rub overnight in cold water to cover' (89). Coughlan reads this recipe as 'a displaced version of sexual prudery and, with the insistent injunction to "cover," of the whole unease with the body that characterised Irish life' connecting this with 'the covering wig: the anxiety about nakedness' (Coughlan, 2004, 185).

Enright's 'menstrual image' is made explicit in the text when Stephen, reading out Grace's horoscope, tells her to 'Clear out the old and sing in the new' (90). Grace then proceeds to follow the horoscope's instructions:

So I tore the room apart, Stephen hovering at my shoulder in a state of celestial agitation. I yanked up the carpet with the newspaper underneath, stuffed it all out the window and when it lodged in the frame, went into the front garden and pulled, like a vet pulling out a dead calf. I fell into the flowerbed when it shot out like a lump and then wrestled it off me, the yellow scraps of paper blowing all over the road, landing in the neighbours' gardens, sticking to the hub-caps of their nice cars and sucking up against the holes in their wire fences. Let them read something for a change. I didn't care what they thought. They had been living with a madwoman for years and never told me. (90)

The menstrual image also becomes linked with one of birth or miscarriage: 'a vet pulling out a dead calf'. A second image of birth occurs when Stephen is painting the attic and falls through the ceiling:

A leg comes through the ceiling. I look at it. Another leg comes through the ceiling. The legs scissor once and the right one kicks. The kick brings a torso down, which hangs briefly at the armpits, before arms, shoulders, head, hands and a can of paint break through. They land on my bed, though the paint also hits the floor [. . .] I look at the lake of white spilling off the edge of my bed and spreading across the floor. (102)

Stephen begins to bleed following this 'birth' as he progressively becomes more corporeal. The textual fragments behind the wallpaper, in this case, include 'a poem about childbirth'. (102)

The image of a pregnant woman swimming is a recurrent one throughout the novel. The final question on Stephen's list is: 'Had I ever seen a pregnant woman swimming on her back' (4). During Stephen's first conversation with

Grace's mother she reveals that 'The summer I was pregnant with this young woman, I swam in the sea every day, in the sun and in the rain. And I said to God that this would be my prayer for the child – whoever it was, whoever it turned out to be' (8). By the end of the novel, Grace has become this pregnant woman; she has taken the place of her mother, and repeats the 'prayer':

> I swim every morning in the sea, in the sun and in the rain and I say to God that this is my prayer for our child, whoever it is, whoever it might turn out to be. I swim on my back and look at the sky, which reminds me of the sky when I was a child. (214)

Shildrick notes the paradox that is insidious in conceptions of the female body: 'while women are represented as more wholly embodied than men, that embodiment is never complete or secure' (Shildrick, 1997, 35). Furthermore, women's capacity in pregnancy to embody both self and other 'is the paradigm case of breached boundaries' (35). The comparisons that Grace draws between herself and her mother's tumour highlight the problematics of the categories 'self' and 'other', given that both child and tumour are of the mother's flesh yet simultaneously alien to it. As Enright asks, 'What's the difference between a woman's own cells and the cells of her cancer?' (Enright, 2000b, 8). Iris Marion Young describes pregnant embodiment in terms of a 'twoness', and argues that it encompasses a subject position that is 'decentered, split or doubled' (Young; 1990; 160, 163). Shildrick holds that historically, and indeed currently, there is a tendency to depict the female reproductive system, the female body, and the pregnant body as essentially connected to corporeality, yet simultaneously dematerialized. Images often portray the female body 'in terms of surfaces and internal spaces' that are largely discontinuous and thus the foetus is represented as disconnected from the maternal body (Shildrick, 1997, 38). It is this unacknowledged connection that is at stake in Grace's rejection of Stephen's removal of her navel and her nostalgia for her previous corporeality that bore the marks of a female genealogy. Enright's depiction of Grace's pregnant body and that of her mother swimming in the sea, subtly highlights connections between mother and foetus in terms of their surroundings, both floating in liquid. It becomes a powerful image of intersubjectivity between the generations.

Grace's new body, as well as reverting to childhood, also becomes similar to Stephen's initial angelic body, as his physique is also influenced by the presence of her corporeality. He thus becomes a type of double to Grace:

'So I realise that whatever is happening through the empty door frame, it is not all one way. The knowledge that the hair on Stephen's body is somehow my fault leaves me mute and glad' (129). Grace experiences strong sexual feelings for Stephen. Her desire affects her own body and increases her awareness of her corporeality: 'His eyes still pull at some vital desire, making my innards and lights feel clotted and strung out' (39). The consummation of this desire occurs at a point when her corporeality is at its least stable: 'My body seems to have forgotten what to do with it all, has forgotten how to cross space, how to complete the surprise. My body is still all in bits, and all different ages' (178). Here Enright configures the body as continuously open-ended and constantly in process both temporally and spatially. Interestingly, what concerns Grace most during this sexual experience are the limits and boundaries of the body; she can only think of 'the gap between us and about the tip of his tongue, through his open teeth, touching the air of the room' and concentrates on his skin (178). Grace remembers his body 'in bits' and the weightiness and lightness of his various body parts: 'the surprising weight of his head, the weightlessness of his mouth' (179). Stephen's corporeality is also at its least stable at this point:

So I made love to him carefully; using my hands carefully to remind him where his body was and where it stopped, to remind him where it stopped and where it turned into something else. Because he was so substantial outside of me but inside there was no end to him. (180)

In contrast to configurations of the body as smooth and intact, or to ideas of the body-self as split into two discrete parts, Enright ends the novel with a proliferation of images which stress the 'leakiness' of the body and its boundaries: 'I woke up grateful and sick with grief, as if I could not carry my heart anymore; it had burst and spread, like an old yolk' (183). The novel concludes with an image of spilt milk. Yet it is not milk to be cried over; it 'makes sense':

Because nothing died when we made love. Apparently that is what it is like for a woman. For a woman, nothing has to die. This makes sense. As much sense as milk staining the road between Furnace and Lettermaghera. (215).

The leakiness of the body implied in this image, which also makes reference to Grace's future lactating self, emphasizes the configurations of the body as fluid and transformative in the novel. Coughlan contends that this image of the leak is 'a figure for the book's theme: that covering and sealing of identities are neither necessary nor possible, and that the impulse to join inner and outer being, self and other, is a human universal' (Coughlan, 2004, 185).

Grace's embodied self at the end of the novel, now a pregnant body, is one that is constantly changing:[9]

> I cannot find the edge of myself, which is why I have to be inside things now, so that the walls will hold me in, so that I can lap into corners and seep into carpets and carry like a bowl the noise of the sea. (182)

For Enright, like De Nooy, making connections insists on the disturbance of ideas of wholeness or enclosed spaces. De Nooy writes of the ovular imagery in Chatwin's twin narrative that the 'isolation of whole eggs is scorned, for friendship depends on breaking the shell' (De Nooy, 2002, 84). The sociologist, Simon Williams, argues against notions of corporeality as closed and bounded and insists on the need to symbolize an embodied subjectivity that is configured, in critic Christine Battersby's words, 'not by repulsion/exclusion of the notself, but via interpenetration of self and otherness' (Battersby qtd. in Williams, 1998, 69). In *The Wig My Father Wore*, Grace's connection with Stephen allows her finally to understand difference:

> Stephen looks up and sees me on the gantry, looking down. He seems scared. He smiles anyway. Pop goes a light, showering the floor with sparks and glass. Bang goes my heart. Pop goes my breast.
> And at last I know the difference between one and two.
> 'One Tchuu,' says Stephen into the mike. 'One Tchew.' (191)

Bodies, in *The Wig My Father Wore*, configure notions of productivity, permit an engagement with otherness and difference, and challenge any idea of coherence or totality. The matter of the body is continuously in motion. Enright expands on her interest in twins and doubles in her next novel, *What Are You Like?* separated twins become the basis of the plot.

What Are You Like?

What Are You Like? is a novel palpable with a sense of absence. It is a novel of the lost, the displaced, and the missing; a novel populated with abandoned children, dead mothers, missing siblings, uncanny doubles, and separated twins. A general sentiment of dislocation unites the many characters in the novel and their relation to the environment in which they find themselves varies from feelings of confusion and disorientation to more complicated interconnections between corporeality and architecture, between the body and the material world that surrounds it. The novel charts the complex relationships made between subjectivities and the material world in order to negotiate feelings of loss, alienation, as well as a desire for connection; the characters variously experience 'a place with no proper map and no way home' (the 'place with no proper map' is the decision made at the beginning of the novel to allow Berts's pregnant wife to die of her brain tumour in order that her twins be born) (7). The impulse to navigate difficult emotions through recourse to the material world and the spatial environment runs throughout the novel, the mapping metaphor is one means by which characters attempt to make sense of the world.

The novel tells the story of identical twin girls, Maria and Rose, separated at birth following the death of their mother, Anna, whose brain tumour goes untreated so as to protect the unborn babies (a decision she does not make and is unaware of); their father, Berts, insists that he can only cope with one child. Thus, Maria is raised in Ireland with Berts and his second wife, Evelyn, while Rose is adopted by a couple in England (who also share their house with boys that they foster for short periods). The novel operates by means of multiple viewpoints and alternates between Berts's life, Maria's childhood and early adulthood in New York, Rose's childhood and early adulthood in England, a brief insight into the life of the nun who was present at Rose's adoption, Evelyn's married life with Berts, as well as the voice of the twins' dead mother, Anna, which is the only instance of a first-person narrative voice in the novel. The girls finally meet towards the end of the novel when Rose accidentally walks into the changing room of the shop in which Maria works. Enright contends that this novel is 'a book about how things get buried' (Padel, 2000). *What Are You Like?* charts the traumatic effects of these buried things on the lives of its protagonists, the hauntings they suffer on account of 'a place with no proper map and no way home', manifested in the off-kilter ways that the characters relate to their environment.

Most significantly, that which gets buried in the novel is Berts's wife Anna, who is dead before the twins are even born, kept 'alive' by a life support machine in order that the babies grow along with the tumour that will kill her: 'What kind of a child comes out of a dead woman?' Berts asks, 'A child with no brain? A child with two heads?', gesturing towards the fact that

Maria is one of twins. Maria and Rose are haunted by each other's loss though they are unaware of the fact that they are one half of twins; Rose 'was born with a hole in her head, a hole in her life. Everything fell into it' (140). Maria unconsciously experiences her lost double: 'Her chest starts to go all stupid and so do her eyes. She has a feeling like there is someone always coming around the corner, who never arrives' (54). Berts's refusal to acknowledge Rose's existence is his second symbolic act of 'burial'. In a vain attempt to erase the presence of two children, Berts only proffers one name, Maria. When registering the abandoned twin, the nun, Sr. Misericordia, alters the last letter of Maria to 'e' – Marie – in remembrance of the loss of the letter from her own adopted name Misericordiæ: 'What she liked best was the way the A and the E stuck together. She was ten at the time. Of course, when it came to it, she had to lose the 'e' – it wasn't grammatical, apparently' (82). Thus, the twins' registered names signal simultaneously their similarity and difference and the conjoined 'æ' in the Latin term for compassion highlights their connectivity; their separation is mirrored in the loss of the letter 'e' from Sr. Misericordia's name and also ironically indicates Berts's lack of compassion.

Twins: Self and Other

Enright's narrative explores the twin's unconscious intersubjective relationship, interconnections between self and environment, and the traumas experienced by efforts to preserve definite borders between self and other.[10] The erasure of the maternal is at the heart of this trauma and the absence of the mother resonates through the narrative both in her haunting monologue from beyond the grave and in the constant imagery of gaps and holes that all characters experience, most often in terms of the landscape that they inhabit.[11] However, the persistence of the gap is experienced differently by Berts and the twins: throughout the narrative, Berts attempts to eliminate the haunting absence of his dead wife, whereas Maria and Rose attempt to find the gaps in their life and to locate the missing origin.[12] This difference between Berts's and the twins' relations to the buried maternal body maps onto Luce Irigaray's work in which she details the ways in which masculine subjectivity is achieved through the separation from and complete erasure of the maternal body, an erasure which returns to haunt: 'once the man-god-father kills the mother so as to take power, he is assailed by ghosts and anxieties' (Irigaray, 1991c, 49). In contrast, Irigaray's model for feminine subjectivity is based on the desire for connection, for intersubjective relations: 'the feminine universe's relationship between two' (Irigaray, 2004b, 13). Enright is passionate about engaging with the traditional silencing and erasure of the mother figure in much of Irish literature. Speaking about *What Are You Like?*, she noted that she had 'split that big iconic mother presence' into two, Anna and Evelyn (Enright, 2003, 61). The mother is both the living person, epitomized in Evelyn, 'a perfectly likable person who is friends with her children, rears the child who is left', as well as 'the omnipresent dead mother in Irish fiction, never explained, never made manifest or real', with whom the living mother must contend (61).

The novel's sustained motifs of twins and doubling gesture toward Irigaray's model of intersubjectivity; recalling De Nooy's observation that twins upset rigid definitions between self and other, displacements of self, inconsistencies in subjectivity, and lack of coherent identities are also highlighted. Maria's first words are ghosted by the distressing events of her birth: 'What could be more monstrous than her birth? Only this: that the first word to bubble up in her throat was her own name – twice' (9).[13] Maria's first words are actually '"Ma Ma". It was enough to break your heart, said the aunts, but Berts understood. "Maria," he said. "Maria"' (9). She consistently fails to secure her identity: 'Maria thinks that she must have been with him all along. Except that it isn't her. It couldn't be. This girl's dress is longer and she even wears tights' (31). Her sense of an embodied self is similarly troubled:

> She lies in bed and tries to tell what size she is. When she closes her eyes her tongue is huge and her hands are big, but the bits in between are any size at all. When she opens her eyes she is the size of the dress. Or she might be. (28)

Maria's vexed relationship with the mirror registers her difficulties with her sense of self ('Maria wanted to take the mirror and throw it across the room' (24)), and both she and Rose at various points fail to recognize themselves in it. Her subjectivity is troubled on two levels – a longing for an engagement with someone other than herself as well as an inability to form adequate connections to location, something which I will come back to below.

In *What Are You Like?*, the unconscious experience of separation, the perceived lack of interconnection between self and other, underpins the psychic trauma of Maria and Rose. Maria's realization that '*We are on our own*', which she repeats twice, leads to her suicide attempt, yet the novel foregrounds the extent to which Maria and Rose are actually intimately connected (152). Maria's '*We are on our own*' finds later echoes in Enright's short story 'Natalie' whose narrator despairs that 'We are not connected', though again this belies her empathetic and intersubjective responses to those she encounters (Enright, 2008b, 50). In 'Shaft', the pregnant narrator laments that, 'We are all just stuck together' (Enright, 2008b, 131). This concern surrounding our connectivity to other people, our intersubjective relations, is a refrain that runs throughout Enright's work. While Maria is attempting to commit suicide, Rose mistakes a lampshade in the house opposite her for a woman hanging herself, 'At two in the morning, her eye was caught by a lampshade hanging over an archway in a flat across the road. For a second it looked like a body hanging there' and Rose shouts 'NO!' (154, 156). The novel also sets itself up as a gothic novel, but without a gothic ending, and the challenges to the autonomous self that the twins highlight are bound up in this gothic aspect. While Berts is haunted by the dead mother, the twins are ghosted by their living others.

Maria's childhood is inscribed with absence, marking out the space of her lost twin and of her mother, absences which become particularly potent during significant rites-of-passage such as her Communion: 'In the photographs you see her [Maria], the extra inch between her and the world' and her eyes 'don't belong to anyone' (26). Maria colours in the photos with crayons to create 'the other girl' (35). The measurements for her communion dress begin at Maria's bellybutton, a corporeal signifier of the mother's present absence but past connection, possibly echoed in Berts's joke, 'Where's it [the bellybutton] gone? Oh, she's lost it' (27). Evelyn's comments hint at Maria's doubleness: 'Like there's a mirror down through her middle' (27). Her neighbour's house is experienced as a mirror image of her own:

> The kitchen goes to the left instead of the right and when you try to go into the dining room there is a massive blank wall. Maria lifts her hand as though there might be a handle in the wallpaper, then turns around in fright, because there is a door open behind her back, like a room in a dream.
>
> Upstairs someone comes out of her bedroom, but it is the wrong bedroom and it is not even a girl who comes out of it, but stupid Ben Quinlan. (34)

The emphasis on the mirror works to underline the absence of Maria's twin and her own experience of herself as inchoate and dislocated. Maria appears to have had an altered 'mirror stage', during which, according to Lacan, we misrecognize in our mirror image a whole and coherent subject in contrast to the fragmented body and self-identity that we actually experience. For Maria, the mirror instead reflects back and reinforces her feelings of loss and incompleteness. Her discovery in New York of an uncanny photograph of 'herself' (actually Rose), at twelve years of age, in the wallet of her lover Anton (who had also been fostered by Rose's adoptive parents in his childhood) heightens this relationship with the mirror: 'She went over to the mirror to check if it was still there. She had been completely robbed' (25). Furthermore, the girl in the photograph appears as her mirror image: 'Her hair was the same, but the parting was on the other side' (37).[14] The mirror reflects absence and her 'robbed' subjectivity.[15] Irigaray argues that the mirror stage is predicated on the position of the mother as infrastructure, as support to the formation of the subject: 'The mother supports the processes of the male imaginary but is not herself represented, a neglect equivalent to matricide' (Whitford, 1991, 34). The twins' difficulties with the mirror image, their inability to recognize themselves in its surface, register the problems for feminine subjectivity inherent in this paradigm that seeks to erase the mother. For them, this is further exacerbated by the actual death of their mother, the state-sanctified matricide which privileges the unborn child's life over that of the mother, though they are, as yet, unaware of the particulars surrounding their birth. Significantly though, Rose's dislocation and experiences of an incoherent subjectivity heighten after she learns of her mother's death from the adoption agency: 'Rose sat on the tube, and watched her shattered reflection in the opposite window, the two faces juddering apart' (191).

Maternal Mirrors?

Irigaray further argues that 'women as body/matter are the material of which the mirror is made, that part of the mirror which cannot be reflected, the tain of the mirror for example, and so never see reflections of themselves' (Whitford, 1991, 34). Anna, the twins' mother, imagines her name as a reflection of itself and operates in the novel as a mirror that fails to reflect: 'I looked at AnnA, who was the same, any way you looked at her. And when I died the mirror went blank' (247). The blankness of the mirror is an explicit comment on the position accorded women, particularly mothers, in the symbolic economy – her pregnant body becomes a 'blank body in the centre of it [her house], like a gap in the middle of a hole' (246). Anna fails to register herself as anything other than a gap, the lack that she is reflected as in the Western philosophical tradition and it is the persistence of this gap that the characters experience throughout the novel, which is often projected onto or, experienced most profoundly, through their environment. Enright is, she says, 'really interested in the gap, but I see it as part of a feminist aesthetic. When women have been silent so long, you have to read the silences really urgently [. . .] the gaps, and the slippages, and the jumps, and the uncertain way of making sense' (Enright, 2003, 63). Re-writing Lacan's Mirror Stage, Irigaray shows that this flat mirror merely represents female embodiment as lack. Furthermore, women themselves form the basis of this mirror. They cannot be reflected within it (Irigaray, 1985b, 151). The failure of the mirror stage for Maria is an effect of the complicated position of the woman in the symbolic order. Anna's death, the failure of the state to treat her as a proper subject, exemplifies her role as foundation for the subject and underlines the erasure of her own subjectivity. Her dead body merely houses the twins and as foundation, as the 'tain of the mirror', she is not reflected in the mirror that guarantees subjectivity. Maria and Rose find themselves reflected as only partial subjects due to this complete erasure of the mother's subjectivity which means that the mirror/mother into which they look in order to secure a 'coherent' (though necessarily illusory) subjectivity is a blank one. The severance of the mother-daughter relationship enacted in order to form the ego is shown here to profoundly affect female subjectivity. This is further exacerbated for the twins by their unconscious sense of each other's loss – another missing mirror image.

Maria's discovery of the photograph of Rose precipitates her nervous breakdown; her feelings of dislocation become heightened and expressed through imagery of the mirror, as if she has travelled to the other side of the looking glass:

> Maria was in the country of the lost. They were everywhere [. . .] It was a parallel world. It was just over the other side. Maria had always known it was there, but, now she was in it, she did not know how to get back out again. (57)

Maria experiences the city as its own mirror image; the city is, like her body, inscribed with doubleness and absence. The geographical manifestation of psychic disturbance continues through Maria's compulsive meandering through the streets of New York City until she

> passed a sad-looking woman who ignored her, and recognized, too late, her own reflection. Even she did not know what she looked like any more.

Finally
She had wiped herself off the map. (145)

Rose similarly reacts to the revelation that her biological mother is dead and father unknown:

> She started to wind through the street for no reason at all. She started to wind through the street, like a ball of string, trying to confuse herself with turns and changes of mind. She crossed from one side of the road to the other [. . .] She had been running on a long leash. All her life, she had been attached by an invisible rope and when, finally, she got around to tugging on it there was no one holding the other end. (166)

Rose merely discovers that she is linked to nothing. This umbilical rope reveals an absence at its origin – the dead body of the mother. Maria too, following her suicide attempt experiences this absence, this 'nothing', 'she lay there untangling herself, the monster and the ball of string. She waited for her life to unravel in the dark, so she could follow the string and slay the monster – which was nothing at all' (163). The labyrinth allusions are worth noting here as Irigarary connects this space with the dislocations of the female subject: 'She is your labyrinth, you are hers. A path from you to yourself is lost in her, and from her to herself is lost in you. And if one looks only for a play of mirrors in all this, does one not create the abyss?' (Irigaray, 1991a, 73). This disorientation here is linked to the complex positioning of women in the symbolic order which becomes an abyss of mirrors, reflecting nothing back.

Maria's impulse, while slitting her wrists, is to put her blood on a mirror, to 'see the sheet of glass between the real blood and the reflected blood. It is very thick. It is very clean and calm' (158). This gesture highlights her desire for the cold, clean separation imposed between the messiness of the blood.[16] But it also makes the mirror itself visible – 'the tain of the mirror' (Whitford, 1991, 34), the unacknowledged infrastructure that supports the subject which is the body of the mother – in this novel an already dead body. Maria and Rose both attempt to reveal the absence that motivates their psychic trauma. This is what they are searching for.

In contrast, Berts's desire is to eliminate this gap completely, to make the absence of his wife fully absent. Following the death of his wife he continuously imagines a voyage around Ireland's coastline. Berts's anxiety concerning the potential accuracy of the cartographic process – 'He worried about piers. Should he travel the length of them, going up the near side and coming back by the far?' (10) – expresses, for Claire Connolly, a 'sharp contrast to the unmapped emotional spaces that the novel charts: adoption, childlessness, sexual loneliness' (Connolly, 2003b, 32–3). Berts imagines his journey on two levels, as a physical expedition and, in more abstract terms, as an imaginary mapping: 'He took an imaginary piece of red wool and wove it around an imaginary map, curling it into coves and wriggling around headlands, then stretching it out along a ruler for miles per inch' (10). The imaginary journey functions as Berts's means of controlling the memory of his wife. The anxiety expressed about the boundaries of Ireland also translates into a concomitant concern about his dead wife's presence in his life:

> The house would be the same when he got back, but it would be better the second time around, or at least different. His wife would be dead, but he would be alive, with a circle inscribed around that life. She would leave him alone. (11)

His imagined cartographies attempt to demarcate boundaries to manage his wife's death but her absence, which becomes in the process a powerful presence, can attach itself to his body and is capable of obliterating the map by inscribing it completely:

> But, as he rolled over the hollow she had left in the mattress, he might catch the edge of her absence like an elastic band on his foot, he might drag it with him around the entire country, until his wife's death had filled the map, emptied the map [. . .] He would have to cross her last, or even not cross her at all, skirting the bed at the end of his trip, leave her outside the circle, on the side of the sea. (11)

His only option is to expel his wife beyond the boundaries of his map and of Ireland (much like he has with Rose). The borders, however, remain too complicated for him to trace and neither the exorcism of his wife nor of Rose is fully secure.

Instead, Berts realizes that a gap exists inside his own head. It is 'the place where he had put his wife' (251), which finally disappears when he confronts the embodied return of his actions when both daughters walk through his door:

For years he had allowed a gap in his head where she could live undis-
turbed, and now it was not even she who was disturbed, but nothing at all.
It was not even she who fled, as the gap closed, but no one at all. [. . .]
How long had he lived here, in the dead self of his wife?
I have been living in a grave, he thought, *I have been living nowhere at all.*
(251–2)

Berts's final exorcism of his wife, following his first sight of the reunited
twins, is configured in terms of an effective rebirthing from the grave, from
a vacuum, from '*nowhere at all*':

The doorbell rang. And the hoover of his wife turned around and sucked
itself up. The house of his wife turned itself inside out for him. The house
of his wife flipped over in space; with the wallpaper showing on the outside and the furniture drifting into the garden, and the lampshades floating off the roof; vomiting Berts out on to the road. (252)

Berts imagines a second exorcism of his wife, closing the 'gap in his head',
pronouncing her dead, and his rebirth is achieved through the erasure of
his wife as she vacuums herself up. However, Anna's voice has directly preceded this in a lengthy narrative speaking from beyond the grave, insisting
that 'I am not dead. I am in hell. And I blame the feet that walk over me'
(248). Thus, Berts's attempted erasure remains troubling and Enright
explicitly draws attention here to the degree to which the maternal body
forms an unacknowledged basis of phantasies of the coherent masculine
subject.

Return of the Mummy

The aimless journeys and incessant recourse to mapping of Berts and his
two daughters operate in sharp contrast to the proscribed spatial possibilities for Anna who is explicitly connected with the domestic space. Berts
notes that he has not seen her outside the house since they got married,
and when she is taken to the hospital, 'The carpets seemed emptied of pattern, the cushions made no sense' (8). His wife and the domestic space
become so inextricably connected that he dreams of 'upholstered breasts'
(8). Domestic spaces are again linked to the pregnant body when his second

wife, Evelyn, conceives. Her pregnancy manifests itself in an obsession with the redecoration of the house, although Berts refuses to change the carpets, associated as they are with his dead wife. In an Irigarayan moment, Berts's first wife, Anna, is relegated to the space of the ground:

> 'I want my own carpet,' she [Evelyn] said, finally, as he knew she would say, now that she had her own child.
> And Berts said, 'my wife chose this carpet. You know that. My dead wife.' (14)

Later, when we encounter Anna's voice for the first time from beyond the grave, she articulates her anger with this positioning: 'I am not dead. I am in hell. And I blame the feet that walk over me' (248). In *Making Babies*, Enright also links the experience of motherhood to a foundational positioning: 'Not just mother, also platform and prosthesis. I'm not sure I feel like a person, any more. I think I feel a little used' (Enright, 2004, 60). Although they cannot articulate it, it is the desire for the living mother that mobilizes Maria and Rose's journeys; journeys, however, that manifest their psychic trauma and dislocations due to the fact that their mother is inaccessible and unrepresentable to them precisely because she is 'a reproductive body in the pay of the polis' (Irigaray, 1991c, 47).

This unrepresentability of the maternal in the patriarchal cultural economy is experienced by Anna herself in her difficulties in articulating her own subjectivity, idiosyncrasies relating to inscription that she has inherited from her own mother. Domestic spaces are used by Anna's mother as a writable surface upon which she can inscribe reminders by rearranging objects in the kitchen:

> The whole room was a reminder to her. There was no telling, when you touched something, what it might mean. 'Who moved the sweeping brush?' she would say. 'When we haven't a sausage in the house?' (234)

Anna, in her narrative, articulates her desire for this kind of inscription: words trouble her. Language and writing, for her, are a source of particular anxiety:

> There is no story to living, and having a child, and dying. Not for me. No matter what order I put them in. So I put vegetables in the wardrobe and buried my clothes. I turned the hoover on itself, all the way up the flex. I rolled along the wallpaper, like Cleopatra coming out of a carpet, and

I wrote lists on the floor. [. . .] I am terrified, here in my grave, by words and what they might want. (235)

Anna's anxiety concerning language also translates to her relationship with her own body. Looking at her naked self for the first time in a cracked eighteenth-century mirror she 'could not find the words for it. Pink. White. Hill. Cunt. Move. You move the tea cosy from the pot to the table, you move it to the side of the range, you turn the cosy inside out' (247). The inability to attach language to the body is deflected onto the house, onto a rearrangement of space that becomes the only means of communication, though unintelligible to everyone else. Anna's hell is the incessant re-emergence of the repressed body as furniture to be moved around a room:

I am in hell. This is what I see, this is what I see, I see the turd, I see the rope, I see my own private parts that I never saw and Berts' private parts that I never saw, I see them clearly. I shift them around the room. I give my husband breasts. I am not ashamed. I shit through the noose and I cry through my backside. I am in hell. (247)

Elizabeth Grosz claims, in her analysis of Irigaray, that 'this appropriation of the right to a place or a space correlates with men's seizure of the right to define and utilize a spatiality that reflects their own self-representations' (Grosz, 1995, 121). Irigaray explicitly connects the female body to the domestic space: 'I was your house. And, when you leave, abandoning this dwelling place, I do not know what to do with these walls of mine' (Irigaray, 1992, 49). Anna's voice from beyond the grave represents the attempt of the repressed and effaced body to speak from what Irigaray terms 'that decorative sepulchre, where even her breath is lost' (Irigaray, 1985a, 143). She speaks from the place of death, from beyond the symbolic order, and from the position of the abject, attacking the processes by which subjecthood is achieved through repression and abjection. Enright brings the psychosis and violence of this space into focus in a way that is missing from Irigaray's account. Enright's novel illustrates that women's relationship to space has been configured in a way that makes their engagement with it seem pathological. The depressions and attempted suicides of Maria and Rose exacerbate an already troubled experience of spatial relations: 'Space had flattened for her, she does not so much cross the room as crawl up the face of the floor' (155). Enright in this novel makes explicit the symbolic murder of the mother – these twins are born from a dead body. The mother here is nothing but a womb, a body to house the twins until born. She is a grave in Berts's imaginary and a vacuum, the gap inside his head, and the constant imagery of holes, gaps, blankness, and loss in the novel make this erasure of the mother explicit. The twins' dislocations, both psychically and geographically, are propelled by this erasure at their origin – the dead body of the mother that births them and Berts's refusal to detail the circumstances of their birth.

The reconciliation between the girls, their connection following dislocation, initiates a sense of possibility: 'Anything was possible, even then' (253). Despite the sense of potentiality that the twins' encounter with each other produces, the narrative highlights the troubling place of the mother in the Irish cultural imaginary and the relation between the female/maternal body and space. Rose expresses her wish to visit her mother's grave, yet Berts's response is merely to mention a tree that Rose's mother had liked, evading questions concerning where Anna is buried. For Enright, narrative itself is bound up in absence:

> Novel narrative is involved in revelation; it's the gap, the awful hole in the text, through which the characters fall. I do think that there is an unsayable thing in the centre of a book, and that if you fill it with something too obvious, then you are lost. You have to fill it with something archetypal that has the possibility of being at least two things at once – that energy has to be maintained. (Enright, 2003, 63)

In *What Are You Like?* the 'unsayable thing' is the erasure of the maternal body, her disconnection from place. Anna later recognizes and articulates her dislocation:

> I was always pregnant. I was never pregnant. I walked from room to room, ambushed by all these things. The past and the future were as big as they ever were, with nothing in the middle, except this empty, waiting house, my blank body in the centre of it, like a gap in the middle of a hole. I was bothered by memories, I was bothered by things that had not happened yet. I was squashed between two unshiftable things and I started to rearrange the house, moving the furniture from room to room. (246)

In Irigaray's words: 'The mother may signify only a silent ground, a scarcely representable mystery' (Irigaray, 1991b, 54). The novel charts the trauma incurred by this silencing of the mother, the relegation of the maternal to the space of the ground, and the mother as infrastructure for the formation of the ego. But the 'unsayable thing' is also everything that is projected onto the mother, the repressed and abjected body. Enright makes the position of the mother within this cultural economy explicit and also gives her a voice, she is not simply 'a silent ground'.

Enright's use of twin and double motifs in the novel initiates an engagement with questions of sameness and difference that refuses to privilege ultimate similarity or opposition, or autonomous selfhood. In *What Are You Like?* this is epitomized in its final sentence concerning Rose's adoptive father's feelings towards the girls: 'he loved them both equally, though he preferred his own' (257). Enright's interest in this type of couple may suggest potential ways of thinking about the positioning of mother and daughter in relation to each other. Enright's fiction contains repeated images of such interconnection: Grace and her mother swimming while pregnant in *The Wig My Father Wore* (subtly highlighting connections between mother and foetus in terms of their surroundings, both floating in liquid), the pregnant Eliza on the boat in *The Pleasure of Eliza Lynch*, the pregnant woman in the lift in 'Shaft'. As Enright says of the images,

> She is in a lift, and I really love the idea of this pregnant woman in this box, it's umbilical really – the rope. So that floated my boat really and the same with Eliza – the pregnant woman on the boat, in a hammock. It was a kind of gyroscope. She herself is a kind of gravity machine, that she was a gyroscope for the child. (Enright, 2011)

These images of interconnectivity are paramount to Enright's literary project and the gyroscope is an interesting metaphor, given its interlocking rings that freely rotate. Neither ring is merely infrastructure, both are mobile and move freely. The gyroscope as mechanism is used, according to the *Oxford English Dictionary*, to 'provide a horizontal or vertical reference direction', to orient. *What Are You Like?* explores the consequences of relegating the maternal to a foundational function – without this interconnecting, mobilized relationship everyone is disorientated, most particularly the mother, Anna, who at the end of the novel remains dislocated – though she is given a voice within the novel, she does not have a narrative, and the ending of the novel leaves her immanent, a 'nothing at all' (163, 251), which haunts.

Conclusion

Enright claims uncertainty concerning the mother-daughter relationship and her engagement with this dynamic in her writing: 'I don't know whether

I want to understand the mechanisms that go on between the mother and the daughter. I don't want to go there yet; there is so much material and kinetic energy' (Enright, 2003, 61). However, *The Wig My Father Wore* and *What Are You Like?* both tackle this complicated relationship. This, for Irigaray, is tantamount to a reordering of a patriarchal cultural imaginary: 'In our societies, the mother/daughter, daughter/mother relationship constitutes a highly explosive nucleus. Thinking it, and changing it, is equivalent to shaking the foundations of the patriarchal order' (Irigaray, 1991c, 50).

Enright's use of twin and double motifs in the novel initiates an engagement with questions of sameness and difference that refuses to privilege ultimate similarity or opposition, which suggests potential ways of configuring mother-daughter relations. Furthermore, Enright's configurations of the corporeal that eschew coherence and privilege connectivity and transformation, (which mirror her narrative style and form), offer alternate paradigms for conceiving the relations between self and other and between generations.

Moving on from the intersubjective and intercorporeal paradigms that *The Wig My Father Wore* and *What Are You Like?* set up, my final chapter will look at fictional biographies written by Colm McCann and Anne Enright. McCann has fictionalized the life of dancer Rudolf Nureyev, whereas Enright has turned to the nineteenth century to explore the life of Irishwoman, Eliza Lynch, who became consort to the future ruler of Paraguay. This chapter will focus on the configuration in these novels of relationships between past and present in relation to corporeality.

Chapter 4

Embodied Histories:
Colum McCann's *Dancer* and Anne Enright's
The Pleasure of Eliza Lynch

Both Colum McCann and Anne Enright have written fictionalized biographies or historical novels. McCann's *Dancer* (2003b) takes the iconic ballet dancer, Rudolf Nureyev, as its focus, whose life spans from Russia during the Second World War to New York in the 1990s. Enright, in *The Pleasure of Eliza Lynch* (2002b), chooses nineteenth-century Paris and Paraguay as her setting and the Irish courtesan Eliza Lynch as her subject. For both writers, historical accuracy is not of major importance; rather McCann and Enright use their subject's lives as structuring principles through which they can engage with questions about storytelling, the creation of iconic figures, the relationship between individuals and historical discourses, and the place of the corporeal in such discourses. Enright's novel looks particularly at the female figure in relation to these concerns. Both novelists profess to an interest in exploring aspects of the past that are unacknowledged by dominant historical discourses: 'The writer', for McCann, 'desires to see inside the dark corners in order to make sense of the room that has already been swept clean (or clean-ish) by historians, critics, and journalists' (McCann and Hemon, 2003b). These 'dark corners', for Enright, are the largely ignored figure of Eliza as well as the body, particularly the pregnant body, in the narratives of history. Corporeality is also of major importance to McCann and it is the image of Nureyev's dancing body that becomes a means for him to reconsider the relationship between history and the present.

Dancer

While McCann's fiction, in general, exhibits a preoccupation with time and memory, no text thus far explores these concepts with such dedication and in such a particular way as *Dancer* does. *This Side of Brightness* engaged with memory and temporalities through a concern for spatial politics as imbricated within the landscapes, subscapes, and skyscapes of New York City. The configuration of temporalities in *Dancer*, while embedded in the landscape to a certain degree, is more particularly situated in the human body which might reflect the choice of subject matter, Rudolf Nureyev, the famous Russian ballet dancer. *Dancer* is a fictional biography of Nureyev, charting his life from his early years in the city of Ufa in Stalinist Russia, through his defection to Paris in the West, his years as partner to Margot Fonteyn, to his death from AIDS in New York in 1993, aged 54. McCann's text is divided into four sections, each dealing with particular locations in Nureyev's life; Book One follows his childhood, ballet training in Russia, and the impact of his defection on those close to him; Book Two charts Nureyev's rise to fame in Europe and America, while Book Three jumps between Nureyev's associates in New York, London, Paris, and Caracas, as well as focusing on old friends in Russia. Book Four looks at Nureyev's final and only visit to Russia after his defection. The text is constructed using a variety of narrators offering a wide array of perspectives.

McCann prefaces his text with an epigraph from William Maxwell's novel *So Long, See You Tomorrow* (1988). This quotation draws attention to *Dancer's* narrative concern with memory. Memory, Maxwell explicates, is 'a moment, a scene, a fact that has been subjected to a fixative'. This implies a break in the movement of time and the removal of an event from the temporal flow. However, Maxwell also delineates memory as 'a form of storytelling that goes on continually in the mind and often changes with the telling', signalling something other than the concretion of an event removed from the flow of temporality, something rather more temporal and metamorphic, something more fictional, in both senses of the word (1). It denotes the act of storytelling as well untruth: 'in talking about the past we lie with every breath we draw' (1).

I would like to focus on the multiplicity and ambiguity of memory towards which Maxwell gestures as a means of exploring how configurations of time and the relationship between past and present are crucial to McCann's novel. Maxwell's use of the term 'fixative' is of particular relevance to McCann's central image in *Dancer*, that of Rudi's balletic jump as an arrestment of time. As Rudi himself notes: 'Nijinsky said it was not difficult to stay in the air, you just have to pause a little while up there' (85). Dancing thus becomes a means of using the body to arrest time; by remaining in the air longer than usual he attempts to create a stasis of movement and to freeze both the body and time. However, the narrative also keeps in clear focus the transformations of the body through time, the impact that dancing has on the physical body, and indeed, the inability of the flesh to halt the process of time. McCann, when explaining the appeal of the subject, expresses this contradiction that is at the heart of the art of dancing and the figure of Nureyev himself: 'What attracted me about dance, though, was again, the violence of it. I mean, there's a tremendous violence committed on the body in order to achieve the appearance of ease' (McCann and Hemon, 2003a).

From the beginning of the text a focus on the bodily is signalled, from the wartime experiences of the soldiers to the cleansing process that the injured must undergo upon their return. Through the first-person narration of a woman volunteer who assisted in the construction of a 'giant metal bath' attention is drawn to the abject physical state of the soldiers and the effects that care of the body elicits:

> I cleaned very carefully, the chin, the brows, the forehead and behind their ears. Then I went vigorously at their back which were always filthy. You could see their ribs and the curve of their spines. I went down towards their bottoms and cleaned a little around there, but not so much that they got uncomfortable. Sometimes they would call me Mama or Sister and I'd lean forward and say: There there there. (16)

Eve Patten suggests that this bathhouse scene is recalled in Nureyev's later visits to gay bathhouses in New York in a 'subtle symmetry' in which 'the invisible patterns of history are suddenly illuminated' that link 'the cataclysm of the second World War' to 'the cultural shallowness of the 1970s onwards' (Patten, 2003). It is also through this woman's narration that we encounter Rudi for the first time, as a boy aged between five and six dancing for the hospitalized soldiers; the sight of his performance heightens their awareness of their wounded bodies.[1] The attention to cleanliness is carried through in a third-person narrative told from the point of view of Rudi; his mother has exchanged picture frames for soap, the aesthetic for the bodily (21). Rudi's perpetual hunger as a child also underscores the prevalence of the physical. Of significance in this text are the links, intertwinings, contradictions, and relations between the body and memory, and between the corporeal and conceptions of temporality. What is particularly important is the question of what is at stake in the relationship between the morphology of the human body and engagements with the past through memory or storytelling. Before approaching these concerns in detail it is worth exploring the construction of the novel and McCann's own attitudes to the text.

The novel, *Dancer*, is a fictionalized account of Rudolf Nureyev's life. McCann stresses that the book is not a biography of the dancer.[2] It is not intended as a 'truthful' rendering of the events that took place in Nureyev's life nor as a faithful explication of his character and personality. Rather, as McCann states, 'It's a book in which a character by the name of Rudolph Nureyev appears as a shadow unto other things that are being talked about. Like stories and story telling, their value' (McCann, 2003a). McCann sees Nureyev, the historical figure, as secondary to concerns of narration and of storytelling. In fact, Nureyev's life seems to become a kind of background to the questions of 'how stories get told and why they get told and how we create stories. Who owns a story and who legislates it?' (McCann, 2003a). The question, nonetheless, arises as to why McCann chooses to explore storytelling and memory through the figure of Nureyev a dancer. What part does the body in movement, or the body of a dancer, play in this? I shall return to these concerns in the course of the chapter.

The importance of stories and of their recitation is borne out in McCann's choice of a multitude of narrators for the text. The narration of *Dancer* continually shifts from third person to first person, and at times to second person, reflecting the perspectives of various characters that touch upon Rudi's[3] life in both major and minor ways. These include, amongst many others, the husband of his first dance teacher, their daughter Yulia, an anonymous rival at the Kirov, Rudi's sister Tamara, his shoemaker, his housekeeper Odille, Margot Fonteyn, and his friend Victor Pareci. The countless stories that surround Rudi's famous one seem more important to McCann's narrative than a faithful delineation of Rudi's history. As McCann claims in an interview, 'no matter how much you are seen on the periphery [. . .] your stories matter' (McCann, 2003a). These perspectives, particularly in the opening sections of the novel, often move from the general to the particular, circling around the subject of the novel, Nureyev. For instance, the opening section of the novel concerns the wartime experiences of the Russian soldiers at the front, following their suffering and eventual return homeward by train, before focusing on the figure of a six-year-old boy, Rudi, watching these trains in expectation of his father's return. In such a way we as readers are always kept at a remove from the central figure; Rudi is glimpsed through the narratives of those around him and we rarely receive an insight into the subjective dimensions of his character. It is not until Book Two of the novel that we hear Rudi's own voice in a diary-like narrative, which forms the centre of the narrative as a whole before it reverts once again to an array of outside perspectives. Thus, the reader is situated as an onlooker at Rudi's life or positioned as audience, though obliquely – the major events of his life, in the terms of celebrity and journalistic reportage, such as his defection, are briefly mentioned in the novel. Interestingly, at the moment in the narrative when he becomes most famous the perspective shifts to that of Rudi.

Ironically, just at the juncture when he becomes most objectified he is given subjectivity. This type of narrative construction emphasizes Nureyev's position as a body that is viewed by other people. His experience is always mediated through the gaze of another: 'Watching people nearby, watching him [Rudi], being watched' (90). This is emphasized in a short section of the narrative which is constructed by means of a repetition of the phrase 'You see him . . . ' (71–4). The idea of Rudi as a dancer, as a body in movement (and as a body that has taken on iconic status, which freezes it somewhat) is intrinsic to novel, to the stories it tells, and to the relations of time and memory that are configured by it.

Novelist Aleksander Hemon, in conversation with McCann, highlights *Dancer*'s subject, 'dance – the body in space and time', which he notes 'is perhaps the human activity least representable and reproducible in language' (McCann and Hemon, 2003a). In contrast, in the novel, dance as the visceral experience of the body in motion is figured as possessing the ability to communicate otherwise: 'It struck me then that Rudik's genius was in allowing his body to say things that he couldn't otherwise express' (50). Furthermore, that which is said to fuel dance in the following passage complicates notions of its artistry as simply a body moving in space and time:

Of course he danced perfectly, light and quick, pliant, his line controlled and composed, but more than that he was using something beyond his body – not just his face, his fingers, his long neck, his hips, but something intangible, beyond thought, some kinetic fury and spirit. (81)

Here, dance encompasses elements that trouble representation, that cannot quite be grasped and that stress the boundaries of thought production. This attitude to dance is constant throughout the novel. Rudi, in his notes to himself, writes 'In an interview Petit[4] says there are certain things that defeat themselves if they are said. That dance is the only thing that can describe what is otherwise indescribable' (145). I would like to link this idea of dance as another means of communication, one that gestures beyond the representable, to Derrida's formulation of dance in his well-known interview with Christine V. McDonald.

Derrida's Choreographies

In 'Choreographies', Derrida evokes a conception of dance as a theoretical tool, or rather, a type of thought or process of conceptual operation.[5]

Dance, as Derrida presents it, is a type of disordering, dismantling, or deconstruction that alters the paradigms through which it moves: 'The most innocent of dances would thwart the *assignation à résidence*, escape those residences under surveillance; the dance changes place and above all changes *places*. In its wake they can no longer be recognized' (Derrida, 1995, 94). This perception of dance, for Derrida, originates in McDonald's evocation at the beginning of the interview of maverick feminist Emma Goldman's famous pronouncement: 'If I can't dance I don't want to be part of your revolution.' The revolution referred to here is the nineteenth-century feminist movement (89). To dance then is to refuse to adhere to the conventions advocated by a particular movement, to insist on querying foundations and assumptions. As Derrida remarks, Goldman's 'ask[ing] of the feminist movement its questions and conditions' is 'a sign of the dance' (90). In this way, dance becomes a term like *différance*, trace, supplement, or *pharmakon*, among others. As Derrida tentatively suggests it could be 'considered (for nothing is taken for granted or guaranteed in these matters) a kind of transformation or deformation of space; such a transformation would tend to extend beyond these poles and reinscribe them within it' (105). In other words, these types of thought open out and warp existing parameters to produce a potential for revision.

Ideas surrounding actual dance in McCann's novel seem to approximate Derrida's delineation of the conceptual movement. Dance is, for Rudi:

> no body anymore no thought no awareness this must be the moment the others call god as if all the doors are open everywhere leading to all other open doors forever no hinges no frames no jambs no edges no shadows this is my soul in flight born weightless born timeless a clock spring broken he could stay like this forever. (168–9)

Yulia describes her first experience of Rudi dancing in terms that highlight his performance as travelling beyond the imagined and the known:

> Rudi had stood upon that stage like an exhausted explorer who had arrived in some unimagined country and, despite the joy of the discovery, was immediately looking for another unimagined place, and I felt perhaps that place was me. (126)

Dance, in the text, is continually compared to journeying beyond borders, to the free movement of the body itself and to the motion of the body across space. Yulia's description of Rudi's performance figures the dancer as always attempting to travel beyond the known and aspiring to 'another unimagined place'.[6] By inhabiting spaces, places, and concepts that have until now been unthought-of, both dance and the dancer operate as powerful inscribers of change, choreographers of the new, also enacting transformations on the level of personal subjectivity. Yulia equates herself to the 'unimagined place'; the performance affects her viscerally.

The attitudes to dance in McCann's novel illustrate Derrida's formulation of dance as a transformative and refiguring process that initiates the radically new:

> [Rudi] talked about how he had begun to believe that there should be no unity in art, never, that perfection embalms it, there has to be some tearing, a fracturing, like a Persian carpet with a wrongly tied knot, for that's what makes life interesting. (209)

However, a further dimension to dance's deconstructive process is stressed in *Dancer*, that of temporality and the relations between past, present, and future: '*If a dancer, he is good,* says Rudi, *he has to straddle the time! He must drag the old forward into the new!*' (209). The dancer here is positioned as a figure that must negotiate these temporal spheres. Combined with the idea of dance itself as 'an experiment, all its impulses going to the creation of an adventure and the end of each adventure being a new impulse towards further creation' (209), the art must also bear witness to the past and draw upon history in this process of invention. Derrida also links the idea of the conceptual dance to histories and pasts that have been occluded but which refuse to remain silent, especially in relation to the record of different feminisms: 'It was necessary to recall the fact that this "silent past" (as that which was passed-over-in-silence) could still reserve some surprises, like the dance of your "maverick feminist"' (Derrida, 1995, 92). Thus, the irruptions of repressed or forgotten histories and pasts also disrupt the dominant narratives through which they move and would permit 'a completely other history: a history of paradoxical laws and non-dialectical discontinuities, a history of absolutely heterogeneous pockets, irreducible particularities, of unheard-of and incalculable sexual differences' (Derrida, 1995, 93). The democracy of storytelling that McCann attempts opens up the text to a proliferation of these competing histories. Rudi's image of the dancer straddling time impacts upon the emphasis on memory and histories that is apparent throughout the novel. Body and dance are conceived of as inextricable from each other in the novel:

> Anna told him that his whole body must dance, all of it, not just his arms and legs. She tweaked him on the ear, saying even his lobe must believe in movement [. . .] Absorb the dance like blotting paper. (48)

How does the image of the dancer inflect the configurations of temporality at work in the text when one bears in mind that it is very much tied to corporeality?

Dance critic, Bojana Kunst, argues that early twentieth-century dance theory focused on the concept of bodily autonomy and also connected it to political autonomy. Dance, then, became connected to political ideologies: 'Autonomy became a privilege of style in American dance. With its expansion in Europe, Russia and other parts of the world, dance became an important export product of a contemporary "free" American culture' (Kunst, 2003, 64). For Kunst, the difference between Eastern and Western cultural embodiments of dance is represented in terms of temporality:

> On the one side there is the western dancing body, completely equipped for the present; and on the other side, a body almost without contemporariness, that of the other unarticulated body with a dark, closed and incomprehensible attraction to the past. (64–5)

Non-western forms of dance and non-western dancing bodies are viewed as anachronistic, lacking in contemporaneity and inextricably tied to the past. This may account for Rudi's discomfort with engaging with the past. For Kunst, '[t]o perform in relation to the present [. . .] is not about being in a certain moment, but about using that moment to reveal a different history, about bringing to light the history of forgotten, overlooked and forbidden bodies' (66). In order to approach this possibility, different conceptions of temporality are required, '*different possibilities of presence and being in the present*' (66). McCann's *Dancer* attempts to address such notions of embodied histories through its multiplicity of narrators and viewpoints as well as through the figure of the dancing body itself.

Memory

Peter Kruth, reviewer for the *New York Times*, points out that 'the images of water and weather, memory, motion and time, are the essence of *Dancer*, because they're the essence of Nureyev' (Kurth, 2003). Issues of memory are particularly important to the first-person narrative of the husband of Rudi's first ballet teacher, Sergei. He and his wife, Anna, have been exiled to the closed city of Ufa from Leningrad, which they remember by its pre-revolutionary name, Saint Petersburg. In their daughter Yulia's words, 'the foothold of their lives was in what they still called Petersburg – the palaces, the houses, the fencing duels, the sideboards, the inkwells, the Bohemian cut glass, the orchestra seats at the Maryinsky' (61). Yulia's metaphor of the foothold highlights a bodily connection to this past. Sergei and Anna, who was a former member of the Maryinsky corps de ballet during Anna Pavlova's career, introduce Rudi to this past prior to the Revolution. Sergei, in particular, meditates on the relationship between the past and the present, between what has gone and what remains. For him the poet Boris Pasternak is of particular significance due to the fact that 'he had learned to love what is left behind without mourning what was gone' (38). However, Sergei also remarks on the difficulty of maintaining such generosity with relation to the past:

I could tell from Anna's face that she had already told him [Rudi] about dancing in Saint Petersburg and that the memory weighed on her heavily. What monstrous things, our pasts, especially when they have been lovely. She had told a secret and now had the sadness of wondering how much deeper she might dig in order to keep the secret fed. (43)

Sergei's comments highlight the painful relationship that encounters with the past often elicit. He and Anna seem to exist more profoundly in the past and in their memories. This is true especially of Anna, who when trying on an old tutu 'looked a bit like a footnote to her past' (41). They are constant reminders for each other of this lost life: 'Once we had filled each other with desire, not remembrance' (41). Their past is further removed from them visually when silverfish are discovered to have eaten the Saint Petersburg photos from their photo album. Yet, they spare the most recent ones taken in Ufa reminding them that their present is both difficult to escape and unpalatable even to a paper-eating insect (40–1). However, as Sergei acknowledges, the past inevitably returns, 'but all dead friends come to life again sometimes', signalling a more complicated relationship between past and present than one of linear succession (48).

Sergei is ambivalent about the value of memory and of engaging with a past:

I have always thought of memory as a foolish conceit, but as the gramophone crackled Anna began to tell him bits and pieces of her past. She glossed over her own youth and quickly settled into her years in the corps. How she yammered on! The costumes, the designers, the trains across borders! [. . .] After a while there was no arresting her – it was like the Dutch boy's dam, except it wasn't only the river that had burst, but the ramparts, the bank and the weeds on the shore also. (47–8)

Memory here is compared to a river, a flow of water that will not be restrained. The motif of trains is important in this context; here they are symbolic of the freedom of movement that characterized Anna's past, both in terms of her own body and of traversing a landscape. In the present both are proscribed and restricted. Trains bring Rudik to Leningrad. He also watches trains at the beginning of the narrative, waiting for his father to return. Rudik spends his time in school drawing 'maps with pictures of trains moving across the landscape. His notebooks are covered with sketches of ballerina legs' (35). This again links the dancing with the idea of free movement.

The novel abounds in references to and images of attempts to resist the flow of time. Sergei says in relation to a portrait of Anna: 'It's our function in life to make moments durable' (131). A related image is that of the china saucer, inherited by Anna from her grandmother, and presented to Yulia by Sergei. As an object, it is 'light' and 'fragile' and disappoints her: 'it seemed to have nothing to do with either of them [her parents]' (135). Despite its apparent fragility it has survived 'Poverty lust sickness envy and hope' (136). The significance of the tiny saucer becomes clearer to Yulia later in the novel when she purchases a 'hand-crafted music box' which 'like the china plate my father had given to me [. . .] seemed to resonate into both past and future' (227). She intends to give the saucer to her adopted son, Kolya, but instead offers it to Rudi on his only visit to Russia. The objects highlight durability and act as vehicles for the ability to connect past to present and future. They become symbols for continuity, connections between generations, and genealogies that persist despite the violent severance of past from present enacted by the Russian Revolution. Indeed, in the list of the auctioned lots of Rudi's property that closes the book one notices 'Lot 1274: Pre-Revolutionary Russian China Dish', sold to Nikolai Mareneov, a character previously unmentioned (290). The dish has outlasted Rudi, has been passed on, and though the familial genealogy has been broken what remains important is the durability of this fragile china saucer. The saucer suggests a link to history and is connected with memory. It is an unbroken object that denotes the persistence of the past into the present and future.

The importance of the image of the china saucer as well as the ambivalences inherent in Sergei's attitude to memory and approaches to the past can be understood more readily if we return to Deleuze's conception of temporality as outlined in my introduction which acknowledges the complex interrelations between past and present. What is important for the configuration of memory and temporalities in *Dancer* is that, in keeping with a Deleuzian conception of time, the past and present are not radically separated but inherently implicated in each other. As Al-Saji writes, 'the present already includes the past [. . .] that presence implies memory and cannot be conceived without it' (Al-Saji, 2004, 208). The characters in *Dancer* frequently experience this coexistence of past and present:

> His [Sergei's] recollections of their life were a jumble – the last days were nudged up against the first days and sometimes the later years seemed to have shaped the earlier ones – as if time had been gripped and squeezed formless. (134)

The past can never be detached from the present and bleeds into it. Time can no longer be thought of in conventional terms and has lost its traditional form. The past cannot be considered as something that is complete and static. Elizabeth Grosz argues that '[r]ather than the past being regarded as fixed, inert, given, unalterable, it must be regarded as being inherently open to future rewritings' (Grosz, 2000, 1019). I would argue that *Dancer* advocates this conception of the past through the figure of the dancing body.

This conception of time initiates a potentializing and transformative function of memory which allies it to Derrida's use of dance as a process of thought that radically alters the ground through which, and over which, it travels. Engaging with a past that produces radical transformation is both embraced and feared by the characters in the novel. Rudi, though insisting that dance '*drag the old forward into the new*' (209), retains a distaste for considering the past: 'If you look back you'll only fall down the stairs' (181). Rudi's rejection of his own history figures the process of retrospection as one that elicits bodily harm.

Doubles, or the Otherness of Bodies

As in Enright's work, the body, despite the emphasis on its materiality, is presented in a way that troubles conceptions of corporealites as coherent, bounded unities. In a reversal of the Lacanian Mirror Stage, it is reflections

in mirrors that provide this recognition of the body as amorphous and incoherent. More particularly, the reflections in *Dancer* emphasize a sense of
otherness in the person gazing in the mirror:

> Erik says that increasingly after performances he feels distanced from
> himself [. . .] He changes clothes, faces the mirror, sees only a reflection.
> He must keep looking long enough until he finally recognises an old
> friend – himself. Only then can he leave. (173)

Yulia experiences a 'feeling of dislocation' when contemplating her mirror
image (62). For her, the reflection highlights the fact that 'We don't ever, I
thought, grow sharper, clearer, or more durable' (62). Temporality seems
to be implicitly bound up in these body images, signalling not only physical
transformation through time and the lack of clear and definite borders, but
also the coexistence of bodily pasts with bodily presents. RosaMaria, Rudi's
Chilean friend, comments: 'The child in him [Rudi] seemed to reflect off
the glass while he watched me in his own reflection' (96). Reflections are
haunted, 'The mirror was smudged with someone's fingerprints and I
[Yulia] had the strange feeling that someone else's ghostly hand was on my
face' (126), and they are also a means of imagining oneself differently and
of projecting oneself out of the body, to cross borders: 'I [Yulia] had often
caught a glimpse of him [Rudi] looking in the mirror, as if he was willing
himself into someone else's body' (127).

As in the mirror's conventional representation, the reflection signals the
emergence of doubling. The invocation of the otherness of the body in its
mirrored reflection feeds into the images of doubles that proliferate
throughout the text, particularly in its second half. Rudi seems almost to
possess the ability to create doubles simply through the power of his dancing. An unnamed addressee who is a colleague of Rudi in Leningrad is
physically affected by his presence:

> and then one day you see him [Rudi] – in class, in the hallway, in the
> canteen, in the fifth-floor rehearsal rooms, it doesn't matter – and you
> believe you are seeing yourself, you want to move but you can't, your feet
> are nailed to the floor, the heat of the day rises through you, it will not
> stop, and you think you have stepped into an acid bath, the liquid is above
> you, below you, around you, inside you, burning, until he moves away and
> the acid is gone, you stand alone and you look down and suddenly realise
> how much of yourself has disappeared. (74)

Rudi, in classic *Doppelgänger* fashion, becomes a double who attempts to destroy the original.[7] This type of relationship between doubles represents, as Juliana De Nooy argues in her study of twins, the resolution of a difficulty with issues of sameness and difference. Doubles, by their nature, cannot be configured as completely similar or radically different. Removing one of the terms of the dialectic by eliminating one half of the double alleviates this dilemma (De Nooy, 2002, 76). However, in *Dancer*, doubles are allowed to proliferate. Only part of Rudi's anonymous rival has disappeared; he has not been destroyed completely.

The figure of the double in this text becomes linked to the past and memory. It is a physical manifestation of memory, an emergence of the past into the present, and the inscription on the present of the past:

> At the party, having drunk too much, I [Rudi] was struck by the idea that, as life goes on, there is a double for everyone, no matter whom [. . .] I looked across the room and saw Sergei was standing by the buffet, minus his hat. He was talking to Tamara (only she never would've been so well dressed). Father sat in a corner. I searched for Mother and found someone vaguely similar [. . .] An older Polish woman reminded me of Anna. (An eerie trip back and forth across the Styx.)
>
> When I saw Sergei's double making his way towards Anna's double it raised the hairs on my neck. (175)

Yet, 'On searching for myself I realised there was nobody' (175). Rudi's double, however, emerges in the form of Victor Pareci, a close friend in New York with whom he visits the bathhouses: 'they were inextricably tied, bound not by money or sex or work or fame, but by their pasts [. . .] they could have been talking to mirrors' (206). For McCann, 'Victor is almost like the shadow image of Rudy' (sic), and his characterization of Pareci is a means to 'deal with all the issues of sex [. . .] a way to glance off and came at Rudy (sic) by glancing off' (McCann, 2003a). Victor exists as a means of exploring Rudi's sexuality; we approach Nureyev's AIDS-related death through exposure to Victor's illness. In such a way, the persistence of doubles throughout the text could be read as a web of allusions to the alternate histories that proliferate beyond official narratives and also represents irruptions of the past into the present in corporeal form.

Body and History

The attitudes of both Rudi and Sergei to memory seem to privilege a breakage model of temporality, one that distinguishes and separates past from present in order to maintain a coherent body-self. However, irruptions from the past within the novel consistently problematize such a paradigm of linear time. In this text, as in Ní Dhuibhne's work, the human body is imbricated in these disruptions. The past's emergence into the present is persistently represented in corporeal form and it is often through bodies that such 'hauntings' are expressed. For instance, Yulia watches teenagers play football with a white ball and using white sticks as goalposts before realizing that their equipment is composed of a skull and arm bones: 'I trembled, wondering whether the bones were German or Russian and then I wondered if it even mattered, and then I thought of my small china dish hidden away and wrapped' (138). As she walks away she glimpses the war veteran, who had admonished the teenagers for disturbing the bones, and reburied them. The bones also become durable objects that persist into the present. However, those who come into contact with the china dish and the bones treat them differently. The bones must be reburied as their emergence brings into focus the fate of the corporeal though history and the discomfort that this reminder elicits. Significantly, this incident occurs on the day that the news blackout on Rudi is lifted. The newspapers' first mention of Rudi parallels the irruption of the past into the present for Yulia. The image prompts her to leave her husband. The ageing of the body, which represents corporeality as unavoidably caught up in the passage of time, is also stressed throughout the novel. The images of an ageing corporeality contrast with the images of Nureyev's dancing body, which signifies attempts to halt the temporal flow: 'One must confront the fact that the face will change and the body is vulnerable. But so what? Enjoy the moment [. . .] When I'm seventy and sitting by the fire, I will take the photos out and weep, ha!' (161).

The novel begins with an explicit focus on the body. Corporeality is visible from the opening pages, which detail the brutality of war and its effects on the embodied self. The narrative focuses on the experiences of the Soviet army during the winters of the Second World War and their attempts to create pathways through the harsh landscape. The wartime experience inscribes itself on their bodies in particular, multiple, and horrific ways:

> Pieces of shrapnel caught them beneath their eyes. Bullets whipped clean through their calf muscles. Splinters of shells lodged in their necks. Mortars cracked their backbones. Phosphorous bombs set them aflame. (9)

Corporeality, violently affected by the war, is also brutally rendered as part of the landscape through which the soldiers attempt to traverse:

> They looked out over the steppe and saw the bodies of fellow soldiers, frozen to death, a hand in the air, a knee in a stretch, beards white with frost [. . .]
>
> They heard the enemy were using the dead to make roads, laying down the bodies since there were no trees left, and they tried not to listen as noises came across the ice, a tyre catching on bone, moving on. (8)

The German literary critic, Leslie A. Adelson, argues for a more explicit understanding of the relationship between history and the human body, in other words, a conception of history that does not elide the 'real' bodies that constitute that history. For her, '[h]istory without bodies is unimaginable' as 'what is history if not the accounts of human bodies in and over time?' (Adelson, 1993, 1). She contends that the body is 'a secret of history' while concomitantly history is 'an even better-kept secret of the body' (1). The image of soldiers' bodies becoming part of the landscape and forming the roads over which they travel is also a brutal reflection of this process of history-making: 'The snow unearthed a history, a layer of blood here, a horse bone there, the carcass of a PO-2 dive bomber, the remains of a sapper they once knew from Spasskaya Street' (10). This history is composed of real bodies and intrudes on the present as a corpse or skeleton refusing to remain buried unlike Con O'Leary's fossilized body in *This Side of Brightness*. The text highlights the significance of the body and foregrounds the corporeal as an important and symbolic site for the production of memories and the re-emergence of suppressed histories. A similar image to that of Con O'Leary's buried body is mentioned in an idea for a ballet about the Berlin Wall:

> A Russian mason who fell into the mortar was not pulled out and so his bones still shore up the wall. He said the Russian mason's lover (call her Katerina) will move along the wall, feeling from brick to brick, trying to recapture the spirit of her dead sweetheart. Against her better instincts, she will fall in love with an American soldier on the other side of the wall. But to cross to the soldier she will have to break through the remains of her Russian lover's body. (176)

Unlike the image in *This Side of Brightness* this interred body must be disturbed. It must be broken through in order for the dictates of this narrative to be fulfilled. The bodies that are buried in the rubble of history cannot remain there, they cannot be enshrined in memory as Con O'Leary's has been and their resting places must be, sometimes violently, breached. However, in contrast to the fragmentation of such disinterred remains, the body in movement, the dancing body, is privileged as a means of engaging with memory and life.

There is no escaping the body in the novel; it is continually visible, in pain, wounded, hungry, and ill. Sergei notes that 'Our bodies are foul things to live inside. I am convinced the gods patched us together so disastrously so that we might need them, or at least invoke them, late at night' (43). But the body is also alive, vital, and triumphant in the novel:

> As the dance begins their [Nureyev's mother and sister] hands are clenched tight in their laps, but soon the women are gripping each other, amazed to see Rudi, not just the dance, but what he has become, whole and full and fleshed, patrolling the stage, devouring space, graceful, angry. (91)

The novel details the impact dancing makes on the corporeal, but throughout the text the body dancing, that is, the body moving through space and time, is figured as exerting an influence over the audience. While dancing, Rudi seems to possess the ability to lend his physical potential to the viewer. Anna's body is altered by her contact with Rudi: 'Her eyes quite honestly sparkled, as if she had borrowed them from the boy' (44). Sergei notes the vitality that such interactions elicit:

> It struck us that he was our new breath and that the breath would last us only a short while, that he would eventually have to move on. It gave us great sorrow yet it also gave us a chance to live beyond any sorrows we had already accumulated. (49)

Furthermore, contact with Rudi's dancing body permits both Sergei and Anna to come to a greater degree of acceptance of their history; in acknowledging the fact the Rudi must leave them and 'move on' they become able to travel 'beyond' their own histories. Rudi's body, associated with movement beyond borders, is this vital 'breath' that propels them forward. Rudi himself seems to distrust excursions into the past: 'But you cannot become a history of what you have left behind' (146). Temporal relationships consistently become related to ideas of movement for the characters of the novel; the past as something that can be travelled away from. Sergei's 'difficulty was that he was unable to move with the change' (79). However, the narrative problematizes such attitudes through irruptions of the past, which predominantly manifest themselves in corporeal form. Furthermore, Rudi's dancing body becomes a central figural representation for the contradictions between a conception of temporality that seeks to deny its flow, freeze a moment, and move on from it, and one that celebrates its movement, heterogeneity, and non-linearity.

Dance: Arresting the Flow of Time

Rudi expresses the desire to arrest the flow of time in order to concentrate more profoundly on dance: 'Rudi wishes sometimes he could just freeze it [life] and temporarily step outside his life, there is so much to do, it takes away from the dance' (217). His physical existence in the text is predominantly linked to dance: 'his body had now accepted dance as its only strategy' (80). In fact, McCann's use of Victor as a type of double for Rudi through whom he can explore issues of sexuality focuses attention on Rudi's body as almost completely imbricated in dance. The text poses a constant juxtaposition between capturing time through the strategy of dance and dance as a temporal movement through space:

> He is told to hold a position as if position is a thing that can ever be held on a floor like this, a sheet at his feet [. . .] Rudi remains in position, his ankle pounding with pain [. . .] there is nothing more Rudi would like than to break the air with movement in the second before the flash erupts, create a blur on the film. (92)

Dance seems to evade and resist any attempt to freeze it in representation. Rudi's dancing body yearns for movement and the creation of 'a blur'. However, the goal that Rudi strives for in dance is to achieve the impression of stillness, to pause time though the body's movement:

> She began working with him on jumps – she told him that above all he must create what his feet wished for and it was not so much that he must jump higher than anyone else but that he should remain in the air longer. (44)

When Rudi jumps from a rock into the water he appears to achieve this in the eyes of Anna's husband: 'He seemed to hang in the air, fierce and white'

(46). Rudi, in his notes to himself, also expresses this goal of resisting gravity and time, by hanging his body in the air: 'Nijinsky said it was not difficult to stay in the air, you just have to pause a little while up there' (85). McCann plays on the paradox mentioned in an interview that 'there's a tremendous violence committed on the body in order to achieve the appearance of ease' (McCann and Hemon, 2003a). This is made explicit in the text: Rudi 'is surprised by the ache, that by remaining still his body is more violently active' (92). The novel constantly highlights the impossibility of achieving a perfect stillness unmarred by movement. If this were ever accomplished the result would be death and thus marketable, as Rudi notes: 'Perhaps one should die in the middle of a dance, *en l'air*, have the performance auctioned, frozen, sold to the highest bidder' (146). When the movement is denied and the representation is frozen, the image of the body becomes a consumable object. If, on the other hand, Rudi 'did his trade, if he really did his trade, the camera itself would not be able to catch him' (92). Movement is privileged throughout the narrative: 'both of them [Rudi and Victor] needing constant motion, since if they stay in one place too long they will become rooted like the rest' (199). Even in aspirations of stillness, motion is implicated: 'as they [Rudi and Margot] walk away the dance is still in their bodies and they search for the quiet point the still point where there is no time no space only pureness moving' (169). Here, 'the still point' is 'pureness *moving*'.

Playing on the etymology of his title, Derrida calls for 'a chorus, for a choreographic text' (Derrida, 1995, 107). 'Chorus' derives from the Greek term *khoros*, which, according to the *Oxford English Dictionary*, denotes 'a dance, a band of dancers' and 'an organized band of singers and dancers in the religious festivals and dramatic performances of ancient Greece or the song sung by the chorus'. The verb *khoreia*, to dance, is the root of the word choreography. Thus, Derrida's appeal for a choreographic text is a demand for a work that dances, in the conceptual terms outlined above. It is a text that challenges, questions, and refigures the ground it traverses while maintaining a chorus of voices: 'No monological discourse – and by that I mean here mono-sexual discourse – can dominate with a single voice, a single tone' (107). The structure of *Dancer* with its multiple narrators, its chorus of voices and stories, could be seen to approximate such a choreographic text. The novel illustrates what Peter Burke descbribes as the move 'from the ideal of the Voice of History to that of "heteroglossia", defined as "various and opposing voices"' (Burke, 1991, 6). Above all, it intimates the crucial role that configurations of the human body play in negotiating conceptions of time, memory, and history. Just as Rudi's masseuse 'can tell the plot of whatever I'm reading just by running his hands along my spine' (187), and Margot can decipher aspects of his past through the movement of his body: 'Sometimes, in the way he moves, she thinks she can discern a whole history of Tatar arrogance' (160),[8] so too does Rudi's body operate within the narrative as a codification of alternate modes and paradigms of conceptualizing time and memory. Rather than representing a still, immobile corporeality that is easily consumed, his dancing body privileges dynamic and affective movement and rather than advocating a relationship with the past that insists it remain 'left behind', *Dancer* instead embraces a Deleuzian paradigm of temporality that resists considering the past as static and, instead, argues for a non-linear relationship between past, present, and future, in which the past remains always open to possible reinscriptions. Thus, to consider the past, and approaches to it, in terms of a dancing body allows the past the potential to constantly disrupt the accepted and conventional narratives at any given historical moment. Movement persists and underlies any appearance of stillness and immobility: 'there was always the thought that water might hide its flowing under ice' (101).

The approaches to the past and to memory that *Dancer* as a text sets up and, in a way, theorizes through the figure of the dancing body and the corporeal irruptions from the past are also thematized in Enright's historical biography, published the year before McCann's novel.

The Pleasure of Eliza Lynch

Anne Enright's 2002 novel, *The Pleasure of Eliza Lynch*, is a fictionalized biography that explores the figure of Irishwoman, Eliza Lynch (1835–1886), who in the 1860s became consort to the future president of Paraguay, Francisco Solano López (1826–1870) and was for a time 'the richest woman in the world'.[9] Eliza's origins belie her eventual status; born in Mallow, Co. Cork and having fled to Paris to escape the ravages of the Irish famine, she encounters the heir to the Paraguayan dictatorship. Eliza then travels to Paraguay with López, pregnant with his child, and upon arrival is rejected by his family and the upper classes of Paraguayan society. Due to her proximity to López during his pursuit of the War of the Triple Alliance (1865–1870), a bloody and disastrous conflict against Brazil, Argentina, and Uruguay, Eliza was much maligned as an instigator of the war. In the 1960s, the morally dubious General Stroessner, who granted asylum to many ex-Nazis during his time as President of Paraguay, rehabilitated her to the status of a national heroine. Thus, although Enright's text is ostensibly motivated by issues of feminist historiography and icon construction, her subject matter could be construed as morally unstable. However, for Enright, it is precisely for these reasons that 'historically speaking [Eliza] is most interesting' and it is also why she has been neglected as a figure (Enright, 2002a). The novel explores questions about the creation of iconic figures, the relationship between individuals (particularly women) and historical discourses, and issues of nationality and migration. Enright's exploration of the figure of Eliza Lynch in this novel begins to uproot and call into question conventional representations of the female body and the pregnant body, particularly in relation to their figurations in the Irish cultural imaginary.

The facts surrounding Eliza's life are minimal and she herself was prone to embroidering the truth of her own origins. As a historical figure, she has been obscured by a tissue of rumour, gossip, and anecdote on account of her extraordinary life, a problem that biographers and reviewers note (McNeil, 2003).[10] For Enright, however, it was the marginalization of Eliza that drew her:

> What is interesting is that she is dismissed by male writers. A footnote in history – someone described her as 'a real Cork woman, overimaginative and oversexed'. And I thought, 'You don't know her; I know her'. And I became interested in the idea of Eliza; of reclaiming her. (O'Flanagan, 2002)

This motivation of uncovering women's lost history is one that she has acknowledged in relation to her previous novels. However, the metaphor of excavation and revelation is not an adequate representation of the processes that are at work in *The Pleasure of Eliza Lynch*. Enright insists on the fictional nature of her text and disavows a consideration of the book as accurate historical biography:

> Eliza Lynch seems to provoke in her English-speaking biographers all kinds of sneering excess. Some facts seem to remain constant and it is around these facts that this (scarcely less fictional) account has been built. This is a novel, however. It is Not True. (231)

Thus, Enright's task is not a direct reclamation of Eliza Lynch from the obfuscations of history, but rather an exploration of the relationships between an individual woman and the historical discourses that surround her, distort her, and attempt to represent or obscure her. A central concern of the narrative is the tension between Eliza's identity – 'Who was Eliza? She was very much herself' (2) – and the Eliza that becomes tangled in history, anecdote, and story:

> She [Eliza] rearranges the story of her life [. . .] You could say she has everything, except the satisfaction of having it. Also, perhaps, that she cannot relax, because she is not real. It must be hard, to be just a story the matrons of Asunción told each other between the hours of three and four. Everything Eliza does to silence them just makes them talk the more. No, the only way she can become real is by getting married, and she cannot get married until old López dies. (58–9)

Enright's novel can be viewed as an engagement with such processes of history, which is facilitated by the choice of such an ambiguous historical figure. Hermione Lee remarks, in her review of the novel, on the deliberate focus on 'so-called women's subject-matter – domestic details, clothes, female bodies, sexuality and pleasure, pregnancy and childbirth' (Lee, 2002, 19). For her, Enright's novel represents a 'very physical narrativ[e]' (19). Patricia Coughlan observes the intertextual relationship of *The Pleasure of Eliza Lynch*'s with Joseph Conrad's *Nostromo*, noting, however, that Enright pays particular attention to the intricacies of gender and colonialism that are neglected in Conrad's work:

> Clearly approaching the available facts otherwise, Enright appropriates and deploys them for a powerful interrogation, not only of the sex-gender system of the West, but of post-colonial versus metropolitan-European reality at the moment of the transition from old colonialism to new imperialism: the two are inextricably bound up together in her vision. (Coughlan, 2005, 353)

Reviews of *The Pleasure of Eliza Lynch* tend to express discomfort with the novel, either in terms of its effect on the reader or its promotion of style over substance. Miranda Seymour declared that 'Enright's Eliza still remains a strangely impenetrable creation', while Alan Massie concluded: 'it seems Enright always wanted to paint pictures rather than tell a story' (Massie, 2002; Seymour, 2003). Stevie Davies 'came away from this extraordinary novel feeling that I had been (like the heroine) on a bizarre and elaborate hiding to nowhere, suffering from an acute case of synaesthesia' (Davies, 2002). Many stress the sensual nature of the prose and content. Thus, Davies proclaimed '[t]he novel is an edible, audible, tactile, odorous fandango of exotica, which at once revels in and recoils from its sensual surfaces' (Davies, 2002). For Seymour, '[e]verything, for Enright's Eliza, is experienced sensually' (Seymour, 2003).

I would argue that when reviewers claim disorientation, discomfort, or bewilderment, this is a direct result of Enright's deliberate engagement with, and renegotiation of, historical discourses and national identity, particularly those that are imbricated in representations of female embodiment. As Lisa Allardice puts it, Eliza 'looms so large over the narrative that she almost entirely obscures the wider historical picture' (Allardice, 2002). Interestingly, this obscuring of the historical facts and details is precisely what troubles certain reviewers (Massie, 2002), though usually a focus on historical details at the expense of a female figure would rarely be commented upon.

Coughlan notes that the setting and subject matter of *The Pleasure of Eliza Lynch* 'perform an implicit rejection of those narratives of masculine identity-formation [...] which until very recently have dominated Irish literary tradition' (Coughlan, 2005, 349). This accounts for the lack of attention afforded the novel in Ireland as well as the reluctance 'to understand it as an Irish novel' (349). However, the novel stages a questioning of the idea of national identity by means of the distancing effect of the South American location: Enright, as Coughlan writes, 'use[s] the *décalage* between Europe and its present or former colonies in the nineteenth century to show the melting away of apparently solid European systems of order and belief in the utter difference of South America' (350). Eliza herself serves in the novel as a means to unsettle categories of nationality, existing in a complex interrelation of Irish, European, and colonial identities, among others. I will explore this in more detail below.

The novel eschews a single narrative perspective. It moves between Eliza's first-person narration and a third-person narrative from the perspective of Dr. Stewart, the Scottish doctor who accompanies Eliza and López on their journey to Paraguay and settles in Asunción. The text begins with an omniscient third-person narrator detailing the first sexual encounter between Eliza and Lopéz and is then divided into four parts, each entitled 'The River' and numbered consecutively. These are then split between Eliza's voice and a version of events focalized through Stewart. This narrative overall takes the reader from Eliza's arrival in Paraguay, through the War of the Triple Alliance, the deaths of Lopéz and his son and Eliza's burial of them, to a final sighting of Eliza in Edinburgh.

Eliza's first-person narration is confined to her time while pregnant on board the *Tacuarí*, travelling down the Río Paraná to Asunción. Once in

Paraguay, Stewart's narration takes over. Enright claims that 'We never see in (sic) inside Eliza's head again because after she reaches Paraguay she becomes an icon, and an icon is unknowable' (O'Flanagan, 2002). Lee, in her review, connects this unknowability with the fate of women in historical discourse: 'Yet, however close we seem to get to her – and we get right inside her skin, her sweat, her blood, her womb – there's still a mystery, the mystery of a woman obliterated and distorted by history' (Lee, 2002, 19). Importantly, Lee notes the foregrounding of corporeality and I would argue that Enright's deliberate focus on Eliza's body is a means of engaging with the particular role of the female body in historical discourse.[11] As Coughlan writes, Enright 'resists the dualistic subordination both of the body and the feminine which underpins Western thought' (367). It is this resistance that permits a rewriting of conceptions of history from a female perspective.

Marina Warner, in her analysis of the female form as allegory, observes that hollowness and blankness are a 'prerequisite of symbols with indefinite powers of endurance and adaptability' (Warner, 1996, 11). Warner discusses the propensity for male symbolic figures to be individuated whereas 'the female form tends to be perceived as generic and universal' (12). However, Eliza, in Enright's imagining of her, is neither hollow nor blank. She is excessive and full and makes explicit her gender, sexuality, and her body, which unsettles the male population around her: 'I remind them of too much – of women. Of the act that made me swell' (33). It is significant that it is while she is on the river, journeying, that we are allowed access to her thoughts – while moving across national borders and landscapes she is accessible to us as a subjective being. One of the effects of the interchange between Eliza's narrative and that of Stewart is that the reader is constantly returned to the journey down the river, 'as if', Coughlan contends, 'to insist upon its defining effect on the travellers' (357).

Pregnant Embodiment

Enright fictionally alters Eliza's pregnancy so that the birth takes place directly after her arrival in Asunción.[12] Through the particular construction of the narrative the pregnancy is sustained for the length of the novel; the last three chapters detail the birth of her child, Eliza's burial of López and her son following their death in the War of the Triple Alliance, and, finally, Stewart's glimpse of Eliza in Edinburgh, 20 years after the voyage to Paraguay. Eliza's pregnant body, then, becomes a central focus of the novel. Despite the initial sentence of the novel, and the opening section, which both signal sexual desire and the sexual act, Enright claims that the novel is 'not so much about sex as about growth, decay, and profusion in general' (Enright, 2002a). One of Eliza's first comments in the novel relates to the landscape through which she travels; 'Everywhere, there is such growth. I think if these people believe anything it would be that the Devil is a vegetable, and God a wonderful big tree' (19–20).

The representation of Eliza's pregnancy is significant in the novel, particularly when situated in an Irish context. Debates in Ireland about the pregnant woman have centred predominately on the issue of abortion and, significantly for the time in which the novel was written, on the hyper-anxiety that the figure of the immigrant pregnant woman elicited in the Irish state and population.[13] In the years preceding the 2004 Citizenship Referendum, the figure of the pregnant African woman became the focus of anxieties concerning a perceived threat to fantasies of racial purity and an intact nation. Both the issue of abortion and the Citizenship Referendum are deeply imbricated in discourses of nationalism and anxieties concerning the body of the reproductive mother focus around issues of borders, both national and corporeal. As Kathryn Conrad writes concerning the 1983 abortion referendum: 'At stake at the time was not only women's agency over their bodies, but also the permeability of the borders between Ireland and the rest of Europe' (Conrad, 2001, 154). The concepts of space and movement became central to the debates: the need to travel to England to seek an abortion, and more recently, the hysteria surrounding the immigration of pregnant women from Africa to Ireland. As Sullivan writes: 'women's bodies – the womb as liminal space, a place of entrance and exit – continue to be symbolic (dis)contents that are a danger to the "integrity" and "wholeness" of the nation' (Sullivan, 2005, 462).

For feminist critics like Imogen Tyler and Iris Marion Young, pregnancy poses important challenges to thinking about the rational subject with a singular identity and to conceptions of the body as whole and unified. For Young:

> The integrity of my body is undermined in pregnancy not only by this externality of the inside, but also by the fact that the boundaries of my body are themselves in flux. In pregnancy I literally do not have a firm sense of where my body ends and the world begins. (Young, 1990, 163)

She argues that pregnancy inherently destabilizes any notion of a unified self as well as disturbing conventional distinctions between self and other, inner and outer: 'Pregnancy challenges the integration of my body experience by rendering fluid the boundary between what is within, myself, and what is outside, separate. I experience my insides as the space of another, yet my own body' (163). In *The Pleasure of Eliza Lynch* this is expressed in terms of Eliza's feeling for her newborn son which is not representable in language: 'It is the inside shape of me – and it is the outside shape of him. It is nothing that you could stick a word between' (214–5). Similar concerns preoccupy Tyler, who argues that '[t]he pregnant subject [. . .] cannot be contained within forms of being constrained by singularity and is at odds with familiar models of the self-other relation' (Tyler, 2000, 292). This accounts for its invisibility within the modes of representation in Western culture; the pregnant body makes visible the instability of systems and paradigms that rely on differentiations between self and other and on narratives of origin that occlude the position of the maternal, such as the Western philosophical tradition. As Tyler writes, 'The pregnant woman can be a challenge to this forgetting of origins, for she embodies gestation and is a sign of, or even for, the absence of maternal genealogies of thought' (Tyler, 2000, 294).

Enright's text foregrounds the embodied pregnant subject in Eliza. Her voice is sustained structurally throughout the narrative and her body is clearly visible. She also refuses to conform to the 'erasure or disavowal of the subject's corporeal and maternal roots' (Tyler, 2000, 293), by making explicit our origins in the maternal body: 'I must love him, because through such narrow gaps in our lives we all must squeeze and crawl [. . .] This is the only way forward, the only way through' (211). What is more, this pregnant woman is on the move, travelling down a river, which Coughlan suggests is 'like a birth canal' (Coughlan, 2005, 364), breaching national boundaries as she progresses into a country which is not her own, bearing a child who will be heir to its ruler in direct defiance of the literal and symbolic positioning of pregnant women in the Irish cultural imaginary.

Hints of an 'internment' of the pregnant subject are, however, suggested in the restrictions to Eliza's movement while on board the boat: 'My belly is huge. They have strung me up in the bow, like a giant tick. I am all caught up in the skeins of muslin they drape around me' (20). Eliza feels imprisoned by the cultural trappings associated with her position as European woman and the clothes she must wear. The significance of costume is continually stressed in the text particularly through the detailed descriptions and naming of her various outfits (29–30, 35, 40, 162–3). This emphasis on cloth and clothing continues throughout the text, representing European values, gender constructions, and Eliza's consumerist power.

Eliza also experiences an erasure of her pregnant morphology within the confines of her room on the boat, which is in some ways a travelling extension of the Europe she has left:

> There is a moon, and watery reflections dance on the walls until it is all about me, a river of broken light, rippling and breaking on the ceiling and on the bed and on my skin. I can not (sic) bear it, this flickering tide on my arms, the way my body disappears under it so that I am just another surface in the dark. (90–1)

However, once outside the walls of her room, she is not subject to such obscuration: 'Outside, under a blank moon, I am free of it. Here is my belly in front of me again, big and hard and round' (91). She comments on the worship of the foetus at the expense of the mother, implicitly referencing the exaltation of the unborn child that has been at the heart of anti-abortion debates in later periods: 'Her belly is quite sacred, you know. And as it grows, poor Dora withers away' (209).[14] Eliza also identifies herself as a tick, an insect who survives by feeding off the blood of other animals and later in the narrative imagines herself as a spider, 'the beastie with my belly huge and my limbs all feeble and waving, and bits gone' (102). I shall return to the construction of Eliza as consumer and to the cannibalistic images that proliferate in the text.

Roberta Gefter Wondrich, in an article on female bodies in contemporary Irish fiction, argues that representations of the pregnant body in texts such as Mary Morrissy's *Mother of Pearl* and Bernard McLaverty's *Gracenotes* tend to emphasize 'loneliness and anxiety' and configure this corporeality in terms of exiled and disordered states (Wondrich, 2000, 141). For Wondrich, this predilection for constructing motherhood as a negative embodiment 'confirm[s] the desexualisation of the female body attached to such a discourse of maternity' (141). Enright rejects such configurations of the pregnant body. Eliza's body is imaged rather in terms of growth, abundance, and sensuality: 'So much I remember: the baby riding high and large under the bone until I thought I might split, not in pain but, as a fruit might, in pleasure at the ripeness of itself' (214). Eliza connects her pregnancy to the profusion of growth that she identifies in the South American landscape:

> I take in the smell of it and think I may well sprout, or rot: some plant will root in my brain. It will flower better than a hat.

My own smell too, has indelicately changed. It is light, and difficult to
match; the smell of grass in the sun; of something green and growing, as
my belly grows. (20)

The imagery of parturition becomes pervasive in the novel; 'They [the men
she has slept with] were still there. They had left their traces inside her' (8).
One in particular, her first, 'was inside her still, between her legs, and
behind her ribs, knocking, knocking to get out. Every time he crashed into
her' (9–10). This imagery represents a defiant contrast to what Sullivan,
after Irigaray, calls 'the culture-wide prohibition of the representation of
the experience of the womb' (Sullivan, 2005, 460).

'A Greedy Girl': Food and Consumption

Combined with the prevalence of images connected with pregnancy and
childbirth are those of food and consumption. In an interview Enright
remarks of her construction of Eliza 'She's a greedy girl. Just a greedy girl.
She consumes all around her; it really is rampant consumerism on a scale
which is hard to imagine' (O'Flanagan, 2002). Coughlan notes the predominance of images of food and eating in the novel, from the titles of the book's
sections, 'A Fish', 'A Melon', 'Asparagus', 'Veal', 'Truffles', 'Champagne',
and 'Coffee', to the prevalence of images connecting food and bodies:

> So pervasive is eating that at times it seems the book's governing concern,
> and Enright anarchically links it with love, beauty, and the ideal, thus
> overriding the immanence-transcendence dualism which structures West-
> ern thought about both women and the body. (Coughlan, 2005, 355)

In *The Pleasure of Eliza Lynch* the material character of eating and food practices interrogates the nexus of interconnecting discourses and symboliza-
tions that Eliza becomes imbricated in, from those of colonialism to those
of sexuality. Each of the titles of the sections refers to a specific instance in
the narrative central to Eliza's life or to particular stories that have attached
themselves to her: 'A Melon' refers to her desire to bite Lopéz's leg 'as you
might into a melon' (38), whereas 'Truffles' relates to 'the story [that] went
about that Eliza ate the flesh of the dead. She said it tasted just like pork,
but gamier – like the truffle-hunting boars you get in the Auvergne' (135).
Both instances connect Eliza with consumption that transgresses regulated

boundaries and with cannibalism. She is the paradigm of consumption and consumerism within the novel, constantly connected with food and eating and expensive possessions; at one point in the narrative her skirts are stiffened with porridge (34). Cannibalism also connotes discourses of colonialism. As Stephen Slemon notes, in reference to cannibalism in *Heart of Darkness,* 'in the economy of the text they [the cannibals] figure as visibly as any marker for the unimprovability of colonialism's Other at the zero degree of History' (Slemon, 1992, 163–4). In colonial discourse the figure of the cannibal signifies the ultimate antithesis of the white 'civilised' European and has been 'central to the construction of the non-European as other' (Probyn, 2000, 92). Eliza becomes caught up in a complex nexus of these discourses.

Coughlan points out that 'these recurring flesh-food and food-flesh motifs' are 'integral to the book's overall argument' (356). For Coughlan, this argument is also related to 'compassionate inter-subjectivity, which is daily betrayed in people's consumption of one another, in war, in the abuse of power, and the struggle between the wealthy and the wretched' (357). The consumption of the female figure by historical discourses could be added to this list. The metaphoric deployment of cannibalism, and flesh as food, is extended to include narrative itself as meat: 'When he [López's first son by his mistress] came to visit, he brought his mother stories from La Recoleta [Eliza's house], as you might bring a caged animal meat' (55).[15] The implication is that Eliza becomes sustenance for the stories told about her; the gossip feeds off her. However, Eliza is not merely a victim or a passive substance ready for consumption. She herself is configured as a consumer *par excellence.* The excessive consumption outlined by Enright's construction of Eliza is also undeniably a comment on the Celtic Tiger Ireland current during the writing of the novel.

In a description of the associations Eliza makes with the different languages she speaks, eating is linked to her origins in Ireland; 'she romped in French, married in English, and she ate in the Irish of her childhood kitchen' (3). This connection between food, consumption, Ireland, and origins is also reflected in a second listing of nationalities and their particular characteristics, this time regarding the relationships between children and their mothers. Thus, Eliza pronounces at a dinner party in her house that the maternal figure in English culture is either non-existent or connected with the inheritance of furniture: French mothers are linked to writing, sexuality, and time-keeping; Spanish mothers are 'an object of terror'; Italian, 'an object of piety absolute', and when questioned on the place of the Irish mother Eliza remarks '"The Irish? Oh we eat them," said Eliza. "You should see it. We start at the toes and leave nothing out"' (146).[16] This ostensibly glib comment is a striking insight into the positioning and symbolization of the mother in Irish culture and such imagery has sustained discourses of nationalism. The body of the mother symbolically nourishes the Irish cultural imagination and yet the mother *as subject* is simultaneously removed from this cultural imaginary. It is akin to the 'maternal and still silent ground that nourishes all foundations' outlined by Irigaray (Irigaray, 1985, 365). As Enright puts it in *Making Babies*, 'the unassuageable hunger for the mother cannot be allowed to run society' as this hunger is fuelled by the anxiety 'that a mother can be elsewhere, that she can look at other things, other people' (Enright, 2004, 107).[17] Enright notes the need to literally erase the figure of the mother due to her foundational status: 'The Irish mother is so strong in Irish fiction that she's always dead' (Enright, 2002a). Enright plays on these associations between mothering, feeding, and the consumption of the mother figure by her offspring in her chapter concerning breastfeeding in *Making Babies*: 'this new drama of being a mother (yes, there are cannibals in my dreams, yes)' (Enright, 2004, 42).[18]

Enright's configuration of Eliza troubles these associations as they are traditionally deployed or configured. Eliza's observations about the Irish mother make explicit and visible her positioning in a dynamic in which she is depicted as a consumable object that is devoured head to foot. Once made explicit, it cannot be ignored by Stewart who fails to separate the meat he eats at the dinner party from either Eliza or his female relations:

> Stewart's mind nibbled along the legs of some poor woman to arrive at a most unthinkable place. The woman was, of course, Eliza, but it was also, a little, his poor rotten aunt, or the clean bones of his long-dead mother, and Stewart felt the violence of it so keenly he wanted to shout 'Whore!' or some other desecration. 'Irish bitch!' was the phrase that sprang to mind. How strange, he thought. And useless. (147)

Eliza's excessive consumerism and her pleasure in consumption not only implicate her in a devouring of the maternal but also complicate her figuration as a passive object-to-be-consumed. She is an active participant in the consuming process. Enright claims that desire is what is at stake in her construction of Eliza. For Enright, 'Eliza's all about hunger, she's a glutton' (Enright, 2002a), and indeed Eliza's desire for 'the meat of [Lopéz's] thigh [. . .] to bite into him as you might into a melon' is fuelled by the fact that 'in the middle of the night I am crazed by hunger. Bewildered by it' (38).

She also 'tell[s] my dear friend that I am turning cannibal' (39). She connects hunger for food with desire for sex: 'I am disturbed in my sleep by such dreams that I wake and must have him. Like food. Now' (41). Desire is consistently connected to consumption and incorporation:

> I want to touch him with the bare tips of my fingers, or with my lips that are all alive, now, with the thought of touching him. I want to touch him where the skin is thinnest so I might drink it out of him, lick it like sweat – a prickling that comes to my mouth from the thought of what lies inside this man. (101)

In Sarah Sceats's psychoanalytic reading of the connections between food and sex, she argues that '[a]n adult urge for incorporation [. . .] reflects both nostalgia for a (mythical) state of union and a degree of ambivalence' in terms of subsuming the other into oneself in an ultimate act of love or desire to annihilate (Sceats, 2000, 39). Literal and metaphorical acts of cannibalism, she argues, are connected to discourses of colonialism. In Eliza Lynch's case, of course, her excessive consumerism and pleasure in consumption mark her as different from and more privileged than the famine victims left behind in Ireland and the natives of Paraguay. She is also distinguished from the soldiers that starve in the War of the Triple Alliance in which hunger and potential cannibalism take on a sobering note:

> But then the hunger moved to his [Dr. Stewart] mouth, and this made him want to wrap his gums around things – all manner of things – in order to assuage it. Or he might, in opening a wounded man, catch a glimpse of his last meal, and find a jealous spittle flood his own maw. (134)

Thus, the figure of Eliza also becomes a source of unease in the novel. She retains her glamour and distance from the war; even when she walks among the people she does not muddy herself:

> Eliza's house was a haven – partly because it was so well back from the arc of bloody muck that was the ballistic limit of the Brazilian ships. Which is not to say that Eliza was a coward; she walked freely out; a distinctive sight – you might even say a target – a swirl of colour with two boys, fore and aft, to lift and lay boards for her feet [. . .] forming an impromptu wheel on whose inside rim she was safe. (133)

Enright deliberately refrains from passing judgement on Eliza throughout the novel. The only time that the reader is permitted an insight into Eliza's subjectivity is during her boat trip. Once in Paraguay, we are privy only to Stewart's perspective and we watch as she becomes subject to the myth-making process, accumulating anecdotes and rumour. The novel ends far from Paraguay, in Stewart's home town of Edinburgh, when he almost encounters Eliza Lynch but instead watches her from afar, his 'heart pounding as though he had escaped some terrific danger' (228). Eliza is in Edinburgh to visit her lawyers due to a court case concerning the contested ownership of some money between Stewart and her. Stewart's feelings toward her seem to be an amalgamation of fear and hatred: 'He did not forgive her anything. Not the war, not the money. He did not forgive her his entire life' (228). However, Eliza appears diminished and out of place in the respectability of Edinburgh's Royal Mile: 'she was the season itself [autumn], all aflame with a rich decay and gloriously sad. She was also an old tart. Perhaps it would pass in Paris, but that gold hair was quite scandalously bright under an Edinburgh sky' (228). By the end of the novel she has become, in Stewart's eyes and in anticipation of her treatment in historical narratives, the 'woman who had taken the gold combs from out of the prostitutes' hair, a woman who had bled the country dry' (229–30). Coughlan observes Eliza's marginal and dislocated status and argues that Enright presents the economic and social aspects of Eliza's life as the driving forces in her attempts for survival:

> Enright vividly represents both the social forces which constrict the development of Eliza's moral life, and the avenging impulses which drive her to seize and consolidate her opportunity for security and prominence. In juxtaposing Stewart's tormented reflections with Eliza's own narrative, Enright represents the dishonesty of the Victorian double standard as indissolubly linked with the ideologies, themselves interconnected, of modernization and the exploitation of the less developed world. (Coughlan, 2005, 362)

Enright's ambiguous characterization of Eliza, then, serves in the novel as a critique of the oppressive and restrictive Victorian ideologies that Eliza engages with, as well as revealing the process by which she becomes obscured by her history, a process that is buttressed by such ideologies. In the novel Eliza is self-aware: 'A woman has no limits, because she may not act. She is all reputation, because she may not act. So, even as we do nothing, our reputations grow more impossible, and fragile, and large' (151). Her protestation that 'I am ordinary *as well* [. . .] As well as being the First Lady of Paraguay,' reveals her positioning as caught between her singularity and the discourses with which she must engage as a 'national Thing' (120, 150).

Eliza's marginal status can also be related to ideas of space and movement. Eliza belongs to the picaresque, she is a traveller and resists anchorage to national or local spaces: 'Eliza's Irishness, for example – was she really Irish? And what kind of Irish, while we were at it?' (141). Although she draws attention to restrictions in movement brought about by European conventions that govern her pregnant body, she still takes part in a journey across national boundaries. Once in Paraguay, the dominant images of her, as filtered through Stewart, are mobile ones: in her carriage or parading through Asunción in all her finery. Her house in Asunción is appropriately depicted as a transitory space; its walls are made from canvas, Eliza calls it her 'field tent' and Stewart finds that the space will not remain stationary: 'the place seemed to dance and recede' (142). Eliza holds two major dinner parties in the novel: one in this house and one on a boat where, when snubbed she throws every morsel of food overboard. Both take place in arguably temporary spaces and even her displays of domesticity are borrowed from elsewhere: 'The centrepiece – those careless flowers in their urn – I copied from an oil by Jensen, the Dane' (149).

The Pleasure of Eliza Lynch offers itself as a powerful critique of the processes of historiography and their relationship to the female subject as well as commenting on Celtic Tiger consumerism. The figure of Eliza draws together these questions with those relating to the position of the female subject as we watch Stewart's attempt to write her out of his own history: 'he was not fine. He wanted a drink. He wanted to get his daughter away from Eliza Lynch. He wanted to go home, and scrape his boots, and see his wife' (230). The final words of the novel hint at the threat that Eliza poses to his respectable Scottish life, and indeed, in a wider context, to the conventional fixing of the pregnant and/or iconic female body.

Conclusion

It is significant that both McCann and Enright chose the fictionalized biography genre as this form reflects their interest in questioning historical discourse. Both revel in the uncertainty surrounding certain anecdotes relating to their subject. Enright signals the ambiguity of the historical past within *The Pleasure of Eliza Lynch*, whereas McCann comments in interviews on the complex relationship between fact and fiction in *Dancer*. The two novels could be read as engaging with the concerns of historiographic metafiction; namely 'de-naturaliz[ing]' that temporal relationship' between present and past (Hutcheon, 2002, 68). However, neither writer is explicitly interested in highlighting the 'epistemological approach' of historiographic metafiction; in other words 'the truth (or falsehood) value of historical and biographical reconstruction' (Niederhoff, 2000, 81–2). Rather, both writers use the lives of their historical subjects to foreground the place of the corporeal within historical discourse and to use reconfigurations of the body as a means to re-imagine relationships between temporalities.

For McCann, it is Rudi's dancing body that represents alternate paradigms for thinking through approaches to the past and to memory. Derrida theorizes dance as a conceptual movement that disrupts and reorients the spaces through which it moves. McCann uses the embodiment of the dancer to consider the past and engagements with it as potentially unsettling to the present moment and to conventional narratives of history. Similarly, Enright uses configurations of the body to examine the historiographical project and its relationship to female embodiment. She creates a past that is disruptive and unsettling in its foregrounding of the types of corporealities that had previously been obscured. For McCann and Enright the prominence of reconfigurations of the corporeal are crucial to attempts to reconsider historiography and temporality.

Chapter 5

Celtic Tiger Bodies:
Éilís Ní Dhuibhne's *Fox, Swallow, Scarecrow* and Anne Enright's *The Gathering*

Introduction

This chapter moves from a discussion of historical fiction to novels set in the years of Ireland's Celtic Tiger, novels that certainly undermine the pronouncements by Gough, Kiberd, and O'Toole that contemporary Irish fiction fails to engage with its own moment. Ní Dhuibhne's novel, *Fox, Swallow, Scarecrow* (2007), published as the Irish economy began its downturn, is acerbic in its commentary on Irish culture during the boom. Anne Enright's *The Gathering* (2007), which won the Man Booker prize that year, also situates itself in the economically comfortable climate of these years but intimately connects present with past, interweaving Ireland of the 1920s and 1960s with its more recent history.[1] Ní Dhuibhne's novel also brings the past to bear on the Celtic Tiger present – she hangs the plot of *Fox, Swallow, Scarecrow* on the skeleton of Tolstoy's *Anna Karenina* and there are constant references in this novel of twenty-first-century Ireland, to the nineteenth century and its literature. Quotations from Yeats litter the novel, which not only critiques the Celtic Tiger but also ridicules an investment in the West, and the 'authentic', as markers of Irishness.

Crucially, in Ní Dhuibhne's novel, the protagonists inhabit a perpetual present, unable to conceive of either future or past, an attitude we might recall from the character in Haverty's novel who claims that Ireland was born in 1994.[2] For the protagonists in *Fox, Swallow, Scarecrow*, the future is inconceivable in the bubble of the Celtic Tiger:

> It was unimaginable, unconscionable, that the civilization to which Anna and Alex belonged could disappear. What could replace it? How could they imagine anything other than what there was now, planes and city

breaks, computers, four-wheel drives, new books every week, concerts and operas and a constant stream of easy entertainment on the television, the DVD, the cinema? Was that what the future would be like? [. . .] Would it be an absence of things, rather than a change or a development, a failure rather than a progression? (Ní Dhuibhne, 2007, 119)

This notion of progression is important here, a notion prevalent in Celtic Tiger culture and which, as I discussed in Chapter One, emphasizes speed and forward-movement away from a past conceived of as 'backward' and/ or marketable. This chapter looks at Ní Dhuibhne's novel before moving on to a discussion of Enright's *The Gathering*. For both novels, the relationships between history, memory, consumption, and identity reveal the complex tensions at work in Celtic Tiger culture.

Fox, Swallow, Scarecrow

Fox, Swallow, Scarecrow deals with the lives of affluent middle-class Dubliners at the height of the boom. Anna, named for her equivalent in Tolstoy's novel, is a writer of children's books, married to an affluent property developer, Alex, and living in a large house in the wealthy suburb of Killiney in south Dublin. As is to be expected from a novel based on *Anna Karenina*, Anna begins an affair with an attractive journalist, Vincy, who moves in the same circles as she does, and later becomes pregnant with his child. The novel details her life in the literary social scene, attending book launches, shopping, and dining in Michelin-starred restaurants. Consumerism is everywhere in the novel; Anna literally throws away money and a superstitious impulse towards charity fuels more consumption:

> she kept loose coins in her pocket so she would always have something small handy [to give to the homeless]. It was a habit that tended to ruin the line of her coat, but that gave her an excuse to buy another one all the sooner. The small coins she would never have spent anyway – often she had to throw them away, those piles of five- and ten- and twenty-cent pieces (8).

She also half-heartedly attempts to write the next *Harry Potter*, and literary worth to her, as, it seems, to all other writers in the novel, is based around monetary value and celebrity. Anna is typical of the apathy and lack of convictions that affect all of the characters that occupy Dublin's social scene:

> Anna formulated no beliefs whatsoever. She was vaguely agnostic, vaguely socialist, vaguely capitalist, vaguely materialistic, vaguely spiritual. The only thing she really believed in was her ambition to be a successful writer, by which she meant some sort of mixture of famous, bestselling and good. (75)

The exception is Leo, an Irish-language-poetry publisher living in Kerry, who falls in love with Kate, Anna's sister-in-law, who is an arts administrator for a small cultural organization called Poetry Plus. Kate however, is initially attracted to Vincy, and his rejection of her in favour of Anna leads to her breakdown and the recurrence of her latent anorexia. Leo's attention to Kate during her illness initiates a romance that quickly leads to marriage and her relocation to his house in the Gaeltacht, where she becomes pregnant and is killed in a road accident due to the state's failure to maintain safety notices on the road. The tragedy of this moment is heightened by Leo's involvement in the protest group, 'The Enemies of the Killing Roads', who lobby for action to be taken to remedy the dangerous state of Irish roads. Leo's parents had also died previously in a car crash. However, even Leo's conviction cannot be sustained: he uses public transport mainly because he cannot drive, his 'protest against the supremacy of the killing car' is merely a secondary factor (55). His apathy towards the movement grows once he marries Kate. Leo, despite his idealism, is also not immune to viewing literature in marketable terms:

> The poems about the orphanages could be a hit, if properly marketed. [. . .] That would have to be his unique selling point. An old shocking story in an old beautiful language (Irish) and a new beautiful medium (the poetry of this woman, which he would insist was beautiful). She was beautiful herself, which helped. And black. The first black Irish language woman poet, he was almost certain, in the world. She had a lot going for her. If he couldn't sell her work, he was worse than useless. (142)

For Leo, and the literary marketplace in which he functions, ethnicity, race, history, and language only signify as markers of consumability and the poet's marketable image is the flip side of predjudice. The fact that a black poet who writes in Irish is viewed as especially marketable also signifies a very particular type of acceptable assimilation.

Travelling in Celtic Tiger Ireland

Infrastructure and public transport play key roles in the novel, and Ireland's roads are a constant source of conversation for the characters. As a Swedish au pair observes of a discussion among her employers: 'it was focused on the kind of issue Irish people were obsessed with, it seemed to Ulla: namely, public transport. That and property values' (31). Roads symbolize the speed and mobility (and danger – they are the 'killing roads') of Celtic Tiger Ireland in the novel and Gerry, Anna's brother, sees the roads as representative of modernization and the new Ireland:

> It was like moving from a Thomas Hardy landscape into a modern American one, where a number – Route 3 – could evoke all sorts of memories and feelings. N11, which used to be the Bray Road, N7 instead of the Limerick Road, these were the brave new symbols of modern Ireland. (29)

It is worth noting that in this modern Ireland, road names no longer signify destinations, symbolizing a lack of connectivity that is also part of this new Ireland in the novel. Wanda Balzano notes in one of the first critical commentaries on the Luas, that the street functions as a 'synecdoche for the city' (Balzano and Holdridge, 2007, 109). For Balzano, 'streets are shaped by social and economic change, and as such they are sites of inclusion and exclusion' (Balzano and Holdridge, 2007, 108). In *Fox, Swallow, Scarecrow*, the street, and indeed all channels of connection, are inscribed with discourses of class that map onto the socio-economic conditions of twenty-first century Ireland. As Aida Rosende Pérez notes in her analysis of the novel, 'The beggar whom Anna constantly bumps into when walking the city for example, acts as a constant reminder, at least for the reader, of the social inequalities and extreme polarization of wealth in contemporary Ireland' (Rosende Pérez, 2010, 42). The middle-class inhabitants of Dublin traverse the city with ease, rarely encountering traffic, and the speed of accessing places is referred to throughout the novel, especially when these are sites of consumerism, such as Dundrum Shopping Centre. Speed is connected with affluence and the points at which mobility is obstructed in the novel symbolize the emergence of tensions that undermine the glossy affluence of the Celtic Tiger patina. One such occasion is the appearance in the novel of the 2005 Irish Ferries protest march, which highlighted the 'exploitation of migrant workers and the displacement of jobs' (O'Brien, 2005). Fittingly in the novel, the march obstructs easy consumerism, 'taking over the shopping streets in the interest of workers' rights' (171).

The Luas (named for the Irish word for 'speed'), Dublin's light rail service which commenced in 2004, becomes symbolic of the Celtic Tiger and becomes almost a character in its own right in the novel.[3] The Luas opens the book, accentuating the wealthy development of Celtic Tiger Dublin as it erotically weaves and glides between its architecture:

From the new glass bridge which spanned the inscrutable waters of the Grand Canal, the tram purred downhill and glided gently into the heart of the city. Like a slow Victorian roller coaster it swerved through Peter's Place, passing chic apartments, their balconies rubbing shoulders with almost equally chic corporation houses, genteel vestiges of democracy that had continued to survive in this affluent area. Then it swung nonchalantly onto Adelaide Road – the modernised version, all windows and transparency, where once there had been high hedges and minority religions. (1)

Zoomorphized as a purring animal, the Luas is the Celtic Tiger itself, complete with a seductively voiced announcer, whose voice reminds Anna of Marilyn Monroe, that lulls the passengers into a state of self-important smugness: 'Confidence and well-being crowned them like an aura' (1). In this purring, self-satisfied depiction of the Celtic Tiger, the opening section introduces the concerns of the book: Dublin's affluence and modernization, its inhabitants' complacency, and the relationships between past and present, urban and rural. In contrast to the efficiency (and implied speed) of the Luas, the train that connects West to East is described as inefficient, slow, dirty, and distant from the Europe to which Celtic Tiger aligns itself economically: 'The TGV from Paris to Bordeaux: two and a half hours. Seville to Madrid: two and a half hours. Stockholm to Gothenburg: three hours. Dublin to Tralee: four hours and forty minutes' (55). This is a mode of transport connected with the past and with death: 'a few old age pensioners waited patiently on the platform with their trolleys, for who knew what? The train to Ballybrophy, maybe, or the death coach, whichever came first' (56).

The Luas also serves to highlight the increasing polarization in Irish society between rich and poor. Ní Dhuibhne has always been incisive in her treatment of class relations in Irish society and nowhere is this clearer than in her portrayal of the Luas, which in the opening section of the novel is the Green Line, connecting the affluent suburbs of south Dublin with the city centre. The Green Line transports and represents the wealthy of Celtic Tiger Ireland:

Travelling by tram, at least on the Green Line, had a bit of cachet. Being seen on it was not necessarily a bad thing, whereas being seen on a Dublin bus, even a most respectable bus like the 7 or the 11, was an abject admission of social and economic failure. Only the young, the old and the poor used the bus. But any successful citizen in the prime of life could travel on the Luas, confident that neither their reputation nor self-esteem would be tarnished. (2)

The sleek and polished Luas operates in the novel as a self-congratulatory mirror for its commuters. Anna herself is consistently associated with the Luas in the novel, frequently travels on it, and her encounter with the Red Line of the Luas towards the end of the novel leads to a derailment of both character and tram, and by implication, a derailment of the Celtic Tiger itself. Balzano's comments concerning the way the Luas, on its launch, was inscribed socially, culturally, and economically echo Ní Dhuibhne's use of the light rail in her novel:

The Luas, fashionable emblem of a social and political reality, functions as a 'nicely polished looking-glass', a modern Lacanian-like mirror of metal and glass held up to the Irish people to have 'one good look at themselves', circulating between the signifier of the street and the imaginary of its citizens. (Balzano and Holdridge, 2007, 107)

The Green Luas line, in *Fox, Swallow, Scarecrow*, is 'sleek' and 'efficient' in direct contrast to the Red Line, which connects the less desirable areas not benefitting from by the boom economy whose inhabitants occupy the margins of Celtic Tiger Ireland: 'the Luas, Red Line, stopped at various places in the middle of nowhere; it seemed to be designed to cause maximum inconvenience to commuters' (49). The priorities of the Celtic Tiger map onto the discrepancies between the two disconnected lines and this detachment between affluence and its underside is highlighted at various points in the novel. For the characters, the working-class suburbs served by the Red Line are ultimately alien. To Anna they are 'more exotic than Seville or Stockholm or Barcelona', they are 'much stranger and more exciting' as she views them merely as locations in which to conduct her affair: 'She turned a blind eye to the odd neglected garden, to the houses with the boarded up windows and broken windows that cropped up on every street' (154). The colours ascribed to the two lines seem symbolic; the Green Line representative of those included in Celtic Tiger Ireland's vision of itself, the Red Line indicative of those excluded from the Celtic Tiger narrative of success and wealth.

David Slattery, in his analysis of the actual and epistemological gap between the two Luas lines, describes the differences between them in temporal terms:

> The Red Line runs on a unique measure as a modern system that transports citizens, in a timely manner, to and from work, otherwise trapping them in the concrete of the modern space of Tallaght. The Green Line is a post-modern simulation of transport that carries consumers through the idealized spaces of consumption suspended in the amber light of ahistorical time. (Slattery, 2008)

Balzano notes the temporal dislocations that the Luas incorporates in its joint symbolisation of Ireland's future and its recalling of Ireland's early twentieth-century tram system:

> As the Luas lines trace both the mark of the future and the past in a present moment which is neither, it is also clear that the origin of this trace is constantly deferred in stripping back the past. There is no absolute past to return to for these tracks, but an endless circulation. (Balzano and Holdridge, 2007, 109)

Dublin's modernization, epitomized in glass bridges and buildings, is haunted by its former selves, 'high hedges and minority religions', or other temporalities. Anna experiences the Donegal Irish of the announcer as 'eerie [. . .] like a voice from fairyland or the world beneath the wave, from some place aeons away from the land of the Luas' (1). The Luas's significations of modernization and futurity refuse to remain stable and the intrusion of the supernatural prefigures the subtle magic realism of the novel, to which I shall return.

Like the socio-economic polarization of Celtic Tiger Ireland, *Fox, Swallow, Scarecrow* also plays on juxtapositions between the rural West as repository of traditional 'authentic' Irish culture and the urban East as indicative of materialism, inauthenticity, and modernization, but as in *The Dancers Dancing*, such associations cannot be sustained. Leo's comparison between a Dublin bar and a pub in the Gaeltacht reveals that an object associated with the consumerism of Celtic Tiger Dublin holds pride of place in the 'traditional' pub in the West:

> How different could two pubs be, he thought, looking at the drinkers seated at their little isolated polished tables and thinking of the pub in

the valley, with the plasma screen television in the corner and the regulars perched on their bar stools, talking about the roadworks or the weather. (104–5)

Leo's Gaeltacht valley shows a layering of different commodifications of the landscape, from a New Age family moving from Dublin in the eighties to build an eco-house there, to a pop star whose mansion included a hot tub but who left the valley when expectations of the local's friendliness are not realized, to a rich family, assumed to be either property developers or dotcom millionaires, who buy the mansion. The locals, as well as holiday makers in the valley, prefer to build new houses, so Leo's own house, purchased from an American lawyer, is neither old enough nor new enough to satisfy the market, though it is a beautiful house, one wall constructed out of glass, mirroring Celtic Tiger Dublin's modern architecture, and also making the house into a display case. This house becomes currency in his courting of Kate; he reasons that once she sees the house and its glass south wall, she 'would be as surprised as anyone else, and this surprise would rapidly transform into lifelong love for the owner of the beautiful house, for Leo' (61). Even Leo, who is the only character in the novel to display any kind of political or social conscience, views nature through the prism of money:

Now the last of the summer flowers, the orange montbretia, had lost their brilliant blossom and all that remained of them was the bladelike foliage, a strange rusty colour, a bit like the colour of a ten euro bill. (94–5)

The Glass Tiger

In the Celtic Tiger Ireland of the novel, money saturates perception and economic structures govern everything including interpersonal relationships, acting as a conservative force rather than a modernizing influence:

Divorce was available in Ireland these days, but it had arrived, strangely enough, at the same time as the big increase in house prices. When people could afford to divorce, it wasn't available, and then when it became available, it became unaffordable. Almost overnight. The free market economy was doing what the Church had done for centuries: reinforcing the institution Joyce had dubbed 'the Irish marriage': couples who stayed together even though they couldn't stand the sight of one another. (45)[4]

Despite the mobility seemingly available to Dublin's inhabitants, everyone is static due to property prices. The economy has caused stagnation among the protagonists of the novel and exacerbated their isolation. As Anna reads Olwen's house as a 'symbol of her sister-in-law's life' so the architecture and material culture of the novel signify the state of the characters' interpersonal relationships. The predominant material of Dublin's architecture in the book is glass. Dundrum Shopping Centre, for many the epitome of Celtic Tiger consumerism,[5] is

> a brilliantly lit palace of glass and mirrors. Everything was shining, reflective or transparent: the lifts were made of glass, so were the sides of the stairs; everywhere she [Anna] went she caught sight of herself, reflected in some bright surface, rubbing shoulders with well-dressed people. [. . .] Only young women with good coiffures and elegant bags bearing the logos of the most fashionable shops. (40)

The glossy surfaces of the shopping centre echo the smooth and shiny Luas and both reflect the 'ideal' Celtic Tiger citizen, the consumer (almost always gendered female). Isobel Armstrong's analysis of glass in the Victorian imagination points to associations with glass still relevant to the consumer-driven Celtic Tiger world. Armstrong notes that glass turns everything into a shopfront, it overlays the 'noise and dirt of existing urban space' with '[a]n "ideal" glassworld' (Armstrong, 2008, 133). For Armstrong:

> The pellucid glass membrane of this double world inevitably generated double meanings – the artificial lustre of consumer experience *and* urban pastoral, the spectacle as visual pleasure *and* reified commodity, economic exploitation *and* communal regeneration. (Armstrong, 2008, 133)

The glass architecture in *Fox, Swallow, Scarecrow* signifies in all these various ways and the modernity that it announces is already dated. The speed at which this image can disintegrate highlights the precariousness of this Lacanian reflection of the Celtic Tiger and the Dundrum experience quickly becomes fragmented and dissonant:

> Its lights no longer dazzled, but irritated. Its heaps of sparkling things no longer charmed, but took on the quality of ephemeral rubbish. The sounds, human voices, ringing registers, clattering crockery, bussing machines, were a cacophony of misery – the voices of the damned. (42)

Glass is also a brittle material, easily cracked, and shows the fragile carapace of the Celtic Tiger's prosperity and comfort.

Glass prioritizes spectacle and surface and its slippery shininess highlights a lack of adhesion. Anna rubs shoulders with (the 'right' kind of) people but this is a sliding, glancing gesture, similar to the Luas's slippery progress though Dublin's glassy architecture. Everyone in Dundrum is sleek and glossy, there are no 'flabby women with streaky orange hair and plastic bags' (40). Indeed, Slattery reads the gap between the Luas lines as indicative of a desire to maintain a physical distance between the classes and refuse the inhabitants of Tallaght access to the affluent middle-class consumerism that Dundrum represents:

> Tallaght (the locus of dense social housing, historical unemployment and low cultural value) could never be linked to Sandyford and the South (with its High Cultural sign-value and expensive housing and hair styles). (Slattery, 2008)

Bodies and individuals constantly fail to meaningfully connect in the novel: even Anna and Vincy's affair is strangely sexless and when they finally do consummate their relationship 'it was successful, but not what she had hoped for' (194). Kate is an expert in superficial relationships: 'she would never, ever, converse with any individual for longer than five minutes before moving on to the next group. Networking was her lifeline' and she revels in this role (68). Her marriage to Leo lacks passion and seems motivated mainly by convenience or lack of resistance due to the medication she is prescribed to deal with her anorexia (she does not seem to be offered any type of psychological treatment for her illness). Despite her constant social engagements and 'infinity of communications with an infinity of individuals', Kate is utterly isolated (121). Her favouring of email communication seems to epitomize the human relationships of Ní Dhuibhne's Celtic Tiger Ireland:

> Emotions engendered by emails, however, were as shallow and swift as the technology itself. Within minutes of receiving or not receiving one, all feeling connected with the transaction would have been deleted and sent to trash. You would move swiftly on to the next communication, or event, or crisis, or emotion of your life. As communications and their concomitant emotions speeded up, so did their quality dilute. (130)

As Bauman writes in *Liquid Love*, these types of communications characterized by speed and surface, constitute the types of human bonds produced
by a liquid modern society governed by consumerism:

> The advent of virtual proximity renders human connections simultan-
> eously more frequent and more shallow, more intense and more brief.
> Connections tend to be too shallow and brief to condense into bonds.
> Focused on the business in hand, they are protected against spilling over
> and engaging the partners beyond the time and the topic of the message
> dialled and read – unlike what human relationships, notoriously diffuse
> and voracious, are known to perpetrate. Contacts require less time and
> effort to be entered and less time and effort to be broken. *Distance is no
> obstacle to getting in touch – but getting in touch is no obstacle to staying apart.*
> (Bauman, 2003, 62, original emphasis)

Fox, Swallow, Scarecrow abounds in such connections. Anna finds it 'impossible [. . .] to empathize with Monica', a mother at the school gate, and
Alex, her husband, 'could not maintain interest in her, or in anyone, for
more than a minute or two' (81, 90). The culture of interpersonal isolation
extends to sociopolitical engagement. Anna's mind glides away from social
and political concerns privileging distant observation: 'Brushing problems
under the carpet was a skill she had long ago perfected, especially if they
were other people's problems. Instead of worrying about the ills of society,
she amused herself by observing them'. (2)

The 'isolated polished tables' of the Dublin hotel bar emphasize the
glossy surface relations that slide off each other and prevent adhesion
(105). The hotel in which the bar is located is also an architectural synecdoche of the novel's relationships, structured as they are purely on a surface level masking a pervasive emptiness:

> Five storeys above was a glass roof: the entire hotel was built around a big
> empty space, a tower of air. The walls all around this looked like exterior
> walls – rendered, with long Georgian windows. The whole effect was
> designed to encourage you to feel you were outdoors, even though you
> were in an interior where the climate was as controlled as it might be in a
> museum. (103)

The commodification of history is also apparent here, emphasizing surface –
the exterior Georgian walls combined with the ubiquitous glass of modernity offer an illusion of European *al fresco* consumption.[6] History as

commodity is also clear in Anna's approach to writing: 'with historical fiction you could pick and choose: invent a bit, copy a bit, steal a bit' (38).

The Luas's and hotel's architectures of separation and slipperiness contrast with the intercity train to Tralee: 'on these intercity trains the rules were different. Many passengers believed it was quite normal to engage strangers in conversation' (57). Despite this gesture towards communality associated with Ireland's traditional West, Leo is just as isolated and lonely in the Gaeltacht. Rosende Pérez comments on the exacerbation of the isolation felt by these rural areas due to the poor public transport system and failure to improve the roads combined with migration to the urban centres and the seasonal population of the area by holiday makers who do not contribute to the community (Rosende Pérez, 2010, 43). Leo finds that the myth of a close traditional community is just a myth and people do not call in unannounced to each other. However, it is on this train that Leo has an encounter with a woman, Charlene, who does just this, moving into his house unannounced and disappearing just as unexpectedly. Charlene is clearly the scarecrow of the title:[7] her hair is like 'burnt straw' and 'she reminded him of a character from a television series he had liked as a child, all about scarecrows' (57, 59). Charlene also signifies as a Cathleen Ní Houlihan-type figure, sending men out to fight, evident in a vision Leo has looking at Connolly railway station in Dublin:

> There in front of his eyes he could see them, lines of marching men in their khaki uniforms, heading to Flanders and the Somme. And among the ranks someone odd marched, a woman who looked like a scarecrow, with black straw for hair and a wide red smile. On her head was a black straw hat with a red rose in the brim, a hat only a scarecrow would wear. I had not thought death had undone so many,[8] said Leo to himself, and this scarecrow waved at him cheerily. (171–2)

Moving into Leo's house, she becomes a symbol for Irish female domesticity, baking bread and apple tarts. Since Charlene can speak Irish but cannot read, she represents the oral culture that Leo is trying to preserve. In Leo's vision, she is also a harbinger of death, and in her last appearance she appears in a field to warn Kate of her impending fatal accident while also seeming to cause it:

> The scarecrow wept at first, and then, as the driver climbed down from his cab and slowly dialled a number on his mobile phone, the scarecrow began to smile. By the time the squad cars and ambulance had arrived on

the scene in a fanfare of flashing lights and blaring sirens, the scarecrow was rigid, and the smile on her red face as fixed as that on a death's head. (340–1)

Rebecca Pelan reads her as a symptom of Leo's mental instability, an 'alter-ego' who signifies 'damage demand[ing] to be dealt with' (Pelan, 2009, 23). However, if Ní Dhuibhne is playing on Cathleen Ní Houlihan tropes, Charlene/scarecrow could function as a deadly aspect of Celtic Tiger Ireland though she is also Cathleen Ní Houlihan made abject, grotesque, and ridiculous. She represents those excluded from Celtic Tiger affluence (her history of being beaten as a child, her illiteracy, and her husband who refuses financial support and is suing her for custody of their children) and is potentially dangerous to the future of the nation (embodied in Kate's pregnancy).

Anna does survive the tram that knocks her down, unlike Tolstoy's Anna, and leaves her affluent life for a writers' retreat to 'write what I have not yet written, something deep inside me, not yet seen, not yet felt, not yet known, to me. Myself. I want to write. Real, I want to write, and unreal' (351). The final words of the novel, 'Lets the words. Lets the words. Lets the words' (354), have been read as offering 'hope and potential of liberation from false life' (Pelan, 2009, 24). However, Anna's removal from Celtic Tiger Dublin, her relocation in a rural space, and her passivity in the writing process ('Lets the words float to the top like spawn on the water' (354)), seem to privilege non-engagement and reinscribe a rural/urban dichotomy in which writing only becomes possible in an idealized rural landscape. Given Ní Dhuibhne's careful undermining of rural idealization throughout the novel, this seemingly redemptive ending is strange. Anna's reinvention of her writing self seems to rely on her loss of memory and failure to remember her daughter's name, which strikes a warning note. In contrast, Enright's *The Gathering*, explores the consequences of forgetting in Celtic Tiger Ireland.

The Gathering

Enright's Booker prize winning novel, *The Gathering*, published the same year as *Fox, Swallow, Scarecrow*, offers us a very different take on the Celtic Tiger world. It is a novel of interiority rather than surfaces, of the unbear-able connections between people rather than terrible isolation, decaying bodies instead of sleek ones, ramshackle homes in place of glass architecture, recourse to past and memory rather than a perpetual present. Where the idiom of *Fox, Swallow, Scarecrow* is glass and shiny surfaces, *The Gathering*'s vernacular is meat and the body. The novel begins with a corpse. Veronica the narrator arrives at her family home to tell her mother of Liam's suicide. Liam is the sibling Veronica is closest to in this large family of twelve children (and seven miscarriages). His death precipitates Veronica's obsessive focus on the past, her own and her grandmother's, to 'bear witness to an uncertain event' of her childhood that may offer answers to her brother's life and suicide (1). The chronology of the novel is not a linear one, moving between the events leading up to Liam's funeral, Veronica's creative reimagining of the life of her grandmother, Ada, and Veronica's own uncertain memories of her childhood, teenage years, and recent past. As Eleanor Birne eloquently notes, '*The Gathering* is a gathering of family members around one of their dead, but it is also a gathering of facts, of evidence' (Birne, 2007, 30). It is also a gathering together of fact and fiction, recollection and recreation, and an attempt on Veronica's behalf to gather herself together in the face of unacknowledged trauma: Liam's abuse at the hands of her grandmother's landlord, Lamb Nugent, the summer they stayed with her, which Veronica witnessed but to which she never bore witness. There is also the suggestion that Veronica herself, as well as her mother and Uncle Brendan, also suffered similar abuse and, for Veronica, a network of collusion, denial, and powerlessness is also at issue.

Veronica seems to belong to the new Ireland that we view in *Fox, Swallow, Scarecrow* but as one reviewer noted, the novel 'shows in wrenching detail how the old Ireland haunts the new' (Tonkin, 2007). Veronica's surface life in her suburban house decorated in 'oatmeal, cream, sandstone, slate' (36), her expensive Saab car, her former job as a journalist who wrote about shopping, becomes haunted by Liam's death: 'I find myself crying on the escalator in Brown Thomas, which is only a shop. And the fact that makes me cry is that there is nothing here that I can not buy [. . .] My brother has just died and I can buy anything at all' (189–90).

The Problem of Distance

In contrast to the slippery non-adhesive relationships of *Fox, Swallow, Scarecrow*, everyone in *The Gathering* is too closely stuck together. Even seemingly exclusive categories refuse to remain separate in the Hegarty family: 'Fact / Conjecture. Dead / Alive. Drunk / Sober. Out in the world that is not the world of the Hegarty family, we think these things are Not The Same Thing'

(26). Indeed, Veronica's narrative shows the extent to which fact and fiction become intermingled and the dead are very much present for her, both in terms of the ghosts that people her consciousness and her constant awareness of the thin border between life and death; her view of her 'child-battered body [. . .] feeding the grave' (79). Love, in the novel, is described as adhesively close: 'There are so few people given us to love and they all stick' (15). A major issue in the novel is this problem of distance which is repeatedly iterated in the narrative, through architecture (Ada's front door opens directly onto the street), in memories (Veronica cannot keep hers separate from those of her siblings), and in desire, 'its awful proximity' (17), which does not respect proper borders in the novel. The problem with distance is expressed most eloquently and intensely through the body:

> Nugent, who feels the eighteen inches between them [him and Ada] more keenly than any other measure of air. Who would push any part of himself into any part of her and find relief in it. Who might put his hands into her belly, to feel the heat and slither of her insides. (32)

Nugent, through this imagery of bodily penetration and invasion, epitomizes this troubling closeness, and the abuse that Liam has suffered is prefigured in Veronica's imagining of Nugent's incestuous desire towards his sister:

> That when he holds his penis in the night-time, it feels like her thin skin; always damp, never sweating. Because, in those days, people used to be mixed up together in the most disgusting ways. (35)

The awful proximity is most potent for Veronica in relation to Liam, who she feels 'at the base of [her] spine' (29). She notes that 'the place Liam worked best was under your skin' (125). Eleven months older than her, Veronica views Liam as an almost-twin, 'Sometimes I think we overlapped in there [her mother's womb], he just left early' (11).

Liam's proximity to her troubles her subjectivity, not only does she fail to distinguish her memories from those of her siblings, but Liam invades her sense of self: 'He is back in my head like an expanding smell – a space that clears to allow him look out of my eyes' (76). For Enright, smell, which is everywhere in this novel, illustrates the close links between the body and memory, but also the degree to which the self is permeable:

In the brain smell and long-term memory are absolutely beside each other. So the flares you get in the brain in response to a smell, the electro-magnetic response in the brain leaks into long-time memory [. . .] Also it is a sense to which we are helpless. You can't *not* smell something. You can *not* touch something, you can look away, but you can't *not* smell some-thing. It is the most open of all our senses. (Enright, 2008a, 18)

The pervasiveness of smell in the novel indicates the degree to which Veronica's subjectivity is invaded by memories, memories of an event char-acterized by a failure to maintain proper boundaries, a violent inability to maintain distance.[9] Nugent is framed as a threat to subjectivity itself, obliquely realized in Veronica's recreation of his meeting with Ada in which she imagines him pushing his way into her stomach, penetrating her through her eyes: 'The shock is the complete self of Ada Merriman. Her pupils open to receive him' (20). As Harte notes, 'one of the cruxes of child sexual abuse, [is] the way in which victims are simultaneously robbed of their subjectivity' (Harte, 2010, 197). Displaced onto Ada here, the reper-cussions of Nugent's destructive force possibly include Veronica's mother's vagueness, Uncle Brendan's madness, Veronica's bodily repulsion, and Liam's life and death in general. Liam himself is constantly referred to by Veronica as a 'messer' (44, 123, 163), a word illustrative of the failure to maintain proper borders and distance that is endemic in the novel.

The architecture of the family home, 'all extension and no house', mir-rors the messy relationships at stake in the novel: 'The house knows me. Always smaller than it should be; the walls run closer and more complicated than the ones you remember. [. . .] I was inside it, as it grew; as the dining room was knocked into the kitchen, as the kitchen swallowed the back gar-den' (4). As seen here, the imagery of invaded spaces is all-pervasive in the novel; rooms do not stay discrete, the outside of the house becomes part of the inside. The abject which, for Kristeva, is expelled from the psyche in order that subjectivity is secured, and which also threatens subjectivity as a reminder of the fragility of its maintenance, suffuses the novel.[10] Veronica constantly invokes the abject. Her narrative abounds in corpses, rotting and decaying bodies, invasive smells, and the collapse of proper borders. Again, the family home, for Veronica, is bound up in this register:

The kitchen still smells the same – it hits me in the base of the skull, very dim and disgusting, under the fresh, primrose yellow paint. Cup-boards full of old sheets; something cooked and dusty about the lagging

around the immersion heater; the chair my father used to sit in, the
arms shiny and cold with the human waste of many years. It makes me
gag a little, and then I can not smell it any more. It just is. It is the smell
of us. (5)

Veronica's reaction to the family home encapsulates the trauma that she is
trying to negotiate, the invasive memory that seeps from under the veneer
of a cohesive subjectivity which both threatens her boundaries, 'makes me
gag', and also structures the family, 'It is the smell of us'. Veronica wonders
'how you might undo all these sheds and extensions, take the place back to
the house it once was. If it would be possible to unbuild it all and start
again' (24). She also fantasizes about gutting Ada's house (the house in
which the abuse took place], ripping the wallpaper, painting the walls white,
'a team of men in boiler suits with tanks on their backs and those high-
pressure steel rods' to fumigate the place of its associations (238). Her own
house, decorated in those clean and neutral colours of 'oatmeal, cream,
sandstone, slate' is an expression of this desire to tidy up the mess of 'the
human waste of many years': 'I spend my time looking at things and wishing
them gone, clearing objects away' (37). But the house, where '[n]othing
settles [. . .] [n]ot even the dust' is also 'nothing to do with me', and this
space offers little security. She spends most of her time in the car driving
aimlessly, pulled towards the airport and the psychiatric hospital where her
uncle was an inmate (36). Veronica seems to realize that the edifice has rotten foundations: 'sometimes I look at my nice walls and, like Liam, I say,
"Pull the whole thing down." [. . .] As if the world was built on a lie and
that lie was very secret and very dirty' (168). In fact, when Liam stays with
her, 'the back of the house was ripped out', and she 'blamed Liam, almost,
and not the builders' (168). Liam's presence highlights the 'dirty secret'
that threatens the clean walls.

Do Not Touch Me

Connected with the lack of distance and messiness of relationships, is the
issue of touch, which is a central concern of the novel, particularly the question of who one can and cannot touch, encapsulated ironically in Nugent's
nickname, Nolly May, playing on the Latin, *noli me tangere*, 'do not touch
me', which Christ said to Mary Magdalene after his resurrection (129).
Veronica poignantly refers to her daughter as 'untouchably fine' encoding

both a sense of warning and hope that her daughter will not suffer inappropriate touch (53). Veronica expresses Nugent's refusal to abide by his nickname somatically, enacting the interdiction on her own body: 'I sewed the tips of my fingers together with one of Ada's needles' (127). Liam Harte reads Veronica's reaction to her witnessing of Liam's abuse (her touching of herself, her 'urge to pee and look at the pee coming out; to poke or scratch or rub when I was finished, and smell my fingers afterwards' (Enright, 2007, 146)) as indicative of 'the way in which her trauma was processed somatically rather than cerebrally, so that the memory of it lodged more in the body than in the mind [. . .] traumatic experience is viscerally embedded, remembered in and through the body' (Harte, 2010, 194–5). The repeated instances of self-harm that Veronica reveals shows the repercussions for her relationship to touch and her own body, leading to her metaphorical construction of the body as receptacle for the traumatic knowledge: 'You know everything at eight, but it is hidden from you, sealed up, in a way you have to cut yourself open to find' (147). Other people's hands are also over-determined in their agency: 'Tom's fingers grip my arm. They are very full of themselves, these fingers of his' (198). The improper touch haunts her body; she feels a ghostly hand at the base of her spine (the place where she feels Liam) at his funeral: 'Who has touched me? I want to say it out loud, but the Hegartys and the Hegartys' wives and the Hegartys' children are some distance away from me: they shift, and talk, and eat on, unawares' (198). The ghostly touch and the family's lack of awareness of it bring into sharp focus the absences and silences that the family is based on which coalesce, for Veronica, in the figure of her mother and the 'mantra of our childhoods [. . .] *Don't tell Mammy*' (9).

Veronica's mother has 'holes in her head' (7), is 'hazy, unhittable, too much loved' (5), is 'forgetfulness itself', but is also 'an agitation behind us, a kind of collective guilt' (3), and the rage leveled at her by Veronica speaks to her symbolization for Veronica of collusion, denial, and failure to protect, which also seems displaced away from Ada onto her. Veronica's mother, 'the loveliest woman in Dublin' (12), and Ada, about whom the neighbours say 'Oh she was lovely' (86), are linked in a public veneer of innocuousness, yet Ada is possibly implicated in witnessing Veronica's abuse and failing to acknowledge it:

This is the moment when we realise that it was Ada's fault all along.

The mad son and the vague daughter. The vague daughter's endlessly vague pregnancies, the way each and every one of her grandchildren went vaguely wrong. This is the moment when we ask what Ada did – for it must, surely, have been something – to bring so much death into the world.

But I do not blame her. And I don't know why that is. (223)

Given Enright's astute awareness of the position of the mother in Irish history and culture, and indeed in the symbolic economy as a whole, Veronica's mother also encodes the lack of subjectivity and invisibility accorded to motherhood in this context: 'when I turn away, she seems to disappear, and when I look, I only see the edges' (3). Her role as mother has erased her: 'My mother had twelve children and – as she told me one hard day – seven miscarriages. The holes in her head are not her fault' (7). The rage directed towards her by Veronica also speaks to her failure as mirror/mother that secures subjectivity. As with the twins in *What Are You Like*, the blankness of the mother in the symbolic economy is shown to negatively affect female subjectivity. Veronica herself expresses her fear that she will also fall prey to erasure if she does not maintain a mother-daughter connection: 'If I don't talk to them I think I will die of something – call it irrelevance – I think I will just fade away' (37–8).

Embodying History

Veronica's desire to take apart the house maps onto her ideal model of narrating the 'crime of the flesh' that she expresses at the outset of the narrative: 'I write it down, I lay them out in nice sentences, all my clean, white bones' (1–2). For Veronica, history, memory, and narrative need to be tamed, boiled clean of the messiness of flesh, and assembled like an obedient skeleton. However, her first act of creative historiography is to re-flesh Nugent's skeleton: 'He must be reassembled; click, clack; his muscles hooked to bone and wrapped with fat, the whole skinned over and dressed in a suit of navy or brown' (14). This reanimated corpse haunts the narrative as a 'slick of horror' that pollutes Veronica's symbolic, her representation of the world and its relations (215). Sexual threat pervades the novel and Veronica's consciousness. She accuses her husband of inappropriate desire and frantically demands to know where the limits of desire are, how to delineate the proper borders: 'I don't know where the edges are, that's all. I don't know where you draw the line. Puberty, is that a line? It happens to girls at nine, now. [. . .] Is there a limit to what you want to fuck, out there?' (176). As Harte observes, so omnipresent are the effects of her traumatic memory that 'a profound alienation from sexual desire, copulation, and procreation has taken root in her since Liam's suicide, fuelling her excremental vision of the fertile world' (Harte, 2010, 195).

The body is everywhere in Veronica's narrative. Her mother is 'benign human meat' (47), and Veronica feels like a 'chicken when it is quartered' following sex with her husband (40). The corporeal here is resolutely not the sleek bodies of *Fox, Swallow, Scarecrow* and Haverty's *The Free and Easy*; this is the abject body, turning itself into meat. The text abounds in rotting and decaying bodies, blood, gristle, and corpses that refuse to stay quiet.[11] This is nowhere more apparent than Veronica's thoughts when she visits Brighton beach, the scene of Liam's drowning:

> An overweight child with breasts – a boy, it seems. An old man with a scab under his nose. A woman with a widening tattoo. A parade of lax flies and stained trousers and bra straps showing under other, shoestring straps. The living, with all their smells and holes. Liam was always a great man for people's *holes*, and who stuck what into which *hole*.
>
> He is back in my head like an expanding smell – a space that clears to allow him look out of my eyes and be disgusted by arse or tit, or 'cold tit', even, by flesh that is never the right temperature or the right humidity, being too *sweaty*, or flesh that is *saggy*, or *hairy*. (76)

History itself becomes subject to this symbolic economy, epitomized by a man whose syphilis writes his history on his face. The memory of his melting flesh leads Veronica to the conclusion that 'History is only biological' (162). The inmates of St. Ita's haunt through a 'residue of skin' (159), and history manifestly refuses to boil down to the clean bones Veronica had imagined in the opening of the novel.

Harte reads the novel as illustrating not just the traumatic effects of child abuse on an individual or family, but as a comment on the state of the nation itself, commending the novel for,

> the subtlety and complexity of its depiction of the trauma of child abuse as a collective as much as a personal experience; its nuanced attempt to build a critical and ethical consciousness in the reader by narrating what was formerly unspeakable; and its scrupulous refusal to redeem history by suggesting that the far-reaching effects of traumatic memory can be completely erased or transcended. (Harte, 2010, 188)

For Harte, Veronica's negotiation of the traumatic witnessing of child abuse and her failure to bear witness to it at the time becomes indicative of Ireland's history of a systemic failure on behalf of the state to protect the vulnerable, the 'prejudices, practices, and institutions that facilitated the perpetration and repression of violence against vulnerable individuals at various state-sanctioned levels' (Harte, 2010, 199). Veronica clearly articulates the connections: 'This is the anatomy and mechanism of a family – a whole fucking country – drowning in shame' (168), and she also links the public discourse about the widespread child abuse to her own ability to remember: 'I never would have made that shift on my own – if I hadn't been listening to the radio, and reading the paper, and hearing about what went on in schools and churches and in people's homes' (172–3). Similarly, Carol Dell'Amico reads Liam as a symbol for all those absented from the Celtic Tiger discourse of boom and prosperity in the present (Dell'Amico, 2010, 68). Liam is associated with Ireland's less affluent past:

> I was sad at the way he had been left behind. Liam existed in the seventies, somehow. [. . .] My emigrant brother makes an old-fashioned ghost, and when he died, I dressed him in worn-out wellington boots, as the Irish seventies dipped back into the fifties in my mind. (Enright, 2007, 191)

His ghostly presence throughout the text, 'like a shout in the room' (10), draws attention to those who haunt the Celtic Tiger, which also includes the unmarked graves of the dead of St. Ita's Hospital: 'the place is boiling with corpses, the ground is knit out of their tangled bones' (160). As Dell'Amico writes, 'in reading Veronica's story we are, in turn, reading part of Ireland's, *The Gathering* is a parable of a nation with the choice either to face or ignore a disturbing past' (73). Liam's 'great talent' is, after all, 'exposing the lie'.[12]

Meaney's reading of the novel insists on its purchase for the present moment:

> The need to bear witness and the uncertainty of the event have a renewed energy in the twenty-first century as anxiety replaces ennui as the postmodern condition. Enright's novel takes a story that has become a cliché, 'yet another miserable Irish childhood,' and makes it unbearable. (Meaney, 2010, 124)

The unbearableness of the story is important. The traumatic event that Veronica is trying to bear witness to constantly evades memory and representation. Veronica continuously reminds us of the uncertainty of her memory, the unreliability of her narration, and her recourse to creative imagination. Yet the narrative also shows that while the event resists representation, it also structures Veronica's symbolic order (decaying bodies, corpses, problems of distance and touch, failure to keep things separate) and signification in the novel is also saturated by it. The event cannot be represented but is signified everywhere. History will not remain in 'nice sentences' or 'clean white bones' (2), but inheres in the flesh of the narrative, which accounts for the predominance of meat, bodies, and flesh in Veronica's narrative and why she 'would love to leave my body. Maybe this is what they are about, these questions of which or whose hole, the right fluids in the wrong places, these infantile confusions and small sadisms: they are a way of fighting our way out of all this meat' (140). The past and history are lived in and through the body just as Veronica comments, 'I do not think we remember our family in any real sense. We live them, instead' (66).

The redemptive ending of the novel marks Veronica's acceptance of this. She cannot run away from her body, from her family, from her history any longer and must learn to live in them instead:

> And I think we make for peculiar refugees, running from our own blood, or towards our own blood; pulsing back and forth along ghostly veins that wrap the world in a skein of blood. [. . .] I am thinking about the world wrapped in blood, as a ball of string is wrapped in its own string. That if I just follow the line I will find out what it is that I want to know.
>
>   Towards or away. (258)

Her decision to follow the blood connection back to her family and her past is illustrative of a potential healing, letting the blood flow rather than to 'default to the oldest scar' (Enright, 2007, 97), aiming to attempt to live in the body rather than forget which brings its own wounds.

Conclusion

The Gathering shows the consequences of turning people into commodities. Abuse turns people into objects, robs them, as Harte notes, of their subjectivity (Harte, 2010, 197). Nugent's economic power over Ada as her landlord 'reinforce[s] his sense of sexual ownership of her and, by extension, her grandchildren' (Harte, 2010, 203, n.4). Both *Fox, Swallow, Scarecrow* and

The Gathering critique the hegemonic Celtic Tiger discourse of consumerism and affluence, and make legible the absences that underpin and haunt it but do so in very different ways; Ní Dhuibhne's novel inhabiting the idiom of glossy surfaces and superficial connections, while Enright forces us to bear witness to the corpses that boil beneath the surface. As can be seen, these two novels, as well as the others discussed in this book, explicitly give the lie to Gough's contention that Irish literature is backward-looking. Contemporary Irish literature engages profoundly and critically with contemporary Ireland in all its complexity.

Conclusion

Pasts, Presents, Futures

This book explores the work of three contemporary writers whose fiction foregrounds the body and its materiality. These authors, who are writing in a specific cultural moment that has been marked by economic growth and prosperity, yet their texts highlight the disturbances and disruptions that complicate linear models of progress. Their fiction reveals the corporeal as a potent locus for explorations of what has been occluded in conventional narratives of history, particularly the embodiment of the mother and maternal genealogies.

These novels convey the extent to which configurations of the corporeal and considerations of our relationship to the maternal body influence temporal models and methods of historiography. These writers formulate connections between the past and the present through the medium of the corporeal. Ní Dhuibhne marks gaps and interruptions in linear temporality through physical hauntings. The body becomes implicated in these disruptions. Her work insists on relationships with the past that preserve its difference and otherness, and she holds traditional models of historiography up for examination revealing the types of embodiment that it obscures.

McCann's earliest works, *Songdogs* and *This Side of Brightness*, depict efforts by young men to come to terms with their own past and the histories of their family. The novels consider these relations between generations through explorations of the connections that are forged between body and landscape. The corporeal is configured through the linkages that it makes with its environment. The texts reveal productive relationships with space and imaginative engagements with images of the body. However, *Songdogs* also highlights the fraught relationship between female embodiment and the spatial.

Enright's novels, *The Wig My Father Wore* and *What Are You Like?* take up this issue of the female body and spatial relations, particularly the reproductive body and the space of the domestic. These texts also offer transformative and productive configurations of the corporeal that contribute to formulations of temporality that stress 'intra-action'. This term is Karen Barad's neologism; it signifies a move away from conceiving of connections as 'linkages among pre-existing discrete' entities to the acknowledgement that spaces, times, and materialities are 'intra-actively produced through one another' (Barad, 2001, 102). Enright's novels highlight the body's connectivity in these terms, as intra-acting productively with its surroundings and other bodies. The configurations of the corporeal in these texts offer dynamic models of relating between self and other, and between generations.

McCann's *Dancer* and Enright's *The Pleasure of Eliza Lynch*, continue an exploration of how conceptualizations of the body underpin and influence the ways we think about historical narratives and the relations between the past and the present. Corporeality is used in these novels to question the project of historiography; Enright particularly foregrounds its relationship to the female body. Both novels question the structures that subtend hegemonic modes of historiography.

In contrast to this historical focus, Ní Dhuibhne's *Fox, Swallow, Scarecrow* and Enright's *The Gathering* both critically engage with their present moment of Celtic Tiger Ireland. Ní Dhuibhne's novel focuses on the sleek consumerism and glossy surfaces of literary Dublin in the early-twenty-first century where the aesthetic is valued in and of its marketability and past and future are unimaginable in an eternal present. The economic and the marketplace are shown to be the paramount structuring principles of this world. The slippery superficial relations between people are revealed to be deeply damaging in the novel which also foreshadows the economic derailment of the Celtic Tiger. The Celtic Tiger forms the background of Enright's *The Gathering*, but this is a novel that incisively explores the dark shadows of the prosperous present and shows the profound dangers of forgetting the contiguities and continuities with the past that persist into the present and affect the future.

These writers all formulate alternative paradigms to describe the relationship between the past and the present in order to reveal the types of embodiment that have been neglected or written out of conventional narratives. Grosz contends that 'the ways we rethink this relation [between past and present] will, of course have direct implications for whatever conceptions of the future, the new, creation, and production we may develop' (Grosz, 2003, 15). Thus, the efforts by these writers to construct paradigms that stress the contiguity between the past and the present, and to emphasize the potential otherness of history, encode new ways of thinking about the future. Their novels do not simply acknowledge the past and the bodies that it formulates, but insist on a connective relationship that propels the present towards thinking materially and discovering what 'matters'. As Grosz writes, 'History is not the recovery of the truth of bodies or lives in the past; it is the engendering of new kinds of bodies and new kinds of lives' (Grosz, 2003, 23). The possibilities that Enright, McCann, and Ní Dhuibhne open up in their configurations of the corporeal emphasize the production of relationships that are intra-connected, acknowledging otherness and difference, and uninterested in preserving wholeness, integrity, and coherence. Their depictions of bodies stress mobility and transformation. They thus rethink the female body and most particularly, maternal embodiment, which have traditionally been subject to constraint and incarceration within the space of the Irish home and the nation. Sara Ahmed, in her essay, 'Feminist Futures', stresses the importance of the concept of movement:

> The relationship between movement and attachment is instructive. What moves us, what makes us feel, is also what holds us in place or gives us a dwelling place. Hence, movement does not cut the body off from the 'where' of its inhabitance but connects bodies to other bodies – indeed, attachment takes place through movement, through being moved by the proximity of others. (Ahmed, 2003, 240)

This is precisely what a novel like *The Gathering* forces us to confront.

This concept of movement suggests alternative ways for thinking about the relationship between body and space. Female embodiment needs no longer to be cut off from place nor become its signifier. Movement stresses the productive value and potential of connectivity in order to open up spaces for radically different futures, ones in which embodiment no longer becomes tied to notions of nationality, wholeness, and integrity.

Generosity

I would like to conclude this book with a short consideration of the concept of 'corporeal generosity', as this has been the ethical consideration informing my readings of the various novels and the bodies they depict. Rosalyn Diprose coined this term to illustrate that generosity is most profoundly theorized through recourse to the corporeal. This type of generosity is the basis for relations between bodies, between generations, and, by implication, between temporalities. It is a relation in which encounters with otherness are crucial (Diprose; 1998, 2002). Diprose's concept of generosity is one that entails transformation and productivity. She defines generosity as 'openness to otherness' and argues that this type of generosity must insist on maintaining difference and alterity; 'generosity is only possible if neither sameness nor unity is assumed as either the basis or the goal of an encounter with another' (Diprose, 2002, 90–1).

This book centres on fictional depictions of generosity with a temporal focus; it focuses on novels that engage with other temporal modalities without reducing them to the terms of the present. It is important to acknowledge the past, and the fact that accepted narratives of history may be forgetful and dematerializing; the relations between generations are multiple and rhizomatic and may not surface in narratives of linear causality. Such an approach to history also implies learning to think about the future in new ways and being open to new and radical possibilities. Being generous implies presents (pun intended), the acknowledgement of the present moment as it becomes future, the acknowledgement of the possibilities of radically new futures. In other words, it is important to engage with the past in new ways in order that the possibility of futurity can emerge.

Thus, generosity between generations, or the generation of generosity, entails a mutual reconsideration of the idea of generation as well as that of generosity. Generosity must entail the possibility of transformation; it involves productive and generative thinking that is self-critical and open to otherness allowing for radically different futures. Reconfiguring the idea of generations in a way that stresses the intra-action of various positionings permits this type of generous thinking to be always in process, always generative.

It is instructive that Diprose theorizes generosity through the body. The Western philosophical tradition that privileges mind over body produces solipsistic thought and relations. However, thinking through the corporeal insists on intra-active relationships as well as what Irigaray has dubbed a politics of touch. Diprose contends that the 'openness to otherness that characterizes generosity is [. . .] carnal and affective, and the production of identity and difference that results is a material production' (Diprose, 2002, 9). This book reads the configurations of the body in the work of Enright, McCann, and Ní Dhuibhne as attempting an ethics of connective corporeal generosity. Enright's depictions of the body formulate paradigms for engaging with questions of difference that do not reduce the other to the same. Her novels offer ways of conceptualizing relations between bodies that are connective and transformative. However, her work also highlights the troubled symbolization of the mother–daughter relationship and the ultimate disavowal of the maternal body that is at the heart of Western culture. McCann's work touches on this problem, but it is the male body and its relationship to the temporal and the spatial that preoccupy his novels. For Ní Dhuibhne, the denial of a relationship to the maternal body is inherently implicated in conventional models of historiography. Her writing forges links between the past and the present that acknowledge the potential of the past to be radically different. Of all the three writers considered in this thesis, Enright offers the most sustained and exploratory engagement with the issue of mother-daughter relations and the inadequate symbolization of the maternal and pregnant body. Her novels consistently raise the problematics of symbolizing female and maternal corporeality. All three writers show that these concerns profoundly *matter* to Celtic Tiger Ireland and highlight the consequences of forgetting the ghosts that haunt. As Enright reminds us in *The Gathering*, 'the place is boiling with corpses, the ground is knit out of their tangled bones' (Enright, 2007, 160), and we must acknowledge their presences and immanences in order to allow the potential for radically different futures.

Notes

Introduction

[1] See also Herron, 1999. Herron's reading of poetry by Heaney, Carson, and Longley suggests culture's dependence on the whole, intact body. This predominant image of wholeness enhances the potency of the horror evoked by disappeared or disrupted bodies. The historical and cultural specificities of Northern Irish poetry largely explain the anxieties connected to violence enacted on a physical or metaphorical body. However, I would argue that issues relating to totality and wholeness in connection to the body articulate a much broader cultural investment in terms of meaning, history, and spatiality. Such an investment is challenged by the representations of the corporeal by the contemporary Irish novelists that I will consider in the course of this book.

[2] Roche justifies his choice of year as follows: 'From an aesthetic point of view, this is the date at which John Banville published his first book of fiction. But from a political perspective, it inaugurated the violence in and the representational emphasis on Northern Ireland, clearly of concern to the writer from there, but a condition to which the South is not immune' (2000, x).

[3] See Neil McEwan's discussion of perspective in British historical fiction, which he takes to mean 'a view of the past adjusted to present interests' (McEwan, 1987, 1). O'Toole had slightly modified his position in 2010, writing that although 'Irish writing (indeed Irish art as a whole) was not very good at reflecting boomtime Ireland' he conceded that 'just because a novel or a play is set in the 1950s doesn't mean it's about the 1950s' (O'Toole, 2010).

[4] See Cullingford, 1990; Meaney, 1991; Meaney, 1998; Sullivan, 2000; Coughlan, 2003; Sullivan, 2005; Meaney, 2010.

Chapter 1

[1] Ní Dhuibhne's date for the Ballylumford Affair, 22 April, closely relates to those of Chernobyl, which took place on 25–26 April 1986.

[2] Jenny christens this woman Elinor, the name of the mother who lived in the Bray House, in an attempt to trick Robin. We later discover that her real name is Maggie. I will refer to her by this name for the remainder of the chapter.

[3] Indeed, she notes that popular opinion in the sixteenth and seventeenth centuries saw fairy tales as subversive gossip engendered by informal meetings of women, most typically in 'public laundries and spinning rooms'. They were linked with

prostitutes, midwives, and wet nurses: 'professions, official and unofficial, those which allowed women to pass between worlds out of the control of native or marital family' (Warner, 1995, 35).

4 As an expression of ruthlessness, she murders Karl in order to get access to information contained in his notebook.

5 This is achieved in a similar manner to the scenario depicted in Leszek Kolakowski's essay, 'Emperor Kennedy Legend', in which future anthropologists quarrel over the historical interpretation of sources that suggest a myth concerning an emperor named Kennedy. An example of the way the article draws historical conjecture into question is the uncertainty of the distinction between Ireland and Iceland: 'He came from a legendary island called Ireland, located in the North; whether this island was identical with another called Iceland and mentioned in another source, has not yet been definitively established; perhaps just a typographic error made two countries of one' (Kolakowski, 2000, 17).

6 For a discussion of the novel, see Heather Ingman (Ingman, 2005, 517–30).

Chapter 2

1 Pultz acknowledges Foucault's observations that the coherent Enlightenment subject was a construct that had to be maintained through various systems of power and control and that photography contributed to such regimes. The scopic order, which legitimated the viewing subject as masterful and the act of seeing as connected to the mind as opposed to the body, is compounded by the invention of the camera – a disembodied eye. For further discussion see Foucault, 1977 and Lalvani, 1993.

2 This view is also confirmed by David L. Pike (Pike, 1998, 18). Pike notes that subway dwellers often view themselves as 'pioneers'.

3 Much of the subway-related incidents that occur in *This Side of Brightness* are, as McCann notes in his acknowledgements, based on historical fact. The story of the forgotten tunnel, built by the entrepreneur Alfred Ely Beach, told by Nathan to Eleanor as a child, and visited by them later corresponds to the fraught beginnings of the subway system and, as Brooks points out, became part of the urban folklore of New York, continuously re-emerging in popular culture such as its incarnation in *Ghostbusters II* (Brooks, 1997, 27).

4 This fictional incident is based on a historical event, which took place on 27 March 1905. In his article on *This Side of Brightness*, John F. Healy notes that McCann's alteration of the year serves to establish a correspondence with the 1916 rising in Dublin but he does not press the implications of this link between the two 'risings' (Healy, 2000, 107).

5 For discussion of artists such as Dan Rico, Harry Sternberg, and Charles Keller, see Brooks, 1997, 145–57.

6 It must be noted that the female members of the Walker family do not possess any profound relationship with the subway and its tunnels. Eleanor is the only woman of the family to descend into the tunnels and although she appears interested in them and their mythology, it is their association with Nathan that provides

the attraction for her. The subway tunnels become part of his personality and part of their courtship rituals. Women themselves are peripheral characters in the narrative; it is the male experience of corporeality with which the novel is concerned. Mary Morrissy, in a review of the novel, argues that 'this is a male book. The women seem to hover tantalising, shadowy and fragmented, filtered through the more powerful interior lives of the two male characters'. (Morrissy, 1998).

[7] For further discussion of the racial implication of subway representations see Pike, 1998.

[8] For a discussion of racial violence in the subways see Brooks, 1997, 183–205.

[9] The liver was commonly viewed, predominantly in the seventeenth century, as the seat of love and violent passions. The earliest recorded instance of this was in the fourteenth century in John Gower's *Confessio amantis*. See reference in *Oxford English Dictionary*.

[10] The term 'haptic' pertains to touch or the tactile. It also signifies a reliance on the sense of touch rather than that of sight. See reference in *Oxford English Dictionary*.

[11] Treefrog also frees a frozen crane from the ice covering the Hudson River at the beginning of the novel prefiguring his own 'resurrection' from a frozen life in the tunnels. The novel contains recurrent images of ice and snow whose fall is represented as positive and beautiful, as opposed to the more negative aspects of falling and descent that are current in the text. Snow is often an image of beauty in the novel, particularly in squalid surroundings. Such a contrast is captured by the image of snow falling through the grates of the tunnels. The image operates according to Brooks's idea of the subway as a place that 'now embraces extremes. It is both sordid and transcendent. Moreover, the sordidness and the transcendence are nearly indistinguishable' (Brooks, 1997, 207).

[12] One such example is Eleanor's denial of her son, Clarence. She describes her memory of this rejection as 'so heavy I can hardly bear it. [. . .] Sometimes it weighs the whole of me to the ground so much I feel like I'm bending over when I walk' (McCann, 1998, 121).

Chapter 3

[1] *Yesterday's Weather* brings together all stories from *Taking Pictures*, most of *The Portable Virgin* and two stories from Enright's first publication in *First Fictions: Introduction 10* in 1989.

[2] See, for example, Tague, 1995.

[3] Grace Anglicizes her Irish name, Grainne, as she was called Groin at school. For Coughlan, this contributes to an undermining of discourses that link the Irish language and the rural to ideas of authenticity. See Coughlan, 2004, 183.

[4] However, she blames herself and her supposed loss of virginity for her father's stroke: 'The other fact is that I stayed out all night, the night my father's brain sprung a leak [. . .] Never mind that I had spent the night talking and fully dressed [. . .] So my virginity, if I ever had a virginity, was just an idea my parents

had. But it was my father who took the brunt of it, because it was his brain that tore and bled and was transformed' (46).

5 This confusion between pregnancy and the presence of a tumour becomes the focus of the initial sections of *What Are You Like?*

6 Umberto Eco argues that the mirror image is a 'unique case' of the double as it 'sometimes works as if there were a duplication of both my body as an object and my body as a subject, splitting and facing itself' (Eco, 1984, 210).

7 The roundness of the full moon is also a recurrent symbol.

8 The asymmetry of her body following the loss of her right nipple impacts upon her relation to space and language: 'There is no way to get my balance. All day, things fall to the floor, slip out of my hands, the phone is a mess of wrong numbers. I say things like 'I think that's the breast option, don't you?' and people look at me' (132).
   The relationship between the female body and space will be explored in more detail in relation to *What Are You Like?*

9 Coughlan points out that Grace's pregnancy does not merely conform to the traditional figuration of the maternal body: 'Enright markedly refrains from staging Grace's impending motherhood as a capitulation to the idealization by Irish ideology of the maternal and its proper metonymic realm, the domestic. Despite her move away from Dublin and the hip urban world of the TV station to Connemara, it is difficult to imagine the woman who earlier has literally turned her house inside out as in any sense returning to an iconic West as to a foundation' (Coughlan, 2004, 186).

10 Enright's privileging of connectivity mirrors her narrative style and form. Reviewers have remarked on Enright's ability to create innovative connections; for James Wood of *The Guardian* 'she speeds up the connections between thoughts', whereas for Justine Ettler of *The Observer*, the detachment that accompanies the multiple viewpoints, 'leaves the reader free to move backwards and forwards between plot and subplots, making the various associations and connections and observing the novel's numerous parallels' (Wood, 2000; Ettler, 2000).

11 For example, 'Rose looked at the carpet, a swirl of green on brown. She felt that if she took one step away from him she would fall into its gaps and holes' (194). We will see later that in the novel, the carpet becomes intimately connected to the mother, to the place of the maternal. For Berts, 'the city was a subsidence, a slow-stirring trap. The city was full of holes' (72).

12 Rose decides that 'She would write to her father and ask him where he was, or where was her mother's grave. And when he wrote back to her, she would fly to Dublin and rent a car, and leave the car at a cemetery gate, and walk through the confused rows of the dead, until she found the right stone and the name it held' (196–7).

13 Berts's refusal to acknowledge that Maria's first utterance most likely refers to her mother, illustrates his constant attempts to erase the maternal.

14 Enright plays with the word 'parting' here to underline the twins' separation.

15 Rose 'was startled by her own reflection in the coatstand mirror' (167).

16 Effectively this separation is what Berts attempts when he refuses to accommodate twin daughters and takes only Maria home.

Chapter 4

[1] This incident, although related to a reporter by Nureyev as fact, is considered by most biographers to be fictional. McCann relates that he only discovered the unreliability of this story after publication of his novel. Indeed, the anecdote was one that initiated the creation of *Dancer* and McCann revels in the knowledge that he 'spun this fiction out of fiction' (McCann, 2003a).

[2] Most reviews of the novel feel the need to point this out. See Allardice, 2003; Coleman, 2003; Pray, 2003.

[3] I shall refer to the character in McCann's novel by the name of 'Rudi' to distinguish him from the historical figure, Rudolf Nureyev.

[4] The French dancer and choreographer, Roland Petit.

[5] The use of dance as a metaphor for thought is prevalent in early-twentieth century philosophy and aesthetics. For Friedrich Nietzsche, the idea of dance becomes the paradigm for philosophy: 'I wouldn't know what the spirit of a philosopher might more want to be than a good dancer. For the dance is his ideal, also his art' (Nietzsche, 2001, 246). His concept of dance is one that 'does not submit to external regulation', rather, it is 'autonomous, yet never fixed, non-repetitive, never beheld in its entirety' (Docherty, 2003, 32; Kunst, 2003, 62). In Symbolist aesthetics and for writers such as Stephen Mallarmé and Paul Valéry the metaphor of dance becomes a means to theorize 'the problematic relationships between the artist and the work of art, the ideal and the material, as well as the mind and the body' (Townsend, 2005, 127). Frank Kermode reads the use of the image of the dancer by Symbolists as a way to insist that 'As in the dance, there is no disunity of being' (Kermode, 2002, 58). This is epitomized in W. B. Yeats's question in 'Among School Children': 'How can we know the dancer from the dance?' (Yeats, 1997, 115).

[6] Yulia's description of Rudi as an explorer directly precedes her discovery of his defection.

[7] See such works concerning *Doppelgängers* and doubles as James Hogg's *The Private Memoirs and Confessions of a Justified Sinner* (1999); Hans Christian Anderson's, 'The Shadow', (2003); Edgar Allan Poe's, 'William Wilson', (1998); Fyodor Dostoyevsky's, *Notes from the Underground and The Double*, (1972); Henry James's, 'The Jolly Corner', (2004).

[8] Rudi's shoemaker Shoemaker, Tom Ashworth, also possesses the ability to decipher Rudi's past that has been inscribed on his body: 'and just by the sketches alone he intuits the life of this foot, raised in barefoot poverty and – from the unusual wideness of the bone structure – barefoot on concrete rather than grass' (106).

[9] For information regarding Eliza Lynch see Dunkerley, 2000; Leuchars, 2002; Lillis and Fanning, 2009; Plá, 1976; and Rees, 2003.

[10] Interestingly, the year after Enright's novel was published, two separate biographies on Eliza Lynch appeared in bookshops: Nigel Cawthorne's *The Empress of South America* (2003), and Rees's, *The Shadows of Eliza Lynch* (2003). A further novel also appeared: Lily Tuck, *The News from Paraguay* (2004).

[11] The text also makes explicit the differences in terms of representation that afflict linguistic constructions of male and female bodies: 'And so, Francisco put his

penis, *son pénis, su penis*, into the nameless part of Eliza Lynch. He put that thing, which is the same in English, French or Spanish, into a part of Eliza Lynch that is, in any language, obscene' (3).

[12] Siân Rees notes that Eliza gave birth while still travelling and arrived in Asunción with her baby (Rees, 2003, 38.).

[13] See Conrad, 2001; Lentin, 2004; and Sullivan, 2005.

[14] A sailor on the ship calls Eliza 'Dora' while she tends him on his deathbed. She then adopts this name as an alter ego: 'I step forward and want to say . . . what? That I am here – that I am his Dora, or not his Dora' (91), and later: 'All this while, I lean over the side – his Dora. I press a handkerchief to my eye and dream of a cottage in Portsmouth or Plymouth where I would feed a man mutton and forget to bring his washing from the line. It is not a bad dream' (94).

[15] La Recoleta is also the name of the cemetery in Buenos Aires, Argentina, in which Eva Péron is buried as is Cándido López, the Argentine painter who is renowned for his paintings and drawings depicting the War of the Triple Alliance. I would argue that the anachronism of the connections between Eva Péron and Cándido López feeds into Enright's concerns with the processes of historical discourse and representations of war and women. The name of Eliza Lynch's actual estate was Patino Cué. See Leuchars, 2002, 12.

[16] It is also important that this discussion takes place at a sumptuous dinner party. The conversation is held over the meat course and it is the pork that causes Dr. Stewart to remark on his aunt, again continuing the flesh-food metaphorical drive of the novel.

[17] The cultural anxiety surrounding the mother who cannot nourish or feed is also part of this positioning of the symbolic mother as sustenance for various discourses. Margaret Kelleher argues that the dominant imagery associated with disasters tends to focus on the female figure, and more particularly, on the mother: 'famine scenes are very frequently depictions of the failure or collapse of this primal shelter, of the mother's inability to nourish or protect her child' (Kelleher, 1997, 7).

[18] Enright also hints playfully at the devouring or murderous mother, naming of one of Eliza's costumes, 'The Medea' (35).

Chapter 5

[1] *The Gathering* also engages stylistically with Joyce's *Dubliners* (Meaney, 2010, 123–4).

[2] See Chapter 1 of this book.

[3] The Luas replaces the train in *Anna Karenina*, and also symbolizes 'death, illicit passion, upper-class society, and the power of public opinion' (Jahn, 1981, 2).

[4] Capitalism here replaces the conservative social force of the Church and at several points in the novel, the accoutrements of Celtic Tiger society are shown to be more potent than the religious institutions: silver service in a Michelin-starred restaurant is 'more ceremonious than Mass' (89).

[5] Frank MacDonald wrote in 2009 that 'Of all the new developments that encapsulate the Celtic Tiger, Dundrum Town Centre is probably the most potent. Designed by BKD for Joe O'Reilly's Castlethorn Construction, it perfectly expresses Ireland's

conversion to Mammon in much the same way that 19th century Gothic cathedrals once symbolised our devotion to God' (MacDonald, 2009).

[6] This is also the case in Claire Kilroy's *All Summer*, in which the hotel is built over the medieval city wall, part of which is kept on 'display' in a glass room.

[7] Anna seems to be connected with the fox, and Kate with the swallow; Kate is often associated with birds in the novel and her anorexia plays on the alternative meaning of 'swallow'.

[8] Leo quotes from T. S. Eliot's *The Wasteland*, which underlines the sense of alienation here.

[9] The novel also speaks to the problems inherent in not being able to resist inappropriate touch and not being able to help seeing this abuse. Both become linked in the novel to the smell of Germolene, 'which will remain with me, for evermore, the smell of things going wrong' (146).

[10] See Kristeva, 1982.

[11] Liam's job was as a hospital porter, who 'put cancerous lumps into bags and carried severed limbs down to the incinerator' (39), and he talks about rot and 'how long it took corpses to go off these days' (125).

[12] Mills Harper makes the important point that although the novel is concerned with the period of time from which Ireland became an independent nation, the novel focuses on domestic and personal history, rather than political: 'the Irish history that forms the backdrop for the book is that of issues that impinged on the lives of women, children, and men in their individual, domestic lives. War and politics, from the Emergency to the Troubles, do not haunt its pages, but other public shifts certainly do' (Mills Harper, 2010, 85).

Bibliography

Adelson, L. A. (1993), *Making Bodies, Making History: Feminism and German Identity*. Lincoln: University of Nebraska Press.

Adigun, Bisi and Roddy Doyle (2007), *The Playboy of the Western World*. Dir. Jimmy Fay. Arambe Productions. Abbey Theatre, Dublin, 29 September–24 November. Performance.

Ahmed, S. (2003), 'Feminist futures', in M. Eagleton (ed.), *A Concise Companion to Feminist Theory*. Oxford: Blackwell, pp. 236–54.

Al-Saji, A. (2004), 'The memory of another past: Bergson, Deleuze and a new theory of time', *Continental Philosophy*, 37, (2), 203–39.

Allardice, L. (2002), 'Heartless harlot', *The Telegraph*, 28 September.

— (2003), 'The Beckham of the barre', *The Telegraph*, 4 January.

Anderson, H. C. (2003), 'The shadow', in D. Crone Frank and J. Frank (eds), *The Stories of Hans Christian Anderson*. Boston and New York: Houghton Mifflin, pp. 225–39.

Anonymous. (1989), *First Fictions: Introduction 10*. London: Faber and Faber.

Armstrong, I. (2008), *Victorian Glassworlds: Glass Culture and the Imagination 1830–1880*. Oxford: Oxford University Press.

Arrowsmith, A. (2005), 'Photographic memories: Nostalgia and Irish diaspora writing', *Textual Practice*, 19, (2), 297–322.

Balzano, W., and J. Holdridge (2007), 'Tracking the Luas between the human and the inhuman', in W. Balzano, M. Sullivan, and A. Mulhall (eds), *Irish Postmodernisms and Popular Culture*. Basingstoke: Palgrave, pp. 100–12.

Barad, K. (2001), 'Re(con)figuring space, time, and matter', in M. DeKoven (ed.), *Feminist Locations: Global and Local, Theory and Practice*. New Brunswick: Rutgers University Press, pp. 75–109.

Barthes, R. (1993), *Camera Lucida: Reflections on Photography* (trans. R. Howard). London: Vintage.

Battersby, E. (1998), 'Coming up for air: Interview with Colum McCann', *The Irish Times*, 15 January.

Baudrillard, J. (1991), 'Paroxysm: The Seismic Order.' <www.egs.edu/faculty/jean-baudrillard/articles/paroxysm-the-seismic-order/> accessed 7 February 2011.

Bauman, Z. (2000), *Liquid Modernity*. Cambridge: Polity Press.

— (2003), *Liquid Love: On the Frailty of Human Bonds*. Cambridge: Polity Press.

Birne, E. (2007), 'What family does to you', *London Review of Books*, 29, (20), 30–1.

Bolger, D. (ed.) (2000), *The New Picador Book of Contemporary Irish Fiction*. London: Picador.

Bourke, E., and B. Faragó (eds) (2010), *Landing Places: Immigrant Poets in Ireland*. Dublin: Dedalus Press.

Braidotti, R. (1994), *Nomadic Subjects: Embodiment and Sexual Difference in Contemporary Feminist Theory*. New York: Columbia University Press.

Brandes, R. (1994), 'The dismembering muse: Seamus Heaney, Ciaran Carson, and Kenneth Burke's "Four Master Tropes"', in J. S. Rickard (ed.), *Irishness and (Post) Modernism*. London and Toronto: Bucknell University Press, pp. 177–94.

Brewster, S. (2009), 'Flying high? Culture, criticism, theory since 1990', in S. Brewster and M. Parker (eds), *Irish Literature Since 1990: Diverse Voices*. Manchester: Manchester University Press, pp. 16–39.

Brooks, M. W. (1997), *Subway City: Riding the Trains, Reading New York*. New Brunswick: Rutgers University Press.

Brown, T. (2004), *Ireland: A Social and Cultural History 1922–2002*. London: Harper Perennial.

Burke, P. (1991), 'Overture. The new history: Its past and its future', in P. Burke (ed.), *New Perspectives on Historical Writing*. Cambridge: Polity Press, pp. 1–24.

Cawthorne, N. (2003), *The Empress of South America*. London: Arrow.

Chan, S. (2006), '"Kiss my royal Irish ass." Contesting identity: Visual culture, gender, whiteness and diaspora', *Journal of Gender Studies*, 15, (1), 1–17.

Coleman, S. (2003), 'A brilliant leap of imagination: Exuberant account of dancer Nureyev's life seems as true as biography', *The San Francisco Chronicle*, 12 January.

Connolly, C. (2003a), 'Introduction: Ireland in theory', in C. Connolly (ed.), *Theorizing Ireland*. Hampshire and New York: Palgrave, pp. 1–13.

— (2003b), 'The turn to the map: Cartographic fictions in Irish culture', in V. Kreilkamp (ed.), *Eire/Land*. Chestnut Hill: McMullen Museum of Art and University of Chicago Press, pp. 27–33.

Conrad, K. (2001), 'Fetal Ireland: National bodies and political agency', *Éire-Ireland*, 36, (3–4), 153–73.

Coughlan, P. (2003), '"Bog Queens": The representation of women in the poetry of John Montague and Seamus Heaney', in C. Connolly (ed.), *Theorizing Ireland*. Hampshire and New York: Palgrave Macmillan, pp. 41–60.

— (2004), 'Irish literature and feminism in postmodernity', *Hungarian Journal of English and American Studies*, 10, (1–2), 175–202.

— (2005), '"Without a blink of her lovely eye": *The Pleasure of Eliza Lynch* and visionary scepticism', *Irish University Review*, 35, (2), 349–73.

Cronin, M. (2007), '"Is it for the glamour?": Masculinity, nationhood and amateurism in contemporary projections of the Gaelic Athletic Association', in W. Balzano, A. Mulhall, and M. Sullivan (eds), *Irish Postmodernisms and Popular Culture*. Basingstoke: Palgrave Macmillan, pp. 39–54.

Cullingford, E. B. (1990), '"Thinking of Her . . . as . . . Ireland": Yeats, Pearse and Heaney', *Textual Practice*, 4, (1), 1–21.

Davies, S. (2002), 'Excess all areas', *The Independent (UK)*, 26 October.

De Certeau, M. (1988), *The Writing of History* (trans. T. Conley). New York: Columbia University Press.

De Nooy, J. (2002), 'Reconfiguring the Gemini: Surviving sameness in twin stories', *AUMLA: Journal of the Australasian Universities Language and Literature Association*, 97, 74–95.

— (2005), *Twins in Contemporary Literature and Culture: Look Twice*. Basingstoke: Palgrave.

Deleuze, G. (1994), *Difference and Repetition* (trans. P. Patton). New York: Columbia University Press.

Dell'Amico, C. (2010), 'Anne Enright's *The Gathering*: Trauma, testimony, memory', *New Hibernia Review*, 14, (3), 59–73.

Derrida, J. (1984), 'No apocalypse, not now (full speed ahead, seven missiles, seven missives)', *Diacritics*, 14, (2), 20–31.

— (1988), 'The deaths of Roland Barthes', in H. J. Silverman (ed.), *Philosophy and Non-Philosophy Since Merleau-Ponty* (trans. P. –A. Brault and M. Nass). Stanford: Stanford University Press, pp. 89–108, 281–2.

— (1994), *Specters of Marx: The State of Debt, the Work of Mourning, and the New International* (trans. P. Kamuf). London and New York: Routledge.

— (1995), 'Choreographies', in E. Weber (ed.), *Point . . . Interviews, 1974–1994*. Stanford: Stanford University Press, pp. 89–108.

Diprose, R. (1998), 'Generosity: Between love and desire', *Hypatia*, 13, (1), 1–20.

— (2002), *Corporeal Generosity: On Giving with Nietzsche, Merleau-Ponty, and Levinas*. Albany: State University of New York Press.

Docherty, T. (2003), 'Aesthetic education and the demise of experience', in J. J. Joughin and S. Malpas (eds), *The New Aestheticism*. Manchester: Manchester University Press, pp. 23–35.

Dostoyevsky, F. (1972), *Notes from the Underground and The Double* (trans. J. Coulson). Harmondsworth: Penguin.

Dunkerley, J. (2000), *Americana: The Americas in the World, Around 1850 (or 'Seeing the Elephant' as the Theme for an Imaginary Western)*. London and New York: Verso.

Dwyer, J. (1991), *Subway Lives: 24 Hours in the Life of the New York Subway*. New York: Crown.

Eco, U. (1984), *Semiotics and the Philosophy of Language*. London: Macmillan.

Ellison, R. (1952), *Invisible Mann*. New York: Random House.

Enright, A. (1991), *The Portable Virgin*. London: Vintage.

— (1995), *The Wig My Father Wore*. London: Jonathan Cape.

— (2000a), *What Are You Like?* London: Jonathan Cape.

— (2000b), 'What's left of Henrietta Lacks', *London Review of Books*, 22, (8), 8–10, 50, 131.

— (2002a), 'Interview with Mark Lawson', *BBC Radio 4*, 26 September.

— (2002b), *The Pleasure of Eliza Lynch*. London: Jonathan Cape.

— (2003), 'Interview with Caitriona Moloney', in C. Moloney (ed.), *Irish Women Speak Out: Voices from the Field*. Syracuse: Syracuse University Press, pp. 51–64.

— (2004), *Making Babies: Stumbling into Motherhood*. London: Jonathan Cape.

— (2007), *The Gathering*. London: Jonathan Cape.

— (2008a), 'Muscular metaphors: An interview with Hedwig Schwall', *The European English Messenger*, 17, (1), 16–22.

— (2008b), *Taking Pictures*. London: Jonathan Cape.

— (2008c), *Yesterday's Weather*. New York: Grove Press.

— (2011), 'Interview by Claire Bracken and Susan Cahill', in C. Bracken and S. Cahill (eds), *Anne Enright*. Dublin: Irish Academic Press.

Ettler, J. (2000), 'The twins of the father', *The Observer*, 16 April.

Ewing, W. A. (2000), 'Form, fragment and flesh', in W. A. Ewing (ed.), *The Century of the Body: 100 Photographs 1900–2000*. London: Thames and Hudson, pp. 13–28.

Faragó, B., and M. Sullivan (eds) (2008), *Facing the Other: Interdisciplinary Essays on Race, Gender and Social Justice in Contemporary Ireland*. Newcastle: Cambridge Scholars Press.

Fernández Vázquez, J. S. (2002), 'Recharting the geography of genre: Ben Okri's *The Famished Road* as a postcolonial *bildungsroman*', *Journal of Commonwealth Literature*, 32, (2), 85–106.

Flood, A. (2010), 'Julian Gough slams fellow Irish novelists as "priestly caste" cut off from the culture', *Guardian*, 11 February.

Fogarty, A. (2000), 'Uncanny families: Neo-gothic motifs and the theme of social change in contemporary Irish women's fiction', *Irish University Review*, 30, (2), 59–81.

— (2002), '"The horror of the unlived life": Mother-daughter relationships in contemporary Irish women's fiction', in A. Giorgio (ed.), *Writing Mothers and Daughters: Renegotiationg the Mother in Western European Narratives by Women*. New York and Oxford: Berghahn Books, pp. 85–118.

— (2003), 'Preface', in É. Ní Dhuibhne, *Midwife to the Fairies: New and Selected Stories*. Cork: Attic Press, pp. ix–xv.

Foster, A. (2000), 'When blood runs thicker than daughters', *The Times*, 24 February.

Foucault, M. (1977), *Discipline and Punish: The Birth of the Prison* (trans. A. Sheridan). London: Allen Lane.

Fuss, D. (1992), 'Introduction: Inside/out', in D. Fuss (ed.), *Inside/Out: Lesbian Theories, Gay Theories*. New York: Routledge, pp. 1–10.

Gilsenan Nordin, I. (ed.) (2006), *The Body and Desire in Contemporary Irish Poetry*. Dublin: Irish Academic Press.

Gough, J. (2010), 'The state of Irish literature'. <www.juliangough.com/journal/> accessed 7 February 2011.

Graham, C. (2001), *Deconstructing Ireland: Identity, Theory, Culture*. Edinburgh: Edinburgh University Press.

Grosz, E. (1994), *Volatile Bodies: Toward a Corporeal Feminism*. Bloomington and Indianapolis: Indiana University Press.

— (1995), *Space, Time, and Perversion: Essays on the Politics of Bodies*. New York: Routledge.

— (1998), 'Thinking the new: Of futures yet unthought', *symploke*, 6, (1), 38–55.

— (1999), 'Bodies-Cities', in J. Price and M. Shildrick (eds), *Feminist Theory and the Body: A Reader*. Edinburgh: Edinburgh University Press, pp. 209, 381–7.

— (2000), 'Histories of a feminist future', *Signs: Journal of Women in Culture and Society*, 25, (4), 1017–21.

— (2003), 'Histories of the present and the future: Feminism, power, bodies', in J. J. Cohen and G. Weiss (eds), *Thinking the Limits of the Body*. New York: University of New York Press, pp. 13–23.

Hand, D. (2000), 'Being ordinary – Ireland from elsewhere: A reading of Eilís Ní Dhuibhne's *The Bray House*', *Irish University Review*, 30, (1), 103–16.

— (2001), 'The future of contemporary Irish fiction'. <www.writerscentre.ie/anthology/dhand.html> accessed 3 December 2003.

— (2005), 'Éilís Ní Dhuibhne', in A. Roche (ed.), *The UCD Aesthetic: Celebrating 150 Years of UCD Writers*. Dublin: New Island Press, pp. 218–28.

Harte, L. (2009), '"Tomorrow we will change our names, invent ourselves again":
Irish fiction and autobiography since 1990', in S. Brewster and M. Parker (eds),
Irish Literature Since 1990: Diverse Voices. Manchester: Manchester University Press,
pp. 201–15.
— (2010), 'Mourning remains unresolved: Trauma and survival in Anne Enright's
The Gathering', *LIT: Literature Interpretation Theory*, 21, (2), 187–204.
Haverty, A. (2007), *The Free and Easy*. London: Vintage.
Healy, J. F. (2000), 'Dancing cranes and frozen birds: The fleeting resurections of
Colum McCann', *New Hibernia Review*, 4, (3), 107–18, 154–5.
Herr, C. (1990), 'The erotics of Irishness', *Critical Inquiry*, 17, (1), 1–54.
Herron, T. (1999), 'The Body's in the Post: Contemporary Irish poetry and the
dispersed body', in C. Graham and R. Kirkland (eds), *Ireland and Cultural
Theory: The Mechanics of Authenticity.* London and Hampshire: Macmillan,
pp. 168–91.
Hirsch, M. (1997), *Family Frames: Photography, Narrative and Postmemory.* Cambridge,
MA: Harvard University Press.
Hogg, J. (1999), *The Private Memoirs and Confessions of a Justified Sinner.* Oxford:
Oxford University Press.
Houston, N. J. (2007), 'Celtic Tiger Ireland: Free and Easy?', *World Literature Today*,
81, (1), 12–15.
Hunt Mahony, C. (1998), *Contemporary Irish Literature: Transforming Tradition.* London:
Macmillan.
Hutcheon, L. (2002), *The Politics of Postmodernism.* London: Routledge.
Ingman, H. (2005), 'Nature, gender and nation: An ecofeminist reading of two
novels by Irish women,' *Irish Studies Review* 13, (4), 517–30.
Irigaray, L. (1985a), *Speculum of the Other Woman* (trans. G. C. Gill). New York: Cornell
University Press.
— (1985b), *This Sex Which is Not One* (trans. C. Porter and C. Burke). New York: Cornell
University Press.
— (1991a), *Marine Lover of Friedrich Nietzsche* (trans. G. C. Gill). New York: Columbia
University Press.
— (1991b), 'Volume without contours', in M. Whitford (ed.), *The Irigaray Reader.*
Oxford: Blackwell, pp. 53–68.
— (1991c), 'Women-Mothers, the silent substratum of the social order', in M. Whitford (ed.), *The Irigaray Reader.* Oxford: Blackwell, pp. 47–52.
— (1992), *Elemental Passions* (trans. J. Collie and J. Still). New York: Routledge.
— (2004a), *An Ethics of Sexual Difference* (trans. C. Burke and G. C. Gill). London:
Continuum.
— (2004b), 'The wedding between the body and language', in L. Irigaray (ed.),
Luce Irigaray: Key Writings. London and New York: Continuum, pp. 13–22.
Jahn, G. R. (1981), 'The image of the railroad in *Anna Karenina*', *The Slavic and East
European Journal*, 25, (2), 1–10.
James, H. (2004), 'The Jolly Corner', in J. Auchard (ed.), *The Portable Henry James.*
London: Penguin, pp. 283–318.
Jay, M. (1993a), *Downcast Eyes: The Denegration of Vision in Twentieth-Century French
Thought.* Berkeley and Los Angeles: University of California Press.

— (1993b), *Force Fields: Between Intellectual History and Cultural Critique*. London and New York: Routledge.

Kellaway, K. (1995), 'A hairy tale', *The Observer*, 12 March.

Kelleher, M. (1997), *The Feminization of Famine: Expressions of the Inexpressible?* Cork: Cork University Press.

— (2003), 'The field day anthology and Irish women's literary studies', *Irish Review*, 30, 2–94.

Kenny, J. (2000a), 'Ferociously-paced magical surrealism', *The Irish Times*, 4 March.

— (2000b), 'Slim book, substantial issues', *The Irish Times*, 29 April.

— (2003), 'Mantra for the future subopolis', *The Irish Times*, 24 May.

Kermode, F. (2002), *Romantic Image*. London: Routledge. [Original publication date 1957.]

Kiberd, D. (2005), *The Irish Writer and the World*. Cambridge: Cambridge University Press.

Killeen, T. (2000), 'Converting difference to inferiority', *The Irish Times*, 7 November.

Kilroy, C. (2003), *All Summer*. London: Faber.

— (2006), *Tenderwire*. London: Faber.

— (2009), *All Names Have Been Changed*. London: Faber.

Kolakowski, L. (2000), 'Emperor Kennedy legend: A new anthropological debate', in T. Spargo (ed.), *Reading the Past: Literature and History*. Basingstoke: Palgrave, pp. 1, 12–17.

Kristeva, J. (1982), *Powers of Horror: An Essay on Abjection* (trans. L. S. Roudiez). New York: Columbia University Press.

Kunst, B. (2003), 'Subversion and the dancing body: Autonomy on display', *Performance Research*, 8, (2), 61–8.

Kurth, P. (2003), 'A story with legs', *The New York Times*, 19 January.

Lacan, J. (2001), 'The mirror stage as formative of the function of the I as revealed in psychoanalytic experience', *Écrits: A Selection* (trans. A. Sheridan). London and New York: Routledge, pp. 1–8.

Lalvani, S. (1993), 'Photography, epistemology and the body', *Cultural Studies*, 7, (3), 442–65.

Lee, H. (2002), 'All reputation', *London Review of Books*, 24, (20), 19–20.

Lentin, R. (2004), 'From racial state to racist state: Ireland on the eve of the citizenship referendum', *Variant*, 2, (20), 7–8.

Leuchars, C. (2002), *To the Bitter End: Paraguay and the War of the Triple Alliance*. Westport: Greenwood.

Lillis, M. and R. Fanning (2009), *The Lives of Eliza Lynch: Scandal and Courage*. Dublin: Gill and Macmillan.

MacDonald, F. (2009), 'Celtic Tiger era earned some architectural stripes', *The Irish Times*, 26 March.

Massie, A. (2002), 'Travels with a not-so-great dictator', *The Scotsman*, 28 September.

Maxwell, W. (1988), *So Long, See You Tomorrow*. London: Secker & Warburg.

McCann, C. (1994a), *Fishing the Sloe-Black River*. London: Phoenix House.

— (1994b), 'Interview with Stephen V. Camelio'. <www.albany.edu/~lk9827/xml/dtd_assignment/mccann.xml> accessed 25 August 2006.

— (1995), *Songdogs*. London: Phoenix House.

— (1996), 'An Irishman in Harlem', *The Irish Times*, 10 August.

— (1997), 'The mole people', *The Irish Times*, 27 September.

— (1998), *This Side of Brightness*. London: Phoenix House.

— (2000), *Everything in This Country Must*. London: Phoenix House.

— (2003a), 'Colum McCann, author of *Dancer*, talks with Robert Birnbaum'. <www. identitytheory.com/people/birnbaum89.html> accessed 7 February 2011.

— (2003b), *Dancer*. London: Phoenix House.

— (2006), *Zoli*. London: Weidenfeld & Nicolson.

— (2009), *Let the Great World Spin*. London: Bloomsbury.

McCann, C., and A. Hemon (2003a), 'A good story is facts, imagination and language rolled into a tight bouncing ball', *The Guardian*, 1 July.

— (2003b), 'The writer sees in the dark corner swept clean by historians', *The Guardian*, 30 June.

McEwan, N. (1987), *Perspective in British Historical Fiction Today*. London: Macmillan.

McGahern, J. (1990), *Amongst Women*. London: Faber.

McNeil, J. (2003), 'A vicious adventuress has inspired two biographies and a novel', *The Independent (UK)*, 18 January.

Meaney, G. (1991), *Sex and Nation: Women in Irish Culture and Politics*. Dublin: Attic.

— (1992), 'Beyond eco-feminism: A review of Éilís Ní Dhuibhne's *The Bray House* and *Eating Women is Not Recommended*', *Irish Literary Supplement*, 11, (2), 14.

— (1998), 'Landscapes of desire: Women and Ireland on film', *Women: A Cultural Review*, 9, 237–51.

— (2010), *Gender, Ireland, and Cultural Change: Race, Sex, and Nation*. New York: Routledge.

Mills, L. (1996), *Another Alice*. Dublin: Poolbeg.

Mills Harper, M. (2010), 'Flesh and bones: Anne Enright's *The Gathering*', *The South Carolina Review*, 43, (1), 74–87.

Morris, C. (1996), '*The Bray House*: An Irish critical utopia', *Études Irlandaises*, 21, (1), 127–40, 136.

Morrissy, M. (1998), 'The sky above, the mud below', *The Irish Times*, 31 January.

Mulvey, L. (2000), 'Visual pleasure and narrative cinema', in T. Miller and R. Stam (eds), *Film and Theory: An Anthology*. Malden: Blackwell, pp. 483–94.

Nash, C. (1993), 'Re-mapping and re-naming: New cartographies of identity, gender and landscape in Ireland', *Feminist Review*, 44, 39–57.

— (1994), 'Re-mapping the body/land: New cartographies of identity by Irish women artists', in A. Blunt and G. Rose (eds), *Writing Women and Space*. London: Guilford, pp. 227–50.

— (1997), 'Embodied Irishness: Gender, sexuality and Irish identity', in B. Graham (ed.), *In Search of Ireland*. London: Routledge, pp. 108–27.

Negra, D. (ed.) (2006), *The Irish in Us: Irishness, Performativity, and Popular Culture*. Durham: Duke University Press.

— (2007), 'Fantasy, celebrity and "family values" in high-end and special event tourism in Ireland', in W. Balzano, A. Mulhall, and M. Sullivan (eds), *Irish Postmodernisms and Popular Culture*. Basingstoke: Palgrave Macmillan, pp. 141–56.

Ní Dhuibhne, É. (1981), 'With his whole heart'. Dublin, University College Dublin Ph.D.

— (1988), *Blood and Water*. Dublin: Attic Press.

— (1990), *The Bray House*. Dublin: Attic Press.

— (1991), *Eating Women is Not Recommended*. Dublin: Attic Press.
— (1993), 'Interview with Donna Perry', in D. Perry (ed.), *Women Writers Speak Out: Interviews by Donna Perry*. New Brunswick: Rutgers University Press, pp. 245–60.
— (1997), *The Inland Ice and Other Stories*. Belfast: Blackstaff Press.
— (1999), *The Dancers Dancing*. Belfast: Blackstaff Press.
— (2000a), 'One woman's writing retreat: Interview with Nicola Warwick'. <www.prairieden.com/front_porch/visiting_authors/dhuibhne.html> accessed 3 September 2004.
— (2000b), *The Pale Gold of Alaska and Other Stories*. Belfast: Blackstaff Press.
— (2003a), 'Interview with Caitriona Moloney', in C. Moloney and H. Thompson (eds), *Irish Women Writers Speak Out: Voices from the Field*. New York: Syracuse University Press, pp. 101–15.
— (2003b), *Midwife to the Fairies: New and Selected Stories*. Cork: Attic Press.
— (2007), *Fox, Swallow, Scarecrow*. Dublin: Blackstaff Press.
— (2010), 'Irish literary writers "cut off" from current of culture', *Irish Times*, 11 March.
Niederhoff, B. (2000), 'How to do things with history: Researching lives in Carol Shields' *Swann* and Margaret Atwood's *Alias Grace*', *Journal of Commonwealth Literature*, 35, (2), 71–85.
Nietzsche, F. (2001), *The Gay Science: With a Prelude in German Rhymes and an Appendix of Songs* (trans. J. Nauckhoff). Cambridge: Cambridge University Press.
O'Brien, C. (2005), 'Thousands join protest marches', *The Irish Times*, 9 December.
O'Flanagan, M. K. (2002), 'Reclaiming Ireland's Eva Peron: Interview with Anne Enright', *The Sunday Business Post*, 3 November.
O'Toole, F. (2001), 'Writing the boom', *Irish Times*, 25 January.
— (2010), 'We live in the 19th century as well as the 21st', *Irish Times*, 6 March.
Olkowski, D. (1994), 'Nietzsche's dice throw: Tragedy, nihilism, and the body without organs', in C. V. Boundas and D. Olkowski (eds), *Gilles Deleuze and the Theater of Philosophy*. London and New York: Routledge, pp. 119–40.
Padel, R. (2000), 'Twin tracks and double visions', *The Independent (UK)*, 26 February.
Parker, M. (2009), 'Changing history: the Republic and Northern Ireland since 1990', in S. Brewster and M. Parker (eds), *Irish Literature Since 1990: Diverse Voices*. Manchester: Manchester University Press, pp. 3–15.
Patten, E. (2003), 'Dancing in the dark', *The Irish Times*, 4 January.
— (2006), 'Contemporary Irish fiction', in J. W. Foster (ed.), *The Cambridge Companion to the Irish Novel*. Cambridge: Cambridge University Press, pp. 259–75.
Patterson, C. (1995), 'Angel delights', *The Independent (UK)*, 19 May.
Pelan, R. (2009), 'Introduction', in R. Pelan (ed.), *Éilís Ní Dhuibhne: Perspectives*. Galway: Arlen House, pp. 9–28.
Perkins Gilman, C. (1892), 'The yellow wallpaper', *The New England Magazine*, 11, (5), 647–57.
Peter, C. St. (1999), *Changing Ireland: Strategies in Contemporary Women's Fiction*. Basingstoke: Macmillan.
Pike, D. L. (1998), 'Urban nightmares and future visions: Life beneath New York', *Wide Angle*, 20, (4), 8–50.
Plá, J. (1976), *The British in Paraguay 1850–1870*. Richmond: Richmond.

Poe, E. A. (1998), 'William Wilson', in V. Leer (ed.), *Selected Tales*. Oxford: Oxford University Press, pp. 66–83.

Pray, J. (2003), 'Nureyev's story gets a novel turn', *USA Today*, 15 January.

Probyn, E. (2000), *Carnal Appetites: FoodSexIdentities*. London: Routledge.

Pultz, J. (1995), *Photography and the Body*. London: Weidenfeld and Nicolson.

Purkiss, D. (2000), *Troublesome Things: A History of Fairies and Fairy Stories*. London: Penguin.

Reddy, M. (2005), 'Reading and writing race in Ireland: Roddy Doyle and *Metro Eireann*', *Irish University Review*, 35, (2), 374–88.

Rees, S. (2003), *The Shadows of Eliza Lynch: How a Nineteenth-Century Irish Courtesan Became the Most Powerful Woman in Paraguay*. London: Headline.

Ricoeur, P. (1988), *Time and Narrative* (trans. K. Blamey and D. Pellauer), vol. 3. Chicago: University of Chicago Press.

Riddick, R. (1990), 'The right to choose: Questions of feminist morality'. *Lip Pamphlet Series*. Dublin: Attic.

Roche, A. (2000), 'Introduction: Contemporary Irish fiction', *Irish University Review*, 30, (1), vii–xxvii.

Rosende Pérez, A. (2010), 'Éilís Ní Dhuibhne's *Fox, Swallow, Scarecrow*: Visions and revisions of (and from) a changing nation', in D. Clark and J. Álvarez (eds), *'To Banish Ghost and Goblin': New Essays on Irish Culture*. Oleiros: Netbiblio, pp. 39–45.

Scarry, E. (1988), 'Introduction', in E. Scarry (ed.), *Literature and the Body: Essays on Populations and Persons*. Baltimore: Johns Hopkins University Press, pp. vii–xxvii.

Sceats, S. (2000), *Food, Consumption, and the Body in Contemporary Women's Fiction*. Cambridge: Cambridge University Press.

Seymour, M. (2003), 'First mistress of Paraguay', *The New York Times*, 23 March.

Shildrick, M. (1997), *Leaky Bodies and Boundaries: Feminism, Postmodernism and (Bio) Ethics*. London: Routledge.

Slattery, D. (2008), 'Minding the gaps (epistemological and modern) on Dublin's new Light-Rail System', *International Journal of Baudrillard Studies*, 5, (1). <www.ubishops.ca/baudrillardstudies/Vol5_1/v5-1-article17-slattery.html>accessed 7 February 2011.

Slemon, S. (1992), 'Bones of contention: Post-colonial writing and the "cannibal" question', in A. Purdy (ed.), *Literature and the Body*. Amsterdam: Rodopi, pp. 163–78.

Smyth, G. (2001), *Space and the Irish Cultural Imagination*. Basingstoke: Palgrave.

Spargo, T. (2000), 'Introduction: Past, present and future pasts', in T. Spargo (ed.), *Reading the Past: Literature and History*. Basingstoke: Palgrave, pp. 1–11.

Stallybrass, P., and A. White (1986), *The Politics and Poetics of Transgression*. Ithaca: Cornell University Press.

Stoekl, A. (1998), 'Lanzmann and Deleuze: On the question of memory', *symploke*, 6, (1–2), 72–82.

Sullivan, M. (2000), 'Feminism, postmodernism and the subjects of Irish and women's studies', in P. J. Mathews (ed.), *New Voices in Irish Criticism*. Dublin: Four Courts, pp. 243–51.

— (2005), 'The treachery of wetness: Irish studies, Seamus Heaney and the politics of parturition', *Irish Studies Review*, 13, (4), 451–68.

Tague, J. (1995a), 'A traveller's tale', *Times Literary Supplement*, 22 September.

— (1995b), 'Glowing from the cathode-ray tube', *Times Literary Supplement*, 31 March.

Tallone, G. (2004), 'Elsewhere is a negative mirror: The "Sally Gap" stories of Éilís Ní Dhuibhne and Mary Lavin', *Hungarian Journal of English and American Studies*, 10, (1–2), 203–15.

— (2008), 'Past, present and future: Patterns of otherness in Éilís Ní Dhuibhne's fiction', in P. Coughlan and T. O'Toole (eds), *Irish Literature: Feminist Perspectives*. Dublin: Carysfort Press, pp. 167–84.

Tóibín, C. (1999), *The Penguin Book of Irish Fiction*. London: Penguin.

Tonkin, B. (2007), 'The fearless wit of Man Booker winner Anne Enright', *The Independent*, 19 October.

Toth, J. (1993), *The Mole People*. Chicago: Chicago Review.

Townsend, J. (2005), '*Synaesthetics*: Symbolism, dance, and the failure of metaphor', *The Yale Journal of Criticism*, 18, (1), 126–48.

Tuck, L. (2004), *The News from Paraguay*. New York: Harper Perennial.

Tyler, I. (2000), 'Reframing pregnant embodiment', in S. Ahmed, J. Kilby, C. Lury, M. McNeil, and B. Skeggs (eds), *Transformations: Thinking Through Feminism*. London: Routledge, pp. 288–302.

Wall, E. (2000), 'Winds blowing from a million directions: Colum McCann's *Songdogs*', in C. Fanning (ed.), *New Perspectives on the Irish Diaspora*. Carbondale and Edwardsville: Southern Illinois University Press, pp. 281–8.

Warner, M. (1995), *From the Beast to the Blonde: On Fairy Tales and their Tellers*. London: Vintage.

— (1996), *Monuments and Maidens: The Allegory of the Female Form*. London: Vintage.

Whitford, M. (1991), *Luce Irigaray: Philosophy in the Feminine*. London and New York: Routledge.

Williams, R. (1990), *Notes on the Underground: An Essay on Technology, Society, and the Imagination*. Cambridge, MA: The MIT Press.

Williams, S. J. (1998), 'Bodily dys-order: Desire, excess and the transgression of corporeal boundaries', *Body & Society*, 4, (2), 59–82.

Wondrich, R. G. (2000), 'The pain within: Female bodies, illness and motherhood in contemporary Irish fiction', *Textus*, 12, 129–48.

Wood, J. (2000), 'To thrill – a mockingbird', *The Guardian*, 11 March.

Wright, R. (1969), 'The man who lived underground', *Eight Men*. New York: Pyramid, pp. 22–74.

Yeats, W. B. (1997), 'Among school children', in E. Larrissy (ed.), *W.B. Yeats: The Major Works*. Oxford: Oxford University Press, pp. 113–5.

Young, I. M. (1990), *Throwing Like a Girl and Other Essays in Feminist Philosophy and Social Theory*. Bloomington: Indiana University Press.

Ziegler, G. (2004), 'Subjects and subways: The politics of the third rail', *Space & Culture*, 7, (3), 283–301.

Index

Lightning Source UK Ltd.
Milton Keynes UK
UKOW031922181011

180526UK00001B/37/P